Women World Leaders

Great Politicians Tell Their Stories

———————

Laura A. Liswood

THE COUNCIL
Press

Reprinted from First Edition:

Women World Leaders: Fifteen Great Politicians Tell Their Stories

Copyright © 1995 by Laura A. Liswood

ISBN 0 04 440904 4

Published by Pandora, An Imprint of HarperCollins*Publishers*

Printed in Great Britain by HarperCollinsManufacturing Glasgow

Updated Edition:

Women World Leaders: Great Politicians Tell Their Stories

Copyright © 2009 by Laura A. Liswood

Printed by The Council Press

One Dupont Circle NW, Suite 700, Washington, D.C. 20036 USA

ISBN 978-1-4276-2395-9

ISBN 978-1-4276-2395-9

53000

9 781427 623959

*"There is no democracy in our
beautifully democratic countries.
Why? Women have not the same part
in decision making as men have."*

VIGDÍS FINNBOGADÓTTIR
President of Iceland (1980-1996)

*"We are not yet there, but it's
very important that we see that
more and more countries are appointing
women as their political leaders, as
prime ministers, as presidents, and
I think that's a very important
development."*

MARIA LIBERIA-PETERS
Former Prime Minister,
The Netherlands Antilles (1984-86, 1988-93)

To Benazir Bhutto
Friend and leader
June 21, 1953 - December 27, 2007

Table of Contents

Acknowledgements

It is impossible to list all of the wonderful, supportive individuals who helped make this project possible. Many were government employees, United States Information Agency cultural affairs officers, U.S. State Department country desk officers, U.S. embassy personnel--including ambassadors and their staffs who guided me--all provided crucial information, listened with interest, and kept me company. The D.C. office of Senator Ted Kennedy kindly contacted the embassies of Pakistan and Bangladesh on my behalf. Overseas, many people in the countries I visited helped to ensure that interviews occurred and were always friendly, no matter how busy.

I want to thank UNIFEM, a division of the United Nations which deals with women's and children's issues, and the Kongsgaard Foundation for their initial financial assistance. Also, my grateful thanks to Adrienne Arsht Feldman for her continual wise counsel; to Dr. Christine di Stefano of the University of Washington, Seattle, for my political science education; and to Laura Boydston, for working so tirelessly. Patricia Coburn was also an essential part of this undertaking. My thanks also to Kristina Veirs for research assistance and word processing of the manuscript.

Editors always deserve to be recognized: Belinda Budge and Sara Dunn, of Pandora, and Rebecca Lewis, of HarperCollins, certainly do. My thanks to Dana for being on the other end of the long-distance telephone calls so many times. Finally, to friends and family around the world who believe in women as leaders--my warm appreciation.

The updated edition required a lot of work and research; special thanks to the staff of the Council of Women World Leaders.

Original Introduction

This book, one aspect of the Women's Leadership Project, is the result of many fascinating journeys. The interviews with women prime ministers and presidents of the world on which the book is based carried me to countries as disparate as Iceland and Sri Lanka, Ireland and Bangladesh, Poland and the Philippines.

As background were questions that had been in my mind for some time regarding women and governance. I had read essays by feminists and political scientists about why more women should be in politics. When women--one-half of the world--are as severely underrepresented in governing, across the world, as they currently are, something is very wrong. Why, I asked myself, are qualities that we often identify as feminine--qualities of nurturing and cooperating, among others--not more active ingredients in world politics? And how could I get actual proof that women's leadership makes a difference?

One day in late 1992 I read a short study published by the Center for the American Woman and Politics (CAWP) located at Rutgers University. It was a survey, done by Debra Dodson, of women elected to state legislatures. "Women are diverse and some are more likely than others to reshape the policy agenda and work on women's rights bills," noted Dodson, "but it is clear that, overall, women lawmakers do more to help women than their male colleagues." The survey showed that women do reshape the policy agenda through their legislative priorities and their work on women's rights bills.

It also provided evidence that women public officials are changing the way government works. The women legislators were more likely than men to bring citizens into the political process, to favor government in public view rather than government behind closed doors, and to be responsive to groups previously denied full access to the policymaking process.

No matter that the study was narrowly focused on state legislators. It was the first quantitative research I had seen that went beyond general ideas of the need for gender balance and greater roles for women in politics. My M.B.A. "need for statistical proof" was satisfied; there was a difference, and it was not merely academic theory that said so.

I was in my studio overlooking Elliott Bay in Seattle, Washington, and that year I had co-founded a group called May's List in Washington State. We wanted to emulate the highly successful national model of EMILY'S list--to bring power fundraising for women candidates to the local level and "bundle checks" for women running for city council, mayor or state representative. We understood that we had to "fill the pipeline," help women run at all levels, if we were to have more women leaders.

So I was primed and delighted to read the CAWP report. As I watched the ferries float by on the bay, I thought: How can I find out what it is like, this women's leadership? Where are women exercising power at the very top?

I cannot say I saw my opening journey from that moment. It was only a concept in my mind to ask those who were in power what it was like. But I was thinking about something else as well. I wanted to go to the Fourth World Conference on Women, to be sponsored by the United Nations in Beijing in September 1995. I knew little about it, but in another example of how "you find what you need when you are ready to learn it," I read in *Ms.* magazine in 1993 that a Mrs. Gertrude Mongella of Tanzania had been appointed by UN Secretary-General Boutros Boutros-Ghali to be the Secretary-General of the Fourth World Conference. So I called. And wrote. And finally got an appointment with her. (Thanks to two supportive UN secretaries, Elizabeth Ellers and Juliet Kiswaga, who helped make it happen.)

I proposed the idea of a video of women world leaders to be shown at the conference. Would Mrs. Mongella support that? Neither of us quite knowing what "that" meant. She said "Yes, why not?"

From that slim but crucial bridge, I approached Madame Corazon Aquino through the help of old and new friends. She said yes, she would meet me. Such excitement, such amazement! The fax from her came on a Friday. What was I to do? I rushed and called and faxed. My luck held as an Undersecretary of Tourism, Ms. Mina Gabor, graciously offered to arrange for the camera crew and to personally attend in support my effort. A *Seattle Times* reporter, Eric Nalder, suggested interview techniques.

I was so busy that there was little time for self-doubt. I wanted to know about leaders' styles, about family backgrounds and values, about how women did their jobs. Was the public's expectation of them different than for men? Let them talk of power; let them just talk!

Before I left for the Philippines, I spoke with State Representative Velma Veloria, the first Filipina-American woman elected to Washington state office. She gave me the names of her college friends. So did others. I was armed with a list of women to meet. And I did meet them. Women who had organized to help other women.

A similar process occurred each time I wanted to approach a woman leader. I never expected to meet nearly every living woman president or prime minister who served for at least nine months.[1] I just kept asking. Explaining. Being scrutinized. Who was I with? What purpose did I have? Who would see my video?

I received immense help from U.S. State Department desk officers who were used to journalists' requests for interviews. They directed me to the United States Information Agency (USIA) press officers, whom I would fax, who would then send the request on. In the meantime, I would talk with country-specific embassy press officers to further my requests. All were courteous, though not all were encouraging. Imagine the impossible number of requests each leader gets! And who was I? Not Barbara Walters or CNN or Oriana Fallaci (with whom I once spent a glorious three hours talking of Golda Meir, Indira Gandhi, and her own life of "writing plays"--Ms. Fallaci's term for interviewing). However things were going, I just stayed at it. Never *demanding*, so I avoided getting a complete 'No.' Was I a nuisance? Probably. But no one said so to me. I was sometimes warned with a laugh by USIA personnel that if I got an appointment, the exact time would come suddenly without warning, and I must be prepared to react. Other appointments, I was told, would be given in a more Nordic style--exact time, length of stay, all very firm. There would be, as it turned out, long waits in hotels around the world, camera crews on standby.

I can now say this: Had I known the enormity of my undertaking in advance, how much I should have known in order to do it, this project would not have gotten done by me. In the end, I just did it. The impossible became the inevitable.

Some comments on the interviews: The list of questions that I put to each woman leader can be found in Appendix A. Interviews were from thirty to seventy minutes in length. I would have loved more time, but time is something that women ruling at the top have far too little of. Sometimes it was natural to ask a few questions that deviated from the standard list.

The heart of what I was after was how the responses of women leaders compared across an issue--both the divergences and similarities of responses. To me that would be of most interest. Once the interviews were on videotape, transcripts were derived and major themes organized. The Women's Leadership Project produced both a film and this book.

I should point out that since history moves on and politics change constantly, some of the women I interviewed may be out of office when the reader engages my pages. A few of the women regularly move in-and-out of prime ministerships as the political parties which they head win or lose elections. In 1995 one more woman, Chandrika Bandaranaike Kumaratunga of Sri Lankamay qualify for inclusion in this book by virtue of being in power for at least nine months.

What struck us? What did we learn? My chapters are organized by theme, and messages will become clear as the reader progresses. I would note my awe at what some of these women have taken on. Because there have been so few women governing at the top throughout history, all are pathfinders. Role models for them are few, and many have experienced events unlikely for us to imagine in our own lives. And yet even Benazir Bhutto talks of the burdens of being a mother, and Maria Liberia-Peters says her children always want mommy. So they are flesh and blood, as we are. And their numbers will increase. I particularly anticipate the first woman president of my own country, the United States. I hope that by the time the reader finishes this book, it will have become obvious what it takes to bring more women to the top. There are many ways in which the resources necessary can be helped along by every reader.

At the outset, it may be useful to turn to my biographic section and read each woman leader's brief biography. And study her face in the photograph, too. In addition, I have tried to provide some sense of the milieu in which each must function, in a section on geography and gender and country backgrounds. Obviously, leading a country in which many women are still illiterate is not the same experience as its opposite, nor is leading a wealthy and stable nation the same as leading a poor country with a history of military takeovers. Many, many factors will make a difference in what a leader, female or male, can hope to achieve. My section on geography and gender tries to introduce some of this necessary background.

It has been a great privilege to be in the company of so many out standing women. I now know that it is not impossible for a woman to lead a country.

Laura A. Liswood
Seattle, Washington
October, 1994

Revised Introduction

Over ten years have passed since I started my journey to meet 15 women leaders who were Presidents and Prime Ministers of their countries. Over ten years have also passed since the UN Conference on Women in Beijing. My quest was to find out what it was like to have a woman running a country and to learn what it would take to have a woman President of the United States. The quest of the Beijing conference was to gain equality for women around the world. These two journeys were two sides of the same coin.

Today, there are over 38 current and former women Presidents and Prime Ministers, heads of state and government, in so many places around the world: on a continent that had never seen a woman elected head of state, Liberia elected Ellen Johnson-Sirleaf as President in 2006. That same year Chile, a culturally and religiously conservative country, elected Michelle Bachelet as President. And in 2005, in a country that once had the slogan for women, "Kinder, Kirche, Kuche" (children, church, kitchen), Angela Merkel, an East German leader, became Chancellor of Germany. (See Appendix B for list of current and former leaders.)

Much has happened to me, to the women's movement and to the condtion of women and girls over this period. For my journey, it was unforeseen, the sequence of events that were triggered by my first interview with Corazon Aquino through my last with Margaret Thatcher. Personally, I moved from my long-time home of Seattle to Washington, D.C. and then to Boston and back to Washington, D.C. Some of those women I interviewed became friends, probably the least expected and most treasured outcome of this work. I went from being a corporate executive to being the head of an organization I created, and to advising Goldman Sachs, the premier investment bank in the world, on leadership and diversity.

Most journeys have a known destination. Mine has not. I never expected to be where I am now and it is only through the rearview mirror that I see how my path came about.

The women's movement blossomed post-Beijing. Tens of thousands of non-governmental organizations emerged, each with their own energy and passion, ranging from women's health to micro-financing, from political participation to research and business organizations. Women connected through the internet with each other and networked furiously. Women came together to support and advise others with common goals, from Africa to Mongolia and from Chile to Canada. Conferences, workshops, seminars, and retreats are frequent and energizing.

Women have learned to gather together to share their learning, to join for collective action, and to advocate for themselves and those for whom they can speak. Women want to "hurry history" as I put it when Barbara Lee, Marie Wilson, and I started The White House Project in 1998. We see what is possible and yet our dreams and visions are not complete.

During my journey to meet the 15 world leaders, I kept hearing so many similar stories: experiences were the same, though the leaders were from different nations, cultures, and backgrounds. They felt treated in very similar ways as women, not as leaders. They seemed to have received the same treatment from reporters and their readers-- over-scrutiny and excessive critique of their clothes, hair, hand bags and scarves. Their policies seem to sit second chair to their person. They felt a familiar feeling of less tolerance for mistakes than what they saw for the male counterparts.

Ironically, my interviews stretched in time; each leader wanted to hear what the others had said and their stories. It seemed reassuring to learn that what happened was not due to personal defect but to gender. I learned that these women, like most women, began to think what happened to them as pathological to themselves when they were not aware that similar experiences were occurring to their sister leaders.

They were much relieved to hear the stories and realize that it was not them, but who they represent that caused this disparate treatment.

So after several interviews, I started observing that this increased conversation was not an interview so much as a way of creating a virtual network with me as the linking lines. I finally asked them if they wanted to meet each other.

Thus, what I thought would be a finite project—to interview, video document and create a book and documentary—became much more than that. In 1996 the Center for Strategic and International Studies (CSIS) agreed to partner with my Women's Leadership Project to create a summit in Stockholm of these world leaders. It would be the first time that many of them had met their counterparts. We invited other women leaders as well and the results were amazing. Twelve women heads of state and government came to the Summit and the Swedish women loved being a part of history.

Not knowing what might happen at this Summit, I researched what organizations existed for current or former heads of state and government. There were two at the time. One was the InterAction Council chaired by Helmut Schmidt composed of many former prime ministers and the other was U.S. President Jimmy Carter's Council of Freely Elected Heads of State.

The group of women leaders who met in Stockholm decided they wanted to create their own group, the Council of Women World Leaders, made up of any woman who holds or has held the position of president, prime minister, or head of state or government. There were not many then (15) and the number is still small today, though it has more than doubled to 38. The only qualification is that they be freely elected and subsequently take office.

Then President of Iceland, Vigdís Finnbogadóttir, agreed to take on the role of Founding Chair, at the request of President Mary Robinson of Ireland who chaired that first gathering. They gave me the honor of asking me to be the Secretary General. Over the next year President Vigdís (as she is known in Iceland) and I met with several leading institutions and, at the invitation of Dean Joseph Nye, Jr., we moved our Secretariat to the Kennedy School of Government at Harvard University. The work of creating a new organization started in 1997 with the gracious support of Dean Nye and the Women's Leadership Board of the Kennedy School, led by Holly Taylor Sargent.

Our first task was to create a mission: to mobilize the highest-level women leaders globally for collective action on issues of critical importance to women and equitable development. It was most important for these leaders to become more visible and more well-known. To make normal that women lead countries.

I have come to realize what I call the "power of the mirror." It is hard for any one of us to know what we can be unless we actually SEE it. How does a little girl know she can grow up to be president of the United States? She can be told it, but without the role model, the physical picture of another person who has had that position, she must stretch her imagination to see herself there.

This power of the mirror is what made so many celebrate the appointment of U.S. Secretary of State Madeleine K. Albright to that powerful job under President Bill Clinton. It was the first time that a woman had held one of the highest level spots in American political life. As she said, "it didn't matter if I were a woman or a man when Air Force One flew into a country. I had the power of the United States behind me." In her autobiography, *Madame Secretary*, Secretary Albright tells many stories about how she was treated and the challenges she faced. It was also clear that when she walked into a room, she noticed if there were other women leaders there, something men would not necessarily do. (Dr. Condoleezza Rice later took the same position—the second woman and the first African-America woman.)

Secretary Albright, along with then First Lady Hillary Clinton, would visit women's clinics to meet with women in the communities to hear their stories, acknowledge their accomplishments and recognize their needs. Other male secretaries of state would not be so inclined or see that as part of their job.

Role models are essential for girls and young women while growing up and for women rising in corporations or political life. One of the biggest roadblocks that women in corporations face is the steep pyramid that exists and impedes their advancement. Women begin to wonder whether they can make it to higher levels of corporate responsibility and position when they look up and see so few others who have been able to make it.

The new Council we created in 1997 caught the imagination of people. Most had no idea there were so many women leaders. If you played a game of naming them, a few could identify Margaret Thatcher, Corazon Aquino, or Benazir Bhutto, as they had made headlines in their country and around the world. But who knew of Hanna Suchocka of Poland, a major figure in the Solidarity movement and a key player along with Lech Walesa in transitioning Poland to a democracy? Or others such as Eugenia Charles, from the small island of Dominica, who was known as the Iron Lady of the Caribbean and who chaired the influential group of countries in the CARICOM (Caribbean Community and Common Market).

Later, when even more women had joined the Council, the former Prime Minister of Canada and previous Chair of the Council, Kim Campbell, would tell the story of a meeting she attended with a number of other prime ministers. She offered $100 to any of them if they could come up with all of the women leaders' names. No one won the money—not even Bill Clinton, who came up with 19 names.

Our Council started with the idea of bringing the women presidents and prime ministers together, to network and share experiences and be provided with new and interesting information on current events and global leadership concepts through the Kennedy School faculty. We soon realized after two summits that although this was a good idea, it is actually quite difficult to get sitting leaders to join in, given their schedules.

However, we found our strength in the enormous convening power of the group. We were able to start a series of meetings of women who hold positions at the ministerial level, equivalent in the United States to our cabinet secretaries. This proved highly useful and our first round started with women ministers of finance during the annual meetings of the World Bank and IMF.

Over the ensueing years we have convened women ministers of finance, justice, environment, women's affairs, and health with powerful results. In truth, there are few organizations with the scope and authority that ours has. In 2002 we actually formalized what we had created: the Council's Ministerial Initiative, with Madeleine Albright as its chair. There are now over 500 women at this high level. I am a strong believer that women need to be at the table to influence policy and the world's agenda. Men have done it forever -- for them it is called the G8, the United Nations, NATO, parliament, Congress.

Often women are exceptionally active and involved at the grassroots level—delivering services or helping other women and girls, whether in health issues, economic empowerment, political participation, clean water, or domestic violence. These activities at the community level are extremely important as women and girls often are underserved. Women now hold many high-level positions but are not organized in the same way that women at the grassroots level are. We are helping to close that gap. Madeleine Albright urges women to create new architectures to deal with the issues of the day. The Filipino women say that "to cook rice cakes you need heat at the top and heat at the bottom." The Council and the Ministerial Initiative have been formed to do that.

I didn't start my journey with the intention of organizing these two bodies. However, it seemed like the natural outcome of that first step-- and the natural evolution of what emerged from the sources of energy that the Beijing conference unleashed for women.

We have been successful-- beyond anything we could have imagined. The small team at the Council—no more than four of us at any time— worked in the office, or in virtual mode, at the Kennedy School. Now we are at the Aspen Institute in Washington, D.C. and Mary Robinson, former President of Ireland and High Commissioner for Human Rights, is the Chair of the Council.

I attribute our successes to pent-up demand. Every time we offered to bring women ministers together, they eagerly sought to join in. The women environmental ministers have created a robust network composed of the women who hold that portfolio. Through the *Joint Conclusions on the Environment,* the network influenced the declaration adopted at the United Nations Rio + 10 Summit which included 39 major references to gender; the original draft had only three minor references to gender. The critical mass of women ministers gave them the power to shape that UN document. (See Appendix C for excerpts from the Joint Conclusions.)

Not all women know or support a focus on gender issues or are looking to see if there is a disproportionate impact from policy on women versus men. For example, poverty is an overarching global issue and yet it affects women more than men since 70% of the poor are women and children and only 30% of the poor are men A similar story is being written about women and HIV/AIDS and its disproportionate impact.

To reach and improve women's lives is a different story than to do so for men. And it requires different policies and resources. For example, universal primary education for all children is a Millennium Development Goal of the United Nations. But more girls than boys are kept from school because of financial cost, the need for girls to take care of younger siblings, or cultural constraints and limitations on girls. To get girls into, and then remain enrolled in, schools demands substantially different resources and strategies than to get boys to school. The Council is now developing the Ministerial Leadership Initiative for Girls' Education to highlight these best efforts and share them globally.

Women ministers are, on the whole, interested in gender, interested in meeting their peers, and desirous of changing policy to guarantee better treatment for women and girls. They may, however, be as uninformed as their male counterparts on gender issues. We have found it valuable to educate these women, too, and not to assume that they will merely know or appreciate the issues by the fact they are women. Having said that, we learned from early experience that women ministers want to create an ongoing network for themselves and to work together when they can.

The ministerial work we do is the most fundamental component of our mission and creates the highest level of tangible product. There are over 500 women who hold these cabinet jobs, usually in the portfolios that have been traditionally seen as "women oriented." Thus, there are larger numbers in ministries such as health, education, and social services. The highest number, not surprisingly, is in the ministries of women's affairs. There are men who hold that job, too, but usually when the women's affairs group has been folded within sports, agriculture or some other odd situation. Not surprisingly also, the ministers of women's affairs speak of marginalization of their department and inadequate funding and resources.

This brings me to another unanticipated product of the Council's work and my journey. Globally, few women sit on boards of directors, or have reached the highest levels of corporate management, or have taken assignments at the senior leadership levels in intergovernmental organizations. Often the lament is heard that when men go looking for women to put in these positions, they can't seem to find them. That is not surprising because "like hires like" men have their networks and they don't necessarily have any need to expand them and therefore most of those networks look a lot alike.

A while ago I received a call from Kofi Annan, then Secretary General of the United Nations. He had heard of our work from his wife, Nan Annan, who is an activist and a person energized around women and women's issues. He requested help in his continuing goal to make his top leadership 50% men and 50% women. But he was having difficulty in identifying possible women candidates for top jobs including special envoys, appointed senior jobs, commission members, etc. Could we help? The answer was, of course, yes, we could. But it highlighted a key fact for me.

Women have been extremely active at the grassroots level with thousands upon thousands of non-governmental organizations working on issues to help women and girls. It is like a world full of mom and pop stores, with all of the personal warmth, touch, and knowledge that comes from a small enterprise in the neighborhood. What was missing were the giant 'big box' stores that had huge purchasing power, a major market position, efficiencies, economies of scale, and the ability to make a huge global impact.

When I thought of the major 'brands' in the non-profit world, names like Greenpeace, Amnesty International, and Doctors without Borders all came to mind. The only worldwide women and girls organization that I could think of with that widespread impact was Girl Scouts/Girl Guides.

I think the next frontier for women is to be able to create means of collectively working together, linking up to create a huge impact, and marketing issues to gain a much larger footprint on the world's agenda. Otherwise we remain scattered, fragmented, and unable to use our critical mass to shape change. One step would be to have a large database of women's groups and leaders that could be a source for institutions like the United Nations to use. We need to harness our resources at the grassroots and at the tree tops. The Council of Women World Leaders is hopeful that it can play one of those roles.

I am proud to say that at least one other organization came to being because of the journey I took. In 1998, three women, all of us eager to harness women's power and leadership, came together and formed the White House Project. Barbara Lee, a tireless social activist and founder of the Barbara Lee Family Foundation, Marie Wilson, then head of the Ms. Foundation, and I formed this project. We wanted to focus on shaping the culture of the United States to make it feasible for a woman to become president of the United States. As I said, we wanted to figure out how to "hurry history." All three of us remain dedicated to that vision and the White House Project, under Marie's strong leadership, has undertaken groundbreaking research, convened women's summits, and even produced a Barbie for President!

Questions still continue to form in my mind regarding women and governance. When women—one half of the world—are as severely underrepresented in governing and leadership roles across the world, something is very wrong. The United States stands 59th amongst all countries in its level of women in national representation in its Congress (Rwanda is first, Sweden second). The U.S. stands 23rd in the World Economic Forum's Global Gender Gap Report 2006, which measures the size of the gender gap in economic participation and opportunity, educational attainment, political empowerment, and health and survival for 115 countries.

Because there have been so few women governing at the top throughout history, all are pathfinders. Role models for them are still few. Only four have followed another woman as the leader of her country (Ireland, Bangladesh, New Zealand, and the Philippines).

I heard almost all the women leaders I interviewed tell me that it takes passion and a clear vision of where they want to go to persevere under the challenges they faced as women leaders. Edith Cresson, Prime Minister of France, told me that when she got out of the car, the press photographers would be lying on the pavement waiting to take pictures of her legs! She never saw that for the male leaders. Hanna Suchocka of Poland said she got tired of always reading about her handbags and scarves and what color her coat was. She once wore a red coat and was criticized because it was the former Soviet Union colors.

Today, ten years after those interviews, I often speak to groups about leadership and the lessons from women leaders. It is particularly important for young women to see these images and role models, to understand their entitlement to lead, and to have a voice. Many young women today are energized and concerned about the women's movement -- they understand there are hurdles yet to be overcome. I've met so many eager, enthusiastic, intelligent women who want to become a part of the continuation of the change started, not in Beijing ten years ago, but long before that.

I have learned that women leaders are as essential to our democracy as men leaders and that true democracy will only exist when both men and women are in the seats of power, wherever those seats are.

Women, like men, have much to contribute and our voices provide as much value (or as little) as men's do. Often I tell women that there really is no glass ceiling—it is just a thick layer of men!

We can change the world together. I heard a saying once, "women are like snowflakes: one alone may melt, but together we can stop traffic."

I am sure that if I had known the enormity of the undertaking and the personal funds required or how much knowledge I would have to amass, the project would not have been done by me. Yet change moves from the unthinkable to the impossible to the inevitable.

I never did imagine the path that I would travel on this journey of women's leadership. Perhaps though, I should have had an inkling of my path early on. I was born on March 8 -- United Nations' International Women's Day.

Laura A. Liswood
Washington, D.C.
July, 2007

List of Women Leaders Interviewed for the Book

***The following presidents and prime ministers of the world were
interviewed for this book:***

Corazon Aquino, *President, The Philippines (1986-92)*

Sirimavo Bandaranaike, *Prime Minister, Sri Lanka (1960-65; 1970-77;
1994-2000; d. 2000)*

Benazir Bhutto, *Prime Minister, Pakistan (1988-90; 1993-97; d.2007)*

Gro Harlem Brundtland, *Prime Minister, Norway (1981; 1986-89;
1990-96)*

Kim Campbell, *Prime Minister, Canada (1993)*

Violeta Chamorro, *President, Nicaragua (1990-96)*

Eugenia Charles, *Prime Minister, Dominica (1980-95; d. 2005)*

Tansu Çiller, *Prime Minister, Turkey (1993-96)*

Edith Cresson, *Prime Minister, France (1991-92)*

Vigdís Finnbogadóttir, *President, Iceland (1980-96)*

Ellen Johnson Sirleaf, *President, Liberia (2006-)*

Maria Liberia-Peters, *Prime Minister, Netherlands Antilles (1984-86;
1988-94)*

Kazimiera Prunskiene, *Prime Minister, Lithuania (1990-91)*

Mary Robinson, *President, Ireland (1990-97)*

Jenny Shipley, *Prime Minister, New Zealand (1997-99)*

Hanna Suchocka, *Prime Minister, Poland (1992-93)*

Margaret Thatcher, *Prime Minister, Great Britain (1979-90)*

Vaira Vike-Freiberga, *President, Latvia (1999-2007)*

Khaleda Zia, *Prime Minister, Bangladesh (1991-96)*

Chapter I: Politics Sans Intention

It never occurred to me in my entire life
that I would be here in this position.
--Violeta Chamorro

Roughly a quarter of the women interviewed for this book came to their top leadership positions through one of the most painful and unexpected of all routes: assassins killed their politically-active husbands. Wives were asked to pick up the work of the fallen leader, sometimes after a number of years passed, often more quickly.

It is no small assignment to be given.

In Nicaragua, in the 1970s, Violeta and Pedro Chamorro had been married for twenty-seven years and had four grown children when Nicaragua's leading newspaperman was gunned down in his car--on January 10, 1978--while driving to work at his newspaper. Pedro Joaquín Chamorro--a member of one of Nicaragua's most prominent families--had worked tirelessly and with great courage to rid his country of a series of Somoza-family dictators. His efforts had not been limited to journalism, but had meant organizing political opposition groups and even, for a brief time, taking up arms with a resistance force. He had been imprisoned, fored into exile for a time, and threatened with death. He predicted he would be killed.

So potent was his martyrdom that his widow was invited into a governing coalition when the Sandinista Liberation Front completed the anti-Somoza revolution in July of 1979, nineteen months after Pedro Chamorro's death. Violeta Chamorro's involvement with this coalition was short-lived, but even eleven years later, feuding groups wishing to oust the Sandinistas in the 1990 presidential elections turned to Mrs. Chamorro--Nicaragua's "mother"--as their best hope of a unifying figure.

In the Philippines, in the 1980s, Corazon Aquino played a similarly unifying role. When her husband Benigno returned to the Philippines on August 21, 1983, after three years of political exile in the United States to attempt a renewed involvement in his country's politics of "guns, goons, and gold," he was shot in the head before he could even leave the Manila airport.

Corazon Aquino, still in exile, quickly returned to the Philippines to lead thousands of people in processions of mourning and protest. She then continued on to support several National Assembly candidates who were opposing the policies of dictator Ferdinand Marcos. Within two years, Aquino was seen as a figure who could unify leadership and mobilize the electorate to get rid of her dead husband's persecutor.

In her interview for this book, Aquino--for many years a shy, very private mother raising five children--described the reluctance she felt in taking on such a leading role as challenging Ferdinand Marcos for the presidency of her country. When we met, one of the prominent colors in her multi-flowered dress--the color yellow--reminded me: yellow ribbons had welcomed her husband home from exile, and yellow had been the color she wore to campaign.

Corazon Aquino: *I was a reluctant candidate...as you probably know, and I really was hoping, up to the very last, that it would be somebody else other than me. But the circumstances and the situation called for somebody who would be able to unite the opposition, and it was perceived that I alone would be able to do that. ...Here was a dictator who had really done much wrong to our people, and who, for twenty years, had ruled the country and had robbed the country from a better condition. And here were the people asking, you know, that they be liberated from this dictator and wanting that their rights and freedom be restored.*

My husband had been imprisoned for more than seven years, and then he had been assassinated. And I, at the beginning, I thought I would just support the opposition and not take the lead. But then when the situation, as I said, became such that it was only I who could be perceived as being able to unite the opposition, then there was no way that I could shirk from that duty and that challenge.

Q: That must have been quite the day when you went, in your own mind, from this notion of joining the group to leading the group.

Aquino: *Oh yes. In fact, I kept looking for reasons or excuses to get out of it...but then once I had accepted the challenge, certainly I put heart and soul into it, and I certainly worked feverishly, first of all to win in the campaign, given such a formidable enemy as my predecessor. So it was, for me, not only a challenge, but perhaps a mission.*

Aquino's sense of her *mission* carried her to a dramatic victory--and many challenges as president for one six-year term, a constitutional limitation of the new post-Marcos constitution.

Aquino: *I always thought of myself as just being good for that one term. And, as I said, my mission was to restore democracy, and I was able to do that with the help of the people, of course. So I felt that I had done my part and that it was time for me to move on to other activities. And also to accept the fact that perhaps somebody can do better than I.*

When she let office, the modest Aquino described to a Filipina journalist her relief at becoming a private citizen once again.

> *The heavy burden has been removed from me. I do not have to worry about my decisions, that they will affect many people. Whatever bad decision I make, only me or my family will be affected.*[1]

The strain of being asked to lead was felt by another South Asian woman when Solomon Bandaranaike, Prime Minister of Ceylon (now Sri Lanka), was shot at his home by a Buddhist monk on September 25, 1959. The prime minister had been readying himself for a trip to the United States, where he was to speak at the United Nations and meet with President Eisenhower. He died the next day. The mother of three children, his widow Sirimavo told me of the hardship of taking on the role she was then asked to play.

Sirimavo Bandaranaike: *I had no intention to take up politics during his life. Except after he died, people wanted me. I was more or less forced to take it up competitively...to lead the party after his death. I did not want to. But after much consideration, I agreed to take up the leadership of the party. Because of my discipline, I was able to do that, and take the party forward. And the discipline is all I had to lead the party politically—in 1960—when I became the first woman prime minister of the world, as you know.*

Q: Was it hard for you to become the leader?

Bandaranaike: *It was hard...I was never a politician, and I had no experience. It was not easy. It was a tough time for me, facing up to all these problems and controversies as a politician, to be sure.*

And finally Khaleda Zia, another woman who had led a secluded life and raised children, was also asked--within months after her husband's death--to involve herself in leading his political party. Her husband, then president of Bangladesh, was murdered on May 30, 1981, while he and two aides stayed overnight at a military guest house. President Zia had risen through the military ranks to a political career and leadership role as an elected president. He was shot by a disgruntled army general.

II

Violeta Chamorro, Corazon Aquino, Sirimavo Bandaranaike, and Khaleda Zia could not have foreseen their political roles, nor planned for their political burdens. As Violeta Chamorro put it: "...when I came into the presidency, I did not study to be a president." Aquino, Bandaranaike, and Zia—along with Benazir Bhutto, Prime Minister of Pakistan--are often spoken of as inheritors of a kind of family dynastic politics typical of South and Southeast Asia.[2] Such women--Indira Gandhi is another example--come from prominent families in which power is passed from one family member to the next, and gender is less important than family prominence. When Mrs. Gandhi herself was assassinated, the mantle of power in India passed to her son Rajiv, who was sworn in as prime minister within hours of his mother's death.

It should be noted, though, that a tradition of husband-to-wife succession is not unique to Asia, nor to Latin America. While Brazil—like Nicaragua—has had a variant of the "widow's succession,"[3] so too have the United States and Britain, among other countries. In England, "common routes to political power are as the widow of a member [of Parliament] or as the wife of a member who moves to the House of Lords."[4] In the U.S. it has been pointed out that, "in the first generation after suffrage, some two-thirds of the few women to serve in Congress were there because their husbands had died while in office and their governors had appointed them to finish their late husbands' terms."[5] It seems safe to say that the mantle of power could not pass from a husband to a wife if the woman was not perceived as possessing certain necessary personal qualifications. These might or might not include leadership experience.

What *is* a leader, and what *are* the qualities needed to govern successfully? Leadership is often defined as the ability to move other people--followers--in a direction that is mutually desired.[6] To do so may take many different capabilities--for example, a capacity to argue persuasively; powerful analytical insight; a full grasp of how one's political system operates; the ability to arouse feeling; the knowledge of when to call in one's debts.

Qualities of personality and character may be overriding: Does a person compromise too little or too much? Does a leader's behavior carry moral authority or lack it? Does a leader inspire fear? Reverence? And since all leaders face huge constraints, how can a leader act so as to minimize resistance? One scholar, for example, has described how Indira Gandhi--despite her eminent family tree-- "continually encountered male hostility directed at her gender. The disrespect ranged from despair among some Indians over having a woman leader to sexist overtones in the contempt expressed by her critics, as in Pakistani President Yahya Khan's outburst during the Bangladesh conflict, "If that woman thinks she is going to cow me down, I refuse to take it."[7] So, for a woman political leader, part of her preparation may simply mean thinking through what she could be up against.

As I discovered, most of the presidents and prime ministers interviewed for this book did not plan to be what they became. On the contrary, many found themselves--at some point along an evolutionary pathway--urged into leadership by others because of obvious qualities that they possessed and displayed. Some leaders expressed surprise at where they had, in fact, ended up.

For example, Maria Liberia-Peters, a teacher by profession, became, in 1984, the much-respected prime minister of the island nation of the Netherlands Antilles.

Q: In your background, you were educated [as a teacher]. Presumably you didn't start out thinking about being in politics...

Liberia-Peters: *Definitely not...*

Kazimiera Prunskiene became prime minister of Lithuania and negotiated the future of her Baltic country with Mikhail Gorbachev.

Q: Was there anyone, when you were younger, who had been in politics that you admired?

Prunskiene: *When I was younger I did not admire politics at all. And I was not interested in the politics of that time. I was more interested in books and theatre, but not in politics. And even when I was choosing my profession I thought of choosing one far...from...politics.*

Hanna Suchocka of Poland comes, like Prunskiene, from a country whose fate changed drastically in the late 1980s and 1990s. Suchocka, a highly educated law professor with parliamentary experience, showed some of the same reluctance about coming to the top as newly widowed Sirimavo Bandaranaike or Corazon Aquino.

Suchocka: *I ask myself...was it really necessary for me to be prime minister? I put the question, but it is a question for me.*

Q: I suppose if you were a Buddhist, you're on the path that you're supposed to be on...that there was a reason for you to be prime minister, and it may be a reason you can't see.

Suchocka: *You know, I know a lot of very reasonable answers given me by [a] friend of mine, [by] different politicians, but it's not my own answer...I had to be convinced that it was really needed for me to be prime minister for the country, but now after sixteen months...I'm not so convinced....*

Mary Robinson, the President of Ireland, is also a law professor by background.

Q: You really didn't start out with the intention of having a political career.

Robinson: No, I didn't. I started with the intention of using my skills as a lawyer to influence...legislation, and to use law as a kind of instrument for social change.

Q: Would you say that women get involved in politics usually because of an issue, whereas men often seek politics as a career? And start their careers off that way?

Robinson: *I think there may be a certain amount of broad truth in that, if I'm reflecting on the women that I would know both here in Ireland and elsewhere who have become involved. It's usually for a reason outside themselves that they want to change.*

Norway's prime minister, Gro Harlem Brundtland, explained that the "reason outside herself" in her case had to do with the issue of abortion. She spoke of the "terrible dilemma...of breaking off a pregnancy" and said that she "felt very strongly how the law had to be made." Her feelings led her to become very involved in Norway's abortion debate. She then elaborated:

Brundtland: *Well, you know when I was thirty-five...the prime minister of this country surprised me very much by calling me to his office without saying why. I thought he was wishing to talk to me about the way to treat the abortion issue...But then he said, "I ask you to enter the cabinet," and I was completely surprised...I never planned to become a politician, although I always had a political interest, always was engaged in political debates and thinking; I never saw myself as a politician before I was asked to become one.*

Maria Liberia-Peters is another woman who was invited in, as was Vigdís Finnbogadóttir, the president of Iceland, when friends and acquaintances pressed her to agree to run for her "apolitical" post.

Q: Some people say that women get into politics because of an issue that's very important to them, maybe it's health care or child care or something like that. That men get into politics because it's a career. What do you think?

Liberia-Peters: *Why do women get into politics, really? If I can say from my own experience, before getting actively involved in politics, I was very active in the social field. I'm a teacher, and in that way you were confronted with certain--let's say social problems--of your students, problems in family life, in the neighborhoods, certain needs and necessities of your students, which, at times, hinder them in making progress. And then at a certain moment, from your position as teacher and educator, you start to become the ears, and the eyes, and the feet of those who cannot walk, hear, and see. And then at a certain moment...that's the way I walked right into politics. Because I was then approached at a certain moment in 1975...International Women's Year...I was approached by the board of the political party to which I belonged, saying, "well, you know, why don't you get closer to the party, and why don't you get closer to politics, because it is through politics and getting involved--in being a member of the island council, being a commissioner or, you know, getting involved--that's when you can really bring about changes." At first, I said, "uh um, I think I can do my work best away from politics, outside of the political arena." Until I decided, well, let's see what it's all about. And if I don't like it, I'll step out--that's* *what I thought. Until you realize that once you have stepped into politics, it's a one-way street.*

Eugenia Charles of Dominica, a British-educated attorney, exemplifies a certain idealism that is typical of many of these women leaders.

Charles: *...we had had this march to present the petition on what you call the "shut your mouth" bill. The leader of the country then...came out and said that "we are here to rule and rule we will." And...you know, that was the sentence that put me into politics. Before that, I was very loud-spoken. I felt [I] was a taxpayer and I had a right to express my view. I was paying for it! But I found that [his] reply was wrong. I mean three thousand people had signed the petition, and that's a lot for Dominica, with its literacy, with its lower population, with a population that had been not very aware politically before, and I think that he could have at least said, "We'll look at this petition and we'll see whether anything can be done about it. We don't offer any hope. But we'll at least consider it." He could have said that much. But without reading it, without looking to see what the number of names was on it...to say, "we have to rule and rule we will." I thought, "Well then, well then, we'll do everything we can to take you out of the ruling position." It took us ten years to do it.*

Q: That was your defining moment.

Charles: *That's when I decided that we had to be much further than just being concerned citizens.*

My finding that a majority of the women presidents and prime ministers I interviewed came to politics "by accident" or by invitation is not a new finding concerning women leaders. It fits with other research on women who have played political roles, perhaps not at the *very* top, but during recent generations.[8]

Increasingly, however, women are not waiting to be asked to dance. They are putting aside hesitation, learning how their systems work, and, as did Margaret Thatcher, actively seeking out a political career. In my home state of Washington, in 1992, nearly one hundred women announced their candidacies for the state legislature, and women ran for secretary of state, attorney general, insurance commissioner, land commissioner, and justice of the state Supreme Court, as well as for the U.S. Congress and the U.S. Senate.[9] Many of these women won: Patty Murray, a "mom in tennis shoes," scored an upset victory to become one of Washington's two U.S. senators.

The challenges these successful women faced were only getting underway, as the presidents and prime ministers I interviewed could have told them.

Chapter II: Backgrounds

What you can pass on to your children is very, very important, and I say that to everybody who asks me about this...
--Violeta Chamorro

The women leaders interviewed for this book have been willing to bear the heavy burden of governing; too, they come from backgrounds providing some of the resources needed for such demanding effort. Almost all come from well-off or professional families, some from families of very great wealth (one exception is Margaret Thatcher). A consequence of this is the opportunity for education. Many are highly educated indeed: they are attorneys or law professors (four); they hold doctorates in economics (two) or some other field of study (demography); one is a medical doctor. If from the Third World, they are likely to have studied in North America or England at some point in their lives. In some cases, their histories suggest that an academic career is a rout into political power.

it may also be important that, in certain families, expectations were high not only for sons but for daughters as well. If we look, for example, at comments made by the prime minister of Norway, and by the presidents of Ireland and Iceland, we find high family expectations.

Gro Harlem Brundtland: *The things they expected from me and from my brothers were the same. Of course I was also the oldest child, but there was never any thinking that my younger brother, because he was a boy, would in any way be asked to do different things than I was being asked. We were just treated like equals from the beginning.*

Mary Robinson spoke of how her parents, both doctors, encouraged all five children to develop their potential--and made her brothers do housework too (her brothers even "claimed that I was the one who did

33

less [housework] because I was the only girl"). Equal treatment was the standard in this "very professional family." Similarly, President Finnbogadóttir found that her father "became a dedicated feminist when he had a daughter. Nothing was good enough for the daughter. And the daughter was absolutely capable of whatever my brother was capable of. Never a hesitation of that."

When one thinks of the number of major cultures in the world where the birth of a daughter is still considered a disappointment (e.g., India, Pakistan, China), or at least much less desirable than having a son, the "equality of expectation" in a few of these backgrounds is particularly striking.[1] Benazir Bhutto, for example, has said that "Pakistan is a patriarchal society to the point of caricature."[2] She has also said that because of her father's personal attitudes, there was "no question" that she and her sister would have the same opportunities as their two brothers.[3] Bhutto's father went so far as to insist that his favorite daughter do graduate work at Oxford, one of his alma maters.

In England, Margaret Thatcher's beloved father, Alfred, had no sons, but also believed in a good education for his two daughters. To help Margaret qualify for Oxford, he paid for lessons in Latin and the classics.[4]

It has been written that "just as many forceful male political figures have had strong identification with their mothers (e.g., Lyndon Johnson), so too have most women leaders had very strong bonds to their fathers."[5] While Bhutto and Thatcher are examples, my set of interviews suggests that the group of women leaders from which the analysis was derived was too limited. Without any prodding from me, several presidents and prime ministers brought up their mothers as important forces in their development. Lithuania's Kazimiera Prunskiene, who was exceptionally hospitable, invited me to her home and opened her interview by introducing her mother in person. After her mother left us, Prunskiene commented:

> I can't say that my childhood was easy. I was bereft of my father being one year old, and it was not easy for my mother to

raise three children at the time. But as long as I remember her, she was always helping...other people, and she was providing the best care for us. So, I consider that this is the teacher I took from my childhood and brought into...present life. To take care of other people, to work as much as possible...My mother taught me to work without pressure, and this ability to work I brought into my present day life.

Hanna Suchocka of Poland, interestingly, also noted that her mother showed her how to work hard. She said that her family had a "custom" of working, and that her mother, a pharmacist, provided such a good example of a hard worker that "I was well prepared for much work."

Dominica and the Netherlands Antilles have strikingly different cultures from those of Lithuania and Poland, yet Caribbean leaders Eugenia Charles and Maria Liberia-Peters also spoke of the central position of their mothers in their lives:

Eugenia Charles: *It wasn't just my father. My mother was just as strong...My mother was in control of the family. And he knew it. But it was because I had parents like I had that there was never any doubt in their minds that I was going to do the things I was to do.*

Liberia-Peters said that her mother "had a very central position" in the lives of her five children: "She really was the director." Her mother's presence remains influential with her today:

> *My mother is eighty-eight years of age, not very politically oriented, but the mere fact that I can go to my mother, she's a fat little lady, and rest my head on her chest and--just don't say anything, just keep silent--but just the fact that I can rest my head on her chest, gives me the strength to...restore my confidence and go on...God bless my mother.*

When one examines the literature on women's development, self-confidence or the lack thereof is spoken of over and over again. For example, the United Nations Institute for Training and Research (UNITAR) sponsored a workshop in the early 1980's "to identify the obstacles that prevent women from participating in, and benefiting from, political life in their societies."[6] The published report from the workshop noted:

> *Lack of confidence was identified as one of the major obstacles to women's greater participation in politics. A number of factors inspire, foster, or contribute to this lack of self-confidence. Numerous societal and familial pressures make most women feel that it is not legitimate for them to want more and more out of life, or actively to seek political change. Tradition and culture assign to women demanding roles within the small circles of family or immediate social groupings. Such demanding roles hinder women from gaining experience, and the accompanying self-confidence, outside their small circles.*[7]

Because this topic is so significant, the link that President Vigdís Finnbogadóttir of Iceland made between her mother's modeling behavior and her own ability to shoulder burdens ("responsibility is...something I find quite natural") is noteworthy.

Finnbogadóttir: *I had a mother [who] never hesitated to take on responsibility, and I see...now when I look back how very important it has been in my life. She was very engaged in everything, in social life in general, she was a nurse, head nurse in Iceland, an enthusiast dedicated to everything that she did, and I think that had much influence on my views, so to speak. I was against it as a child because I wanted to have mom at home, but later I see that, indeed, it has been a model.*

Q: Today can you give me an example of how you [were influenced]?

Finnbogadóttir: *Well...responsibility is of course something that I find quite natural, and I wish that more women would not hesitate to shoulder responsibility. I think it's very important in the upbringing of*

*every individual to teach...about responsibility, because it is this
hesitation--"not me"--that has not always a good effect in society.*

Q: What creates that hesitation for women?

Finnbogadóttir: *Lack of self-confidence, of course, of course...they all
have to realize that this is something that women have to surmount,
they cannot continue. We are not morally secure and that's our upbringing.*

Q: We don't get that much reinforcement.

Finnbogadóttir: *No. No. We worry about being judged. Whether it is
in large society or slower societies. Because we all live in onions.
Onions, yes. You are the core of the onion and there are layers around
you. And so you, you--I don't know whether you are like that--they say
we are afraid that those that we appreciate, in the layers in the onion,
will judge us; say silly cow, what's she doing now. And you don't want
to be called silly cow.*

Eugenia Charles described why self-confidence is so important in
governing:

> *...if you're not completely sure of yourself and you're not com-
> pletely sure of what you're doing, the direction you're taking,
> you give up very quickly....you have to know where you're going,
> you have to be sure of yourself, you have to be completely un-
> consumed with other people's opinion. And that sounds con-
> ceited--it isn't. It's just that if you want to be able to succeed, if
> you want to be able to carry out the projects you're thinking of,
> the policies you're thinking of, if you're wanting to do the things
> you think would help your country, you have to be able to be
> sure of yourself.*

Some women actually expressed surprise at what they had, in fact,
been able to do. Kazimiera Prunskiene said she was "amazed".

looking back, at the way in which she had been able to make decisions, despite having to deal with matters "entirely unknown to me from my early experience."

A human being's encouragement--or undermining--begins very early. Family behaviors which support a child's development and self-confidence were described by Benazir Bhutto and Eugenia Charles when they talked of their upbringings.

Benazir Bhutto: *Well, I suppose that the single most important factor in my upbringing is a sense of security and a sense of confidence which my father gave to all his children, and even if I said something foolish, he gave it as much weight as though it were the most wonderful insight. I think this gives a child confidence and enables a child then to develop [a] thinking process.*

Charles spoke of "*the whole spirit of the family where you sat down for meals together, and you argued, and you were never told as a child to shut up, you don't know what you're talking about. You're always allowed your opinion.*"

Thirteen of the fifteen women in this book are themselves mothers (two of them via adoption--Maria Liberia-Peters and Vigdís Finnbogadóttir). While their children are now mostly adults, a few children (Benazir Bhutto's) are still very young, or teenagers (Maria Liberia-Peters'). I believe these heads of government or state would all agree: any parent who is raising children well--laying down a floor of self-confidence--is creating a potential for future leadership.

What else does it take, especially to develop what researchers call a "transformational" leader, one who deeply seeks to alter a status quo? Both Gro Harlem Brundtland and Mary Robinson have been written about as feminist leaders of this transformational kind.[8]

Prime Minister Brundtland described the kind of parental values--"the basic thinking in my...home"--which led to her career as a medical doctor and an eventual politician:

...what I feel in my own upbringing and the atmosphere in my home was to try to do something which was meaningful outside of your own interests. You know, what, how can you do something which...makes a difference? How can you think to do something on behalf of others. This was the basic thinking in my own home, and I was reading the books of the early fights of the Social Democratic movement in this country, the physicians who went out and worked with people and did something, instead of being interested in their own income. People who made a difference in, on behalf of society. This kind of thinking and the right of every individual was always on my mind; it was not own interests, but everybody's interests. This is the atmosphere in my own home, I would say. And I think this is what has to be there if you wish to move things ahead in your own society, and, more widely, in your own part of the world, or the world at large, which has been on my mind since I was small, in a sense.

President Robinson described conversations with her grandfather:

The influence I think that mattered in the sense of altruism was probably the influence of my grandfather, who was a solicitor...he had to retire quite early on for ill health, and I used to talk to him a lot as a teenager, twelve, thirteen, fourteen...he had a great sense of justice for the small person...and the role of law in providing an opportunity for everyone to have their case heard. And he would give me examples, and the examples would generally be cases that he had either been involved in or had witnessed in the local courts. They were very local, small-town stories, but the under-riding value there was, I think, promoting a sense of justice for the individual, no matter what the background of that individual--respect for everyone and the right of everyone to have access to the law and justice. It was quite an idealistic grounding, I think, and it certainly conditioned me in my approach to the law....

She also observed her father at work at his medical practice.

I saw his patients come and go--the elderly, the poor, the young. Nothing was too much trouble for him. He would talk about their problems, many of which were caused by strains and stresses outside the medical [arena], such as poor housing. He injected a very real sense of looking out into the community and being concerned about it.[9]

There is one further factor not to be overlooked in reviewing the leadership potential of these fifteen women. With only two or three exceptions, they had seen relatives active in politics before them. They had watched fathers be ministers or mayors or provincial governors; they had seen grandfathers be senators; sometimes they had even seen a female relative active on the political scene. So while they might still have everything to master concerning the particulars of governance or a specific position, they were like the duck who hatches near the pond and knows that this is water. Politics for them was not like something that happens on the moon.

And certainly, when they themselves came into office, they learned that they were not on the moon, nor on a distant planet. As Tansu Çiller, Prime Minister of Turkey, put it, people "put you under the microscope, and they're looking at you all the time. All the time."

Chapter III: Through a Different Lens

What I find amazing is that, when a man is designated as prime minister, nobody asks the French if they think it is a good thing that it is a man.
--Edith Cresson

In a profile of Poland's Hanna Suchocka that he wrote for *The New York Times Magazine*, journalist Stephen Engelberg tells this story:

> When Bronislaw Geremek, a leading member of the Polish Parliament, called to inform [President Lech] Walesa of Suchocka's selection as Prime Minister, the President was momentarily confounded. "A woman?" he asked. There was silence on the line as he raced through the pros and cons in his head. "A woman," he said, his voice rising. "Now that's smart."[1]

Engelberg goes on to explain that Walesa guessed that Poland's male-led parties would hesitate to intrigue against a female prime minister: "Poland is a country in which men routinely kiss women's hands in greeting, and Polish men live by a rigorous unwritten code of what constitutes 'cultural' conduct. Many observers believe chivalry alone...constrained Walesa from undermining Suchocka, as he has all other rivals from virtually the moment he became chairman of Solidarity in 1981."

Suchocka, when asked by Engelberg if being a woman was helping her govern, replied: "I can't answer." She then went on to say that "my candidacy was accepted unexpectedly well, and...with a lot of hope." She added: "This was most surprising and shocking."

It is not unusual for a woman today to be seen as an asset in some political situations--particularly in circumstances where she is unexpected, or even a novelty, and can be shown to voters as a sign of a party's "modernity" or renewal. Such motives came into play when Turkey's True Path party chose economist Tansu Çiller as party head and eventual prime minister. The choice of the stylish, Western-educated Çiller--who wears Chanel suits and generally shuns the traditional Muslim head scarf--could signal to voters and to the world that True Path was up-to-date and European-oriented, and that Turkey was not some Asian tribal backwater.

But once a woman is actually in office, focus quickly shifts from symbolic value to performance. And on no question posed to women at the top was there more uniformity of opinion than on this one: Are women leaders scrutinized differently than male leaders? From all quarters came a resounding *Yes*.

The fabric of response included the belief that people expect greater honesty from women, and that their publics sometimes have greater expectations that women can solve problems. Here, for example, is Khaleda Zia of Bangladesh:

> *Many people have great expectations from women leaders. They think that when a woman leader comes to power, many problems will be solved quickly and easily. But in countries like ours, I mean the developing and Third World countries, this is rather difficult....*

Corazon Aquino reflected from her own experiences.

Q: Would people go at you more, as a woman, than at a man?

Aquino: *Well, I think in my case that did happen, because here were the people under dictatorship for twenty years, and so, you cannot fault them for having such great expectations. And yet the reality is it'll be very difficult to undo or to change completely the wrongs that have been committed before you...as I said, there were just too many great expectations.*

Among these leaders there was the sense that women must try harder, work harder, than men--whether serving in a country of the developing or developed world.

Maria Liberia-Peters: *I kept telling myself that my work was so important, and you had to put all into it, and everybody expected you to put everything into it, because nobody questions the preparations of a man over [a] female, not even in my community, and I think over the whole world it's the same...when you're a woman, you hear, oh, she's a kindergarten teacher, she's this, she's that and she's the other, and suddenly you are being questioned, so you have to put 100 percent, 200 percent in your work, you know.*

Q: What do you think the standards are that people judge a leader by, the woman leader?

Finnbogadóttir: *We all know that women have to do everything a little better than men. Women cannot afford to make [a] faux pas, as they say in French, that is quite clear. We're all so very, very tolerant when men make mistakes, but I don't know of any society that is tolerant when women make mistakes...there's a tendency to say...well, she's a woman. You'd never say, "Well, he's a man, it's natural that he makes a mistake." You do not say a thing. You only accept it.*

The double burden that women carry in being both leaders and (typically) homemakers and mothers was addressed by Irish President Mary Robinson:

> *If you take public and political life, women still have the main responsibility for family, child rearing, homemaking, and that's not shared in an equal and balanced way. And therefore there is that additional need, to be either more assertive, or better, or more determined, make more sacrifices, get up earlier, get to bed later, or whatever it may be.*

Margaret Thatcher called herself "dead lucky" that her husband's work was in London, her constituency was in London, Parliament met in London--"everything just happened to gel" to make it possible to combine motherhood and politics.

Maria Liberia-Peters explained that children do not understand why a meeting is more important than an appointment that one has with them. She summed up the need to "maintain an equilibrium between...work and family life" by citing a Curaçao proverb: "You cannot...put on the lights in the street and keep your house in darkness."

The question of a woman leader's female role--whether she is obliged to be married or to have children, in order to suit voter preferences--is a complicated one that varies from culture to culture. Benazir Bhutto explained to interviewers that, in conservative Pakistan, she could not function in politics without having a husband.

> *I was under so much scrutiny. If my name had been linked with a man, it would have destroyed my political career. Actually, I had reconciled myself to a life without marriage or children for the sake of my career. And then my brothers got married. I realized I didn't even have a home, that in the future I couldn't do politics when I had to ask permission from their wives as to whether I could use the dining room or the telephone. I couldn't rent a home because a woman living on her own can be suspected of all kinds of scandalous associations. So keeping in mind that many people in Pakistan looked to me, I decided to make a personal sacrifice in what I thought would be, more or less, a loveless marriage [her arranged marriage], a marriage of convenience.*[2]

It has been pointed out that "in the U.S. political system, voters show a clear preference for candidates with presentable spouses and one or more children."[3] In Washington State, in 1994, one of the male challengers to first-term Congresswoman Maria Cantwell repeatedly asserted that her single status and lack of children implied human failings of inner emptiness and over-aggressiveness. The gentleman candidate touted himself as a more appropriate representative to Congress because he is a family man with four children--an oddly outdated position if one knows anything about population growth's geometric progression and the disproportionate claim on world resources of every child born in an advanced country.

Two unmarried leaders I interviewed could see advantages to their single state.

Eugenia Charles: *It's harder for women who have families to take the flack, because it spreads out to their husbands, to their children, and so I think I'm fortunate to have so few relatives. I mean my parents are no longer there to be annoyed by this, I haven't got any children who would suffer because of criticism at school, "look at what your mother is doing"... I think it's easier, quite frankly. I'm not advocating that people in politics shouldn't get married and have families, mind you. I'm just saying that it's less of a burden if you don't have that to contend with as well.*

No one expects a male politician to sacrifice marriage for the sake of his career. It would seem a very strange notion indeed. Yet related ideas have influenced the thinking of President Finnbogadóttir, because of cultural stereotypes affecting women.

> *I'm not married, as you may know, and it is in a way my strength not to be married, because if I had been married, there would have been a great tendency to say: Her husband told her to say this. It was actually one of the elderly men, during the campaign thirteen years ago, who pointed this out: "I'm so happy that you're not married, because everybody would say that her husband told her [what] to say." While a male candidate would never have been accused of being so under the influence of his wife that she was directing him. That is a fact.*

Another lens that these women leaders have had to deal with is the media focus on female clothes, grooming, body parts, and hair arrangements. While men occasionally encounter media reactions to their physical characteristics, such commentary is to be expected for women--as Hanna Suchocka found out.[4]

> *I read such a lot of things in different newspapers on my...personality, my clothes or my handbag, on my foulards. I never would read such a thing for men. It was all so very strange and difficult for me. For example, I like this color you*

have--the jacket. I bought a jacket in this color [hot pink]--I like it very much--and once I read in the newspapers: How is it possible for a prime minister to wear such a color, such a jacket....Why? Why is it not possible? I am first a woman, second I am prime minister. And so it is difficult.

Edith Cresson spoke of how "cameras are not directed the same way if you are a woman....For instance, when you get out of the car the cameras are focused on your legs. It never happens to a man." Cresson went on to explain that there is a fundamental difference, "in France in any case," in the media's approach to women and to men. With women, the media like to discuss "the color of her dress, the way she behaves, details linked to her as a person," rather than her politics or the measures she carries out.

Eugenia Charles, rather amusingly, described the method she uses to deal with male criticism.

> *I really had a tough time, and they tried--it was really a baptismal fire. I mean they were trying everything to denigrate me as a woman. In fact, I couldn't allow it to happen because I didn't think along those lines. So...I just said, "Poor fellows, they don't know what they're talking about." You know, that was the feeling I had about them. Commiserate with them in their ignorance in this respect. I didn't say it to them in those words. But in the back of my mind I was saying "Poor fellows, they don't know what's happening," you know.*

Mary Robinson noted that it is not only men who react critically towards women in public life.

Q: Do you think women get scrutinized or reacted to differently than men do?

Robinson: *Women in public life? Yes, I do, and part of that I think is other women. Scrutinizing, perhaps sometimes very critically, and that I suppose again is because there are fewer women, and they're under a different kind of challenge very often for that reason.*

Edith Cresson pointed out that if anything should validate the competence of a woman in politics, it should be the fact that she convinced voters to elect her, perhaps over and over again. But often, she asserted, even repeated victories are not enough to establish one's right to have a role.

> *...a woman who has a position similar to a man's must always be competent, but this is not only true in politics, it is true everywhere. The fact of her being competent will always be something that, by definition, people will have a tendency to deny her. I noticed that, not only regarding myself, but regarding a lot of women in...French political life. People start with the idea of questioning her competence, whereas for a man they never do, by definition. If he was elected to such a position it is because he is competent. The only thing they cannot question are...elections because after all we are elected people; that is to say that the people voted for us during the elections when we ran....I never heard people say that was acknowledged....She is named prime minister; where is she coming from? A man, who during the course of his life has never been elected anywhere, and who is named prime minister (it was the case with George Pompidou and Raymond Barre, who had never been elected to any position)--everyone found that absolutely normal. A woman who has been elected for ten years at the National Assembly, at the "Conseil General," that is to say at the regional level, who is the mayor of a city, it is as if she were coming out of nowhere. This is the big difference in the way men and women are treated.*

In one or two countries, however, women leaders felt that the prejudiced treatment of women is changing, as women perform as heads of state or government. In Iceland, there is said to be a body of children born since 1980 who think the president of Iceland is supposed to be a woman. And from Norway we hear this:

Q: Do you have a sense that there is any differing expectation or lens by which people evaluate a woman head of state or head of government?

Brundtland: *Well, at least I am convinced that when I started in 1981 and became prime minister it was...something that could be misused in the election campaign of that year against the Labor Party, which I was leading....By playing on people's traditional feelings, cultural backgrounds, historical feelings. Because it was a new thing that a woman was prime minister, so clearly it was possible to play on subconscious, at least, feelings in people that--why is a woman at the helm? But in this country I think by all the years that have passed this has...worn off. It is not so easy, I think, now to mobilize so many in that kind of negative sentiment, but it took many years, and I think we saw something of the same in the United States when Geraldine Ferraro was nominated for the vice presidency.*

Q: But now, with your exceptional leadership, do you remove the fears that people have, or the misconceptions, perhaps?

Brundtland: *I don't think there is much of that now, because people have confidence and have grown used to the fact that women can do the same leading work that men usually have done historically.*

Let's let Benazir Bhutto have a last word on this subject:

> *Let's face it--women really started having careers since the sixties and seventies. Until then it was a very small number of women who worked, so the concept of the traditional ruler has undergone a dramatic change in the last twenty to thirty years. I think as the evolutionary process continues perhaps people will have a new idea of what the new traditions are, but until that occurs, you're still in the transition phase between one kind of society and another kind of society.*

Chapter IV: Leadership Types

*Women cannot lead without men, but men have to this day
considered themselves capable of leading without women.
Women would always take men into consideration.
That's the difference.
--Vigdís Finnbogadóttir*

Do women and men leaders have different leadership styles? According to Michael Genovese, an academic who has studied the subject, some researchers believe so. The style difference has been spelled out in this way:

> ...males use a hard style of leadership that stresses hierarchy, dominance, and order. Women, on the other hand, exercise leadership characterized by a soft style of cooperation, influence, and empowerment.[1]

A great deal of computer paper has been consumed to discuss this highly controversial subject--and many times more to discuss the role of gender in history.

Author Lawrence Stone wrote as follows when reviewing the five-volume *A History of Women in the West*:

> Is gender a useful category for historical analysis? It is certainly correct politically to argue that race, class and gender drive the machinery of history, and woe betide the historian who dares to question this formula, repeated in book after book like a mantra. And yet...a case may be made that gender played a much less independent role in the past than it is now fashionable to suppose. There is little doubt that life as it was experienced by a woman from a family of wealth and high status bore no relation whatsoever, before 1900, to life as it was experienced by a woman from an impoverished, menial family.

Status and wealth were far more powerful controlling categories than gender.[2]

When the *Harvard Business Review* featured a debate on "Ways Men and Women Lead" in its issue of January-February 1991, several researchers pointed out that a great many variables must be taken into account in comparing the behavior of women and men in a particular circumstance or within a specific organization. Jane Mansbridge (Center for Urban Affairs and Policy Research, Evanston, Illinois) commented, "Gender differences are fascinating, but they don't explain much of the variance between one manager and another."[3]

What do the women interviewed for this book think about female and male leadership styles? Certainly they have all observed far more men in action as political leaders than they have women. But do they see a difference?

In a speech in Denver, Colorado, in 1992, Violeta Chamorro clearly placed herself on one side of the issue:

> *As you know, certain studies show that women traditionally lead by means of reconciliation, interrelations, and persuasion, considering the fact that society has traditionally counted on the women to keep the family together, while men usually lead through control and intimidation. When women entered the fields of politics and business, they brought with them the moral values they had learned from home. These values have shown good results; I dare say they have even shown better results than did the traditional model created by men....*
>
> *There are several ways in which men do not understand women. There is evidence of this everywhere. I think it is time that male leaders look to women leaders as role models. They will find that persuasion brings better results than confrontation. And, finally, they will realize that, when dealing with the nations of the world, reconciliation unites people and allows them to work together for the benefit of all.*[4]

However, some women leaders offered other points of view. Hanna Suchocka was one. Suchocka has said that, in her former career as a law professor, she was surrounded almost exclusively by men.

Q: In your experience, from observing leadership styles, have you come to any conclusion that women have a different leadership style than men?

Suchocka: *No, you know I didn't notice such a difference. And, for example, when I analyze the...style of work of Margaret Thatcher, I see no difference....*

The style Suchocka speaks of--she has a picture of Thatcher in her office--has been characterized as follows:

> *Thatcher was generally more ambitious, more of a centralizer, more autocratic, less collegial, more confrontational, and more ideological than her predecessors.*[5]

This biographer then adds: *"This assertive style was essential to her success. Not only did she take her cabinet and party by storm, she also took them by surprise. Thatcher was different, and the difference often worked."*[6]

The comment the Thatcher was "different"--not simply from other women, but from previous British prime ministers, all of whom were male--makes one reflect on the role that expectation plays in leadership. How *much* can one differ, and within what contexts? Thatcher herself reported to me that she found no difference in style between the sexes, but a difference instead between "someone who wants to be in politics and in power because they believe passionately in certain principles" and those whose motives are otherwise.

When I asked Kazimiera Prunskiene for her thinking on leadership, her initial response did not focus on any differences between men and women.

Q: You've met other world leaders, mostly men; what do you perceive about their leadership styles in comparison to yours, or perhaps to other women leaders?

Prunskiene: *Oh sure, I have met lots of the leaders of other states, both of Western states and of Eastern states, and most probably even more from the East from that time, Soviet Union. And they differed a lot. Mainly due to different political systems that they were living in.*

It was interesting, however, to see Prunskiene move on from *this* comment to assert that there are "female" qualities that help women govern. Prunskiene said the following about her efforts to establish the independence of Lithuania from the Soviet Union during all of 1990:

> *I think that what helped a lot [was] being a woman. I was helped a lot in proving our independence, in establishing our independence, being a woman. Being a woman I found a new flexible way to convince the world. I found not such a straight and straightforward way to achieve our aims, which usually is very inherent to men.*

Q: Tell me some more about that, that flexibility and those things that are inherent to women that men don't have.

Prunskiene: *I remember my communication, my dialogue, and it was not one-time dialogue but a continued dialogue, with the president of that time, Soviet Union, Mr. Gorbachev. I never showed that I am underestimating him, I showed that he is important, I showed my understanding of his role even in our matters, but at the same time, trying to present our values and our understanding of the situation. Meanwhile there were certain forces who were inclined to present him as a tyrant, as the one who does damage to our nation. However, I thought that it's useless and even harmful to present him in such a light. I wanted to make him talk with us, to understand our position, and thus, with the help of the Western leaders, too, to achieve our aim.*

What Prunskiene is talking about here is a psychological approach to another person which she identifies as a female approach. It involves acknowledging the significance of the other individual ("I never showed that I am underestimating him, I showed that he is important"), trying to understand his or her position, and asking for understanding in turn ("I wanted to make him...understand our position").

Maria Liberia-Peters similarly turned to a psychological context when asked to talk about leadership style:

I would not like to generalize, right, but leadership styles, the difference in leadership styles between women and men is--I think that as a woman I would prefer the consensus type of leadership. Why? Because, again, going back to my background, in psychology and in pedagogics, it is so that you get the best results when you convince the other partner, why we have to meet each other. The other style would be, that you say well, you know, I feel that this should happen and this is going to happen and I expect you all to let this all happen. But if you can convince people why they have to do certain things and why they have to go along with certain things, then their active participation can be longer lasting. And it could be also more, you stimulate...them to be more creative, also, in adding their little grain, you know, of sand to the finding of the solution. So I would continue to try to manage through the consensus style.

The release of energies that Liberia-Peters sees as an important result of consensus was also brought up by Irish President Mary Robinson.

Q: What have you observed as the differences in leadership styles between men and women?

Robinson: *I think there are broad differences, but it's quite hard to pin them down. I think women instinctively are less hierarchical, and I find that very much at the grassroots level in women's organizations and voluntary organizations here in Ireland that I keep very much in touch with. They're very open and enabling and participatory and they encourage each individual to have a role and an involvement. And I think it's the same when women are--generally--when women are in* *positions of leadership. It's not as hierarchical, it's not necessarily a question of asserting that particular woman as an individual, as much as trying to influence others to come along a particular path, and trying to harness in a cooperative way the energies of those who are like-minded, whether it's a political party or in a professional group or whatever it may be.*

Here's what Norway's Gro Harlem Brundtland responded when asked about women together in meetings.

Q: Do you ever sit back as you're in a cabinet meeting and look with perhaps amusement, or at least observe in a clinical way, that the women communicate differently than the men do?

Brundtland: *Yes, but you know, in a cabinet meeting itself, the communication is always between both men and women. But if you have a group of women sitting alone, it becomes more clear than when they are mixed with men...women are more ready to use personal examples and to couple their principle thinking or political thinking with concrete everyday observations in their own lives and in their neighbor's lives, and that makes the discussions sometimes more concretely based and more substantive, and it adds something to the totality of that discussion.[7] If you don't understand the type of situation that a family in a local community is meeting everyday, then how can you sum up and have a total picture? Every person in a society is a detail, but the sum of all the details, or the sum of all the people, is how society functions.*

Eugenia Charles came at the subject of *details* from a different angle, but one that she still identified as a female angle. Charles saw no difference between women making decisions and men making decisions, but she felt that "women are inclined to...look after the details more than men. Men have the grand vision, and they pass it on to somebody else to put into practice. Women follow the details more, they want to know that it is being put into practice."

Q: Do you think that women could be open to a criticism that they don't have a grand vision?

Charles: *No, I think that you have a grand vision. But you make sure that with a grand vision, it is implemented. And men, I'm not saying that men don't do this, but they do this secondhand, through other people. And I think women have--they keep their hand on the button all the time.*

We have now had more than two decades of research on gender differences in politics, much of it done by women's studies scholars. State legislatures have been one focus, since in some U.S. states women's representation in these bodies has reached the twenty to thirty percent range (or even higher). As with other research, the findings have varied according to how the analysis was conducted.

In a 1992 article in *The Chronicle of Higher Education*[8], political scientist Lyn Kathlene (Purdue University) argues that gender research must become more sophisticated, moving away from "outcome" analysis--"such as final votes or lists of what legislators think are top-priority issues"--towards examining "how legislators conceptualize problems, what and whom they view as legitimate...sources of information, and how they use their positions of power."

In her own analysis of the 1989 Colorado House of Representatives, which was thirty-three percent female, Kathlene found that: 1) women thought differently from men about the origins of crime, and so proposed different kinds of crime bills; 2) women's bills were more comprehensive and "innovative"--and generated more opposition; 3) men and women behaved differently as legislative committee chairs, with women acting more as facilitators and men more as controllers of hearings; 4) men spoke up "significantly earlier" in committee hearings, even when men and women legislators were equal in number on committee panels.

"Speaking up early" is sometimes a way of setting the agenda. Scholars have found it to be one of the ways in which Margaret Thatcher effectively exercised power:

...Thatcher possessed and expressed strong views, and she always completed her homework, which made her well prepared to argue her case. (Indeed, she often appeared better prepared than her cabinet colleagues.) Typically, she would voice her views at the start of cabinet meetings.[9]

Thus, "Thatcher was quick to set the agenda and put her opponents at a disadvantage."[10] And "even when [she] failed to produce an agenda, her ministers sat in silence and waited for her to do so."[11]

Scholar Patricia Lee Sykes has these words to say about Thatcher's "different" style: "The search for similarities among women as national leaders occurs in the context of fundamental contrasts between men and women, which places women in opposition as 'the other.' In a sense, failure to find hard-and-fast rules about women as...leaders could...signal success for those who appreciate diversity and seek to develop their own identities."[12]

Chapter V: The Toughness Realm

On December 3, 1983, a small news item moved on the wires of Associated Press (AP), dateline San Francisco. It concerned a comment made by Charles Wick, then director of the United States Information Agency, to the newspaper publishers attending the winter meeting of the California Press Association.

Wick had been asked by a member of his audience why Margaret Thatcher opposed the U.S.-led invasion of Grenada. According to AP, Wick replied that Thatcher's opposition "was related to the fact that the British Prime Minister is a woman." Wick then requested that his response not be put in print.

What makes this story so strange--and so amusing--is Wick's amnesia about Margaret Thatcher: only the year before, Prime Minister Thatcher's aggressive prosecution of the Malvinas/Falkland war had made her a hero to Britain's citizens and had greatly enhanced her political standing. According to one biographer: "Almost overnight, her hold on power was solidified. Thatcher was now a world figure who [had] halted Britain's retreat [from Empire] and brought victory. Her popularity skyrocketed."[1] Wick chose to forget this history and instead fell back on stereotypes about women. He might have remembered that neither Golda Meir nor Indira Gandhi avoided being, in some phase, a warrior leader.

Issues of war and peace are complicated ones for women politicians. While a portion of their respective electorates want to--and do--believe in the greater "peaceableness" of women, another (often larger) segment is wary that women are not "tough enough" to deal with military situations or defense concerns. Saddam Hussein's invasion of Kuwait, for example, setting off the Gulf War, is said to have hurt women's campaigns for office across the United States, even though women fought in that war and some came home in body bags.[2]

Among the women leaders I interviewed, some felt, as did Vigdís Finnbogadóttir, that "*women in general* [emphasis added] are greater pacifists than men."[3] The president of Iceland explained the difference by saying that women "have this difficulty in facing death, premature death, and in facing wounded people." However, her fuller response was more complicated:

Q: How about the role if a woman leader is also the chief of state, the head of the military, who has to deal with potential military conflict, how does she do that, do you think?

Finnbogadóttir: *It depends, of course, how the woman is brought up. There are countries in this world that bring women in the military to fight, and it depends on the situation, and it depends on the mentality of the culture, of course. In my part of the world, in this part of the world, it seems to me impossible for women to fight, to carry arms, but however, individuals are so different that way....*

The same complexity of response came from Kazimiera Prunskiene:

Prunskiene: *In the younger days, the boys are usually playing war...the girls are differently prepared for their lives...I can hardly imagine a woman, a politician, who is seeking and escalating...war.*

Q: There's a belief by many people that a woman can't be tough enough to be in the top position because she would have trouble dealing with the military or going to war if necessary. What do you think about that?

Prunskiene: *I really think that women are more cautious in adopting such decisions. Surely they would seek for the other means which would enable them to avoid too sharp a conflict.*

Then Prunskiene went on:

> *But I don't think that the woman will ever sacrifice the interests of the nation or the interest of the state due to...weakness....*

Both Sirimavo Bandaranaike and Corazon Aquino were forced to deal with--and did suppress--attempted military coups during their terms of office; Aquino found that, at first, her military command found it "extremely difficult to accept a woman commander-in-chief." [3]

Violence or the danger of military takeover *at home* is more familiar to some women rulers of the Third World than it is to many male leaders of developed countries. Khaleda Zia knows well the history of the military's role in Bangladesh, and it has been suggested that her government is helped by the fact that her assassinated husband was a professional soldier before he became an elected president. Sporadic political violence in Nicaragua and the Kurdish rebellion in Turkey have affected the governments of Violeta Chamorro and Tansu Çiller.

And then there is the case of Benazir Bhutto, who, accompanied by Prime Minister Çiller, made a special trip to Bosnia to show solidarity with victims of the Bosnian War. A journalist has described Bhutto's official airplane:

> *In all the world there cannot be another plane quite like the official jet of the Prime Minister of Pakistan, Benazir Bhutto. The front section is a kind of office-cum-nursery, jammed with toys, briefcases, newspapers, nannies and Bhutto's children, Bilawal (age 5), Bakhtawar (4), and Asifa (1). In the main cabin, political advisers, security commandos and generals are keeping an eye on the Prime Minister they cautiously support. "Hello, gentlemen....Hello, babies," Bhutto calls as she enters the plane. It is both jarring and interesting to see soldier's saluting a woman with children on her lap.* [4]

This rather light-hearted description belies the searing role that the military has played in the life of Pakistan and in the life of Benazir Bhutto. She saw her father deposed and hanged by a military regime, spent six years under house arrest or in prison, and saw her husband arrested when she filed to run for office in October 1990 elections.

> *It was a terrible time. Two officials came to tell me: "Leave the country. If you leave, nothing will happen. But if you stay, your*

husband will be hanged and you will be disqualified [from hold-ing office]." And I said, "I won't go!" Later, some of them told me: "You don't have to go abroad now, but don't file [nomination peti-tions for the October 1990 elections]. Your husband doesn't file and your mother doesn't file. If you do, your husband will be hanged and you will be disqualified and imprisoned."

Forty-eight hours after I filed, my husband was arrested.[5]

Because she really knows what it means to deal with the military, Bhutto talks tough on foreign and defense issues, and makes no secret of Pakistan's possession of nuclear bomb information, although in August of 1994, her government denied that Pakistan had already built a bomb. In Pakistani culture, to talk any other way about these issues would be tantamount to surrendering a political role.

Bhutto, in the course of her life, has demonstrated so much personal bravery, so much real toughness, that it is rather ironic to hear her talk of being accused of softness.

I'm often told, don't be so soft. Be tougher. And I think that is perhaps the distinction between a male leader and a woman leader. I don't wish to sound like a female chauvinist, and I don't mean this as a disparaging remark on men, but just that-- men often say to me that I should be more tough; they don't mean tough, they mean more ruthless. I can't just drop people. I've been accused of being too loyal, of accommodating people who were with me during the period of struggle, but I've always felt that people who did contribute so much of their lives for the restoration of democracy must be rewarded, so that if a democ-racy's under threat, more people can be inspired to fight for de-mocracy.

Women politicians always face the "personal toughness" issue, just as they always face the "military toughness" issue: both are related to the way in which women are socialized. (U.S. Senator Dianne Fein-stein tried to cover the bases when she picked as her 1990 campaign slogan: "Tough, But Caring.")

Bhutto: *I was taught that ladies try to have good manners.*

Q: The opposite of that...is the double edge--that nice is perceived as weak.

Bhutto: *Yes, and that's the problem, because being nice should never be perceived as being weak. It's not a sign of weakness, it's a sign of courtesy, manners, grace, a woman's ability to make everyone...feel at home, and it should never be construed as weakness...*

Bhutto added:

> *Men are comfortable with being intimidating; a woman is not comfortable with the thought that she is intimidating, and therefore perhaps she tries to be a little informal, but that doesn't mean that the woman can't be tough when the time arises...I believe that we should be nice to each other, and I tolerate a lot of nonsense because I like to be nice to people.*

Corazon Aquino found that exercising executive authority and "being a friend" can be a hard combination:

> *In the beginning...when I had to fire a cabinet member, and where that cabinet member really was a friend...I found much difficulty there...as time went on I realized that whatever emotions [you] may have...towards a person, you have to set that aside, because, being president, you're not supposed to be guided by your feelings, but you just have to do what you believe is right, and what will be for the greater interest of the greater number.*

Q: It's hard, though, isn't it, to keep your feelings down?

Aquino: *It is. It's something very different, and yet I guess I didn't completely lose all of my...feminine feelings and ways, because people would tell me later on that when they wanted sympathy they could still go to me...I couldn't definitely change totally--I mean, I am what I am, and maybe I could adjust and do some things differently, but I still* *continue to be very feminine, and I was not about to lose that kind of femininity.*

In governing, Aquino also had to make adjustments to what she had been taught at school:

> *In school you're always taught to be polite, and you always ask--you don't command or you don't order. So, I remember, I guess in the first few months of my presidency, I would call in a cabinet member, or maybe a general or somebody working under me, and I would say, well I would like to ask you to do this. And then, of course I'm sure they were shocked. And then later on, one of my advisors pointed it out to me, he said, "Look, perhaps that was all right when you were not president, you know, to be polite and to ask instead of ordering." So I think that is one of the first things, one of the first differences pointed out to me, where, I guess as president, you're not expected to be polite, or you're not expected to be too concerned about good manners, etc.*

Q: And probably, there might be the perception, that politeness was weakness?

Aquino: *Yes. I think that is it. You know, that you don't ask, you order. And so, well, I certainly learned that fast enough. But in the beginning...I guess from the time I went to school, and during my time, there was always what I refer to as an etiquette class. In fact one day, every week, in the school that I went to in New York, at high school, there was this lady would come to us, and the class was called Lessons in Charm and Good Manners, or something like that. We were taught how to sit and how, what to do in social engagements, which is, of course so very different from what it is when you are president.*

Q: They didn't teach you how to order generals?

Aquino: *No, they did not.*

Two other women leaders, Hanna Suchocka and Mary Robinson, talked in their interviews about how the necessities of governing, or of simply getting involved in a political issue, had made them tougher women.

Hanna Suchocka: *I think that I changed a lot; for example, now, I can say that...I'm not so delicate...when somebody criticized me I used to be upset for one, two hours...then I said, why? Because it was not a just comment...now when someone says I am stupid, I say...you are more stupid than me. It's my lesson...I changed really rapidly.*

Mary Robinson explained that early on in her days in the Irish Senate, where she had worked to legalize contraceptives, she had encountered "hatred at the popular level":

> *I remember being very shocked and taken aback and deeply hurt, that I would get these kind of hate letters, and even have a sense that if people recognized me in the street that there could be a strong reaction, because I hadn't had that in my own background. And then I went through a kind of low period of suffering under that, and I came out strengthened, I think, by understanding that you pay a price for issues if you really believe in them. And I think I was glad I paid that price very early in my involvement in public life, because when you've paid it, somehow, next time it's a lot easier to stand up to criticism or conflict or public outcry.*

President Robinson's willingness to be controversial, and to suffer for it, is certainly the best kind of example of genuine personal strength. One group of analysts of women's outcomes in the 1990 U.S. elections found that "the 'toughness' a woman candidate needs to [demonstrate]...need not be a military record, it can be any story of...personal adversity overcome," and paths of altruism are certainly not excluded.[6]

Three women writers have found that a "tradition of principled, altruistic political service was forged by women throughout the nineteenth century" in the United States--despite the fact that women could neither vote nor run for office.[7] Accordingly, "women typically sought to exert influence through moral persuasion and education rather than in the rough-and-tumble world inhabited by the male politician, with all its partisan maneuvering. The male world might have been morally ambiguous and even corrupt, although not necessarily so, but it schooled its participants to compromise and deliver the goods. In short, while women were creating a political identity predicated on purity, men were learning to think of politics as the art of the possible and to practice compromise...."[8]

Practicing compromise can itself be morally good or bad, depending, but the above analysis came to mind when I reviewed the answers that women leaders gave to this question: What in politics surprised you most? For what were you least prepared? Several answers displayed some discomfort with the political arena.

Gro Harlem Brundtland: *Well, I think...in political life it is hard to live with the lack of integrity, the kind of infighting which is part of political life, because if you have entered this on an ideological basis, it becomes something that you dislike; some women will certainly be surprised at what they learn...there were things happening around me that I felt [were] immoral and [that] should have been different.*

Eugenia Charles: *I think that unfortunately women don't like the hurly burly of politics...you don't get into being a leader in a country unless you go through the nasty role of politics. And it can be nasty. Oh, it's vicious.*

Kazimiera Prunskiene: *Least of all I was prepared for the political game that usually goes on. I never expected it, and I had...to understand [what was] going on...even [when] I couldn't. I, when I came to power, I got into lots of "behind the stage" matters...I feel that I had to know about the political games earlier....*

Vigdís Finnbogadóttir: *I knew beforehand that there is competition in politics, and there is, let's say, negotiation... Other things are very much in the shadow--lobbying and things like that. The only thing I really dislike in politics is when, as we see sometimes, when there is dishonesty, even though it's all over the world. There is [a] kind of dishonesty linked to politics.*

There are now opportunities for women in the United States and elsewhere to study leadership skills in workshops and classes, such as those sponsored by the Leadership Foundation Fellows program. Such classes teach negotiating skills, the management of people, and strategic thinking, along with many other topics. The aspects of politics which these women presidents and prime ministers find disagreeable are certainly good case study subjects for potential leaders, if only as advance warning. As Maria Liberia-Peters stated:

> ...when you step in, you're very idealistic, you want to work for the benefit of the people and for the best interest of the people...until sometimes you realize that there is more to it than just--what had always been said--the interest of the people.

Chapter VI: Heroes and Helpers

It is a somewhat ironic fact that, when asked to name their heroes, their important sources of inspiration, women leaders named mostly men. But the reason is not far to seek. As Prime Minister Brundtland explained:

> There are...men in the picture because I did meet more men as a political leader than I met women...that had more experience than myself, because I was one of the early women who took on the leading positions, and for that reason those I could learn from were men.

Brundtland was to name among her "influences" Willy Brandt[1] and Olof Palme[2]:

> ...you know you stop having heroes when you get older. So now I would rather focus on what people have had an influence, made an impact on my own thinking, and then there are other politicians like Willy Brandt or Olof Palme because he was ten years older than me and I could learn from him.

In her childhood, Brundtland said Joan of Arc [3] and Golda Meir were heroes to her.

Golda Meir was, in fact, the sole specific woman named by these prime ministers and presidents as a hero. Eugenia Charles selected her, and gave several reasons for admiring Meir, the former prime minister of Israel, who took office in March of 1970 and died towards the end of the decade:

> ...she was so down-to-earth and practical. And she really made a lot of sacrifices for the country, you know. She really lost in the way of family life because of that, and that fortunately didn't happen to me.

Down-to-earth--in *Interview with History*, Oriana Fallaci reveals how Meir, if she invited a group of people to dinner, did all the cooking and cleanup herself, even if it took the prime minister until 2 a.m. or 3 a.m., when she was in her seventies.

Sirimavo Bandaranaike, listing Marshal Tito[4] and Gamal Abdel Nasser[5] as among leaders she admired, gave the following explanation for naming Nasser:

Bandaranaike: *He was very kind. As you know, they had a revolution, but not a very bloody revolution. They didn't kill anybody, they did not have a very bloody revolution.*

In a not unrelated vein, Mary Robinson put famous apostles of non-violence on her list of influences.

> *I don't have obvious heroes. I have been influenced by some of the idealistic people, Gandhi[6], Martin Luther King[7], and Vaclav Havel[8], they would be the kind of people--they all happen to be men--who would influence me because they are emphasizing very much important values for our time and for all time.*

Edith Cresson added more names of men.

Q: Who has inspired you, who has been a model for you?

Cresson: *Like anybody else, I have had several models. I admired a lot of people, essentially people of character: De Gaulle[9], Churchill[10], François Mitterand[11]. I also admired some people who are not well known, who were courageous in difficult circumstances....I admired them for their character.*

Q: Sometimes it is difficult for a well-known woman leader because there are not that many women leaders to admire in history.

Cresson: *Women only played a small part in history because we have only given them a small part to play. But there were some women who* *were admirable who, without having access to power, played a very important part in history....Women played a very determining role during the Second World War especially, and despite this only De Gaulle had the idea of giving them the right to vote.*[12]

It is interesting that a number of women leaders spoke of deriving inspiration and psychological support from their collective citizenry-- whom they often referred to as "my people." This terminology--"my people" or "the people"--is a very different language from that used by some U.S. pundits, pollsters, and politicians. Citizens of the U.S. are not unaccustomed to hearing themselves described as "the public," "John Q. Public," or--most alienating of all--"Joe Sixpack." (Somehow one does not aspire to the equality of discourse of becoming "Jill Sixpack.")

For an instance of the identification between some of these women leaders and the people of their countries, here is how Corazon Aquino described her feelings when she realized what "the People" were doing at one of her campaign rallies:

> *...they were poor, and certainly they needed every single peso, and yet, they would be passing out this plastic pail. And at first I was wondering, what on earth are they doing? Here I was giving my speech, and I was seeing this plastic bucket being passed around and it was only later when I realized...they were dropping money there. Because, at the end of my speech, the leader of the Barangay, the town where I was, would...present me with this bucket of money, and, you know, my heart really went out to them, because I thought, if these people are willing to sacrifice for me, then certainly I should also be prepared, you know, to undergo whatever sacrifices are demanded of me. I think in a way it was the people who really inspired me to continue with this. Without them I don't think I would have dared challenge somebody as formidable as Mr. Marcos.*

Violeta Chamorro described a year of campaigning in a somewhat similar way:

...I had a fractured leg, and I learned during that campaign how important it was to be with the people, to touch the people, to listen to them, and for that reason my own campaign was very easy as a result.

Maria Liberia-Peters discussed a strong sense of closeness to her people as it relates to the issue of personal security.

Talking, for instance, about security: I know security is of course very important, right? Because you have a very important job to do, a responsibility, you have to govern a country. I have children and they would like to see me grow very old. But I like to move around freely in the community. I don't like situations where, let's say, security officers keep me at a distance from the people, and that's why I participate...in all kind of folk activities, such as Carnival, such as neighborhood parties, and such...Because my philosophy is, if the people have elected me, then when they're happy I should be happy with them, and when they're mourning I should mourn with them.

Benazir Bhutto said it was the confidence of her supporters that enabled her to go on, to "face a very difficult odds," while Vigdís Finnbogadóttir spoke of her sense that "my people are my friends." Khaleda Zia asserted that she was not "lonely at the top" because "I am with my people, so I do not feel lonely."

Of course these women leaders also turn to those closest to them personally for support and advice. A number mentioned one or more close relatives, a good friend, or a husband who was a source of help. For example, here's Mary Robinson:

Q: And who do you turn to in that moment, you know, where they say, it's lonely at the top?

Robinson: *I would turn, in fact, to my life partner, Nick. One of the great riches I think about [our] marriage is [that] we were friends before we became more serious, and it's that friendship plus our relationship that is an enormous strength, and I draw on it quite a lot.*

Benazir Bhutto has received criticism from some women because she agreed to an arranged marriage, which her critics considered an historically outdated method of taking a husband. Certainly this method has long traditions in both the Western and non-Western worlds[13]. Bhutto once had the following exchange with a *New York Times* reporter.

Q: At the time of your engagement, many women's rights advocates felt betrayed because they saw arranged marriages as part of the second-class status of women.

Bhutto: *Well, I don't agree with that. People today do computer dating. Is that a betrayal? When it's difficult to find a man, for whatever reason, one has to look for mediation.*[14]

Bhutto then explained the role that her husband Asif plays in her life.

> *I feel there is someone to spoil me, to take care of me, comfort me. It's so nice to have somebody who cares about you. I was so lonely after my father died. I felt I was taking care of everybody else. With Asif, for once, I had somebody with whom I'd lay my hair on the pillow and feel I was safe.*[15]

Women in the West may feel that their styles of living are light-years away from situations confronted by women today in the Third World, and in many cases they are. But a return to the history books soon reminds one of sisterhood similarities. We tend to forget, for example, how recently it has been that Western women achieved their legal rights, or even their right to an education equivalent to a man's. One historian has noted that, in Anglo-Saxon countries, "women were denied control over their own property at marriage" until the late nineteenth century, and "equal opportunity for women in the field of education is only about a century old."[16] He commented:

> *In the long, sad history of women under patriarchy, nothing is more striking than their systematic deprivation of education, and it was this deprivation that robbed women of roles in the public sphere....*[17]

Chapter VII: One-Half of the World

In June of 1993, the *Los Angeles Times* published a special series of stories ("Women and Power") on women across the world.[1] The newspaper's reporters drew upon United Nations reports for statistics like these:

- Two-thirds of illiterate people in the developing world are women.
- As many as one hundred million women are "missing" in the countries of the Third World. In other words, normal mortality patterns are not present. Female deaths during childbirth, infanticide, and the "nutritional neglect" of girl children are blamed.
- Thailand alone has eight hundred thousand girl prostitutes under the age of sixteen.

For the "advanced" industrial countries:

- Women hold jobs that make up 40% of total employment, but hold fewer than 10% of parliamentary seats, on average.
- One out of every six American women will be a victim of sexual assault during her lifetime.

The leaders I interviewed are aware of the problems for women in their countries, whether the problem be sexism in France, reproductive freedom in Ireland, illiteracy in Bangladesh, or poverty in the Philippines. Today, many of these problems are increasingly seen not simply as difficulties causing suffering for individual women, but as restraints on national development. Human development, even more than the creation of a physical infrastructure of roads, say, or hydroelectric plants, is seen as key to national success, key to raised living standards. The Prime Minister of Bangladesh, Khaleda Zia, addressed this fact when she spoke as follows:

I can tell the women around the world, particularly from the angle of my new experience in my country, that women are still quite lagging much behind. Therefore, if the world is to develop and if the problems of different countries are to be solved, the women have to be given due importance, there women have to be valued and given recognition.

According to the United Nations, as recently as the early 1970s "there were few indicators available...to answer even the most basic questions" about women's situations throughout the world.[2] This changed, however, in 1991, when the UN published *The World's Women 1970-1990, Trends and Statistics*. Some of the information gathered was sobering indeed:

- "...in most countries in the developing regions, as well as in eastern Europe and the USSR, the economic outlook was far worse in 1990 than in 1970. And world-wide the population living in the poorest countries increased dramatically."
- "...the number of illiterate women rose from 543 million in 1970 to 597 million in 1985, while the number of illiterate men rose from 348 million to 352 million."
- "...governments seldom integrate the concerns and interests of women into mainstream policies. Development policies typically emphasize export-oriented growth centered on cash crops, primary commodities and manufactures largely controlled by men. These policies typically neglect the informal sector and subsistence agriculture--the usual preserve of women."
- Even today, "laws...deny women equality with men in their rights to own land, borrow money and enter contracts. Even when women have de *jure* equality, the failures to carry out the law deny equality de facto."
- "Women still play a very minor role in high-level political and economic decision-making in most countries."

The UN report could find a mere handful of nations with "enough women in decision-making positions to have a strong influence." The countries named were "the Bahamas, Barbados, Dominica, Finland,

and Norway." Dominica and Norway were, again, named as only two of the three countries where women held "more than 20% of ministerial-level government positions." The other country was Bhutan.

In 1776, after John Adams went off to the second Continental Congress, his wife Abigail wrote to him asking that he "remember the ladies" and give them the suffrage. (He was not sympathetic to her idea.) Today women almost everywhere can vote, and they make up more than half of most electorates. Yet their share in the world's elected parliaments remains low, and has even dropped from fairly significant levels (around 25%) in Russia and Eastern Europe in the past few years.

The women I interviewed gave essentially four reasons why there should be more women in politics now. One was: it is women who really understand women's issues.

Bandaranaike: *Yes. It is time for more women to step into parliament. We need more women.*

Q: Why? Why should there be more women?

Bandaranaike: *Because they are not considered. Women's problems are not considered now...women have to work very hard, not necessarily at a desk in an office...they have...family problems that are different than what the men have.*

The physical abuse of women which has now become a part of the human rights agenda across the world, with new groups monitoring the issue and world conferences being held, was one women's issue specifically mentioned.[3]

Eugenia Charles: *Women's problems are becoming--all the violence and abuse of women--I don't think it's a matter for women only to look after. I think that men are the ones [who]...are the inflictors and therefore they're the ones who require correction. But I think that* *women perhaps are taking different approaches to this than...what men do.*

A second reason given for more women in politics was the sense these leaders had that women are better at understanding issues of human support in general.

Vigdís Finnbogadóttir: *We in the Nordic countries...are very proud of the fact that we have used the good economy in the country for the welfare of the people. We have had such a splendid welfare system that it has been...a model for the whole world that knows about it. We have also gained very much in women's rights--for instance, there are more women in the Nordic countries in government, for instance in Norway, than anywhere else. However, when there is a recession, where do they start cutting? They start cutting at the welfare system, and that is where I think also women in decision-making could be of very great use. Women understand how necessary it is to have this welfare system, how necessary it is to have old people's homes and hospitals, and they are very concerned about education--education is the key to everything, especially for them.*

Some might be surprised to find Margaret Thatcher illustrating a "woman's point-of-view" when she asserted that, while people are "not entitled to be kept from the cradle to the grave by the government," they "are entitled to a good education...because that gives them the chance to develop their talents and abilities...also you need a safety net of social services, because life is so specialized these days, you can't have people in great need through no fault of their own."

Kazimiera Prunskiene commented:

> *I think that the feeling of care and responsibility for the children, for the aging parents, for the dearest ones-- all this transfers into her political life. Turning it into a cure for...other people and turning it into care for the state.*

Some leaders expressed, as yet a third reason for more power for women, their belief that women have a different (not necessarily a better) kind of awareness or intelligence than men.

Vigdís Finnbogadóttir: *...there are nuances, differences in...how women think and how men think, and that's quite natural because we are not completely alike....we can put it...that men can be grateful that they are as intelligent as women and women can be grateful that they are as intelligent as men. So there's no difference there. But the difference is physical and the approach is consequently different.*

Mary Robinson saw this difference in awareness from the standpoint, in part, of the roles that women have had to play in the past.

> *...women speak from their experience and work outwards, and do so with increasing confidence as they find that what they are saying is at least as valid as what they're hearing from other sources. I do feel that women tend on the whole to draw more from their experience and to want to play a role in a power structure to influence change--it's part of a whole different reference point. Women in most contexts are coming from a kind of minority, if not marginalized, position into one where they're trying to move nearer the center, and that brings with it all the empathy, the listening, and the sense of questioning, even...whereas if you feel that the center is your natural heritage, you may not be quite as open....*

Finally, some leaders expressed a sense that elementary fairness ought to put women in power in some reasonable proportion to their numbers in a population. Vigdís Finnbogadóttir, Edith Cresson, and Gro Harlem Brundtland stated that since most populations are half female, women should be represented by their own. Prime Minister Brundtland felt that this was necessary for the "right decisions" to be made and for men and women to "grow wiser together."

So how do we come to this kind of integration, where women approximately equal men in cabinets or legislatures? In Norway, one of the few places where it has happened, I had the lucky pleasure of watching Prime Minister Brundtland's mixed cabinet gather together for the announcement of the names of that year's Nobel Prize winners. In place of the usual cabinet cluster of grey suits: some grey suits-- and a lot of bright red dresses!

However, not all women leaders I interviewed were endorsers of the quota method that has been used in Norway to bring more women to parliament. For example, Maria Liberia-Peters said this:

> ...if I may say so, with all due respect, to situations where you have in certain countries, quota systems, there must be so many women in parliament, and there must be so many...I don't be-lieve in quota systems. I believe in trying to identify, because they are there, trying to identify women who can do the job, who can do certain jobs, and give them confidence, give them confidence so that they can do it.

Margaret Thatcher stated that she was "very much against...having a quota of women. It's totally and utterly wrong. In my life it's merit and suitability that count."

Hanna Suchocka, remembering days when Communist parliaments reflected Marxism's espousal of "equality of all citizens regardless of sex," offered this:

> I remember women being in parliament in Communist times. Sometimes I was of the opinion...that women didn't know [why they were] here in the building. Because they didn't understand what...work in parliament [is]. Because they [found] themselves in parliament only because [of] numerous clauses for different political parties...it was written that from this and this constitu-ency it must be women...the women in parliament now...are re-ally active women. And, of course, they very often have different opinions than I have, but they are active, they know how to argue. I think that the problem is not only the number of women, but...the quality of women...in parliament and politics.

While the issue of quotas--wherever raised--seems always to arouse differences of opinion, their successful use by women in Norway has depended upon certain features of the Norwegian electoral system. The country, like most continental European nations, uses a proportional system of voting in which parties (there are several, not simply two) run their proposed parliamentary (or municipal council) candidates in groups (lists) in each jurisdiction.[4] Each party that achieves a certain number of votes will get some representation, and the names of candidates at the top of the lists will be taken first, to serve. This is in contrast to an electoral system like that of the United States, in which candidates run as individuals, each of the two major parties eventually sponsors a candidate, and one major party winner emerges in each contest, regardless of how close the vote was.

Proportional voting systems give women (or minorities) a better chance to be represented; they also involve more coalition building, since more parties (views) are represented in an elected body. In Norway, the parties of the center and the left now reserve quotas on their lists for women. The big breakthrough came in 1983, when the Labor Party, led (not incidentally) by Gro Harlem Brundtland, adopted a 40% women quota for all of its lists.

This achievement did not come out of the blue. Agitation for more women on party lists began in the late 1960s. Prior to that time, Norway's parliament of about one hundred and fifty members had a less than 10% representation of women, no better than most countries today. Continual work by women's organizations led to 1983. This is the larger story of Norway's success, beyond the particular features of its electoral system.

One academic researcher who has studied Norway is Jill M. Bystydzienski, a member of the faculty at Franklin College in Indiana. Her research in 1986 "indicated that women in public offices in Norway contributed to a change in the political agenda and to the climate in government...Once a significant number of women (filling at least 15% of the total number of positions) found their way into government, they began to raise women's issues and concerns."[5] They also made it possible for politicians in general to behave differently:

Whereas fifteen years ago it would have been unheard of for a minister to excuse himself from a meeting because he had to pick up his child from a nursery school, today such an occurrence hardly raises an eyebrow...[6]

However, Bystydzienski has offered two cautions about these significant changes, one concerning Norway and one concerning reform in general: 1) "In addition to economic problems faced by the country, which have led to increasing conservatism and limited experimentation, the structures within which...women must operate are well-entrenched and still largely male-dominated";[7] and 2) the strategies pursued by women in Norway, "where access to public offices is relatively open and official ideologies espouse 'equality,'" may not work elsewhere.[8] Less open societies may require other tactics to give people, and not simply women, more access. The President of Ireland, Mary Robinson, showed her awareness of the need to think through each national situation:

I believe there are various ways in which countries will address these things, discussing issues such as quotas, role models, ways of encouraging, and I think it will be different combinations...depending on different countries. I also think that conferences such as the forthcoming Beijing Conference are very important taking-stock opportunities. It is important to have a whole process of taking stock...

The Beijing Conference to which President Robinson refers, taking place in China in September of 1995, was the fourth international conference on women which the United Nations has held. Others took place in 1975, 1980, and 1985, in Mexico City, Copenhagen, and Nairobi. The "final brochure" for the Beijing conference notes that "only seven of the 184 Ambassadors to the United Nations are women. Only four of the UN specialized agencies and programs are headed by women." The leaders I interviewed called for more women in high positions at the UN.

Q: What role should women be playing in the United Nations that they are not yet performing, in your mind?

Prunskiene: *Well, I think, as far as I know...all the different missions conducted by the United Nations are being led by men exclusively up until the present moment, and I think that this is not good, if we are taught about the development of democracy in the world, because you cannot talk about...democracy as such if you are using only one-half of...humanity.*

While Benazir Bhutto was able to point out that her own mother was active at the UN ("my mother is at present in the United Nations representing Pakistan and the Commission on Women's Rights"), there was a perception that women are under-represented.

Q: Let's turn to the UN for a little while. What role do you think women can--could--play in the UN that they're not playing yet, and what would be the benefit of that?

Peters: *Yeah, I really wonder, I really wonder at times why an organization such as the United Nations, that found it necessary to proclaim a decade to stimulate [the] participation of women, [in] all fields of life, [in] all aspects of life, still in their organization has not yet been able to physically give that example. I find that it is still very much a man's organization.*

In fairness to the UN, Prime Minister Brundtland pointed out that the problem of inadequate female representation has not gone unrecognized in important quarters there. She noted that "the Secretary-General of course has made that an issue and is trying to pursue this..."

Mary Robinson called attention to the way in which non-governmental organizations (NGOs), particularly networks of women's groups, can try to influence and support the work of the UN.

Q: Perhaps we should consider the UN to be precisely one of those models that should include more women.

Robinson: *Yes, and perhaps be influenced by the kinds of structures that are evolved by women, for example, the capacity to network, the* *capacity to link an informal grouping together in very supporting and helpful ways. I think that this way of networking and networking between networks and networking in a way that links grassroots organizations into systems, is very important. And I'm glad that the role of non-governmental organizations is becoming increasingly important...*

Sirimavo Bandaranaike acknowledged that not all women are awake to the role they can play--a fact certainly not unrelated to private difficulties.

Q: The country has much to be proud of: high literacy rates, high health rates. What more would you like to see for women in Sri Lanka?

Bandaranaike: *Women taking a more important place in the country, in the interest of the country. I'm sorry to say most women are not interested in what's happening in the country. They think of their families and themselves, but not enough [of] what's happening in their country. They assume only the men in government can play with the important part.*

Q: Why?

Bandaranaike: *Well...they've never been interested.*

Q: How do you get them interested?

Bandaranaike: *We have to do a little propaganda...we have to wake them up.*

Q: How can more women come into power?

Bandaranaike: *Well...when people work, they can come into power.*

Chapter VIII: A Handbook of Advice

Question: What advice will you give to the future prime ministers of the world?

Well, they must keep in touch with world leaders and know what's happening in the world.
--Sirimavo Bandaranaike

The women interviewed for this book represent a rich bank of political experience. It seemed fitting to ask them for the advice they would give--not only to future women leading at the top--but to any woman, particularly, planning to enter politics.

Their judgments and suggestions ranged over a wide variety of topics, and were sometimes funny, occasionally tinged with bitterness, most often simply serious.

Q: What advice would you give to a woman who wants to go into politics now?

Cresson: *Well, it depends at which level, of course. If a young woman goes into politics, first she has to join a project. Meaning you do not do politics as you do accounting, for instance, or anything like it. She has to join a project, to formulate or have contributed to formulate this project...to want and to agree to sacrifice a lot of things for this project. So I will advise her not to get involved if she does not believe in it.*

Margaret Thatcher's advice was not dissimilar: "Come into politics...because you believe in certain things. That's the only reason for coming in."

Eugenia Charles offered more on being serious.

Q: So what do you say to young women?

Charles: *I think they must know--they must know their minds. You can't do anything half-hearted, in this world. You must know what you want. You must, also appreciate, that this is what will bring out the results, the goal, that you're looking for. And then you must look for the right way to do it and follow it. And not let anybody else interfere with it.*

Hanna Suchocka, having served in different capacities, pointed at the difference between being a member of a parliament and acting as a nation's chief executive:

> *I [had] not been prepared for being prime minister totally; I was a member of parliament, but it is quite different to be...prime minister.*

Suchocka, as a law professor, was used to studying her issues in a particular way.

> *...suddenly I found myself in the position of a person who must know everything...And it was really difficult because I was a professional being in the university...and suddenly I noticed I had to undertake particular decisions without the ability to study or documents...I felt that one of the first things I had to do was to find a group of advisers, because without advisers, it's impossible to be prime minister.*

Edith Cresson stressed the importance of being able to choose advisers whom one knows extremely well--if one can.

Q: How does one know, determine whom to trust, as advisers, as ministers, in a leadership situation?

Cresson: *I think that choosing one's advisers, one's ministers, is one of the most difficult things. You have to know that you are not entirely free to choose the ministers (far from it). As far as I [was] concerned, my freedom was certainly limited. Indeed, it is very important to select* *advisers and ministers, and one must and should stick to people that one has been knowing for a long time (I was able to do so in some occasions); one must also select people one trusts because one knows that they are devoted to the general interest of the country and do not pursue their self-interest. Once again, one does not always have the possibility to choose, but if one does, these are the people that must be selected.*

Corazon Aquino spoke very frankly of the difficulty she had in choosing the right people for her cabinet.

Q: We all learn from our experiences so that, if you could go back knowing what you know now, and start back again, you know, from that point, how would you, how would you have done it differently?

Aquino: *Well, I guess in the choice of cabinet members. Before becoming president...I was being, well, lambasted by Mr. Marcos saying, how can you elect a housewife who knows nothing about running a government? To which I said, yes, it is true, I do not have the experience that he has; I do not--I'm not experienced in cheating, lying, etc. However...I felt confident then that I would be able to get fifteen men and women to help me. And many [said] that this would constitute the nucleus of government activities. Well, I thought that the main qualities that I should look for were honesty and competence in government officials. I did not know until later how necessary it was to have a third quality, and that is the ability to work well with others. I mean, you can have a cabinet full of stars, and really the most brilliant people, but if these people cannot relate to each other, or if they cannot be humble enough to accept that perhaps somebody else has a better way of doing it, then you are in trouble. So, if I had to do it all over again, I would look for men and women who have that ability to work well with others, because it's only in that way that you will be able to effectively carry out the government's programs. Honesty and competence of course are two very desirable qualities, but the third quality of cooperating and working with others is also an absolute necessity.*

Kazimiera Prunskiene also noted the trouble she had, early on in her career, putting together her "team."

Q: How do you decide whom you can trust?

Prunskiene: *It's very difficult to answer such a question, and I think you cannot avoid making mistakes. And also, I made mistakes in relying [on] and trusting...other people, in trusting those whom I invited to take part in my team. But I would say that with experience you learn somehow, and intuition helps you a lot. To see the person and to know that he's the one you can rely on. You see the other person and you find something strange about that person and you know immediately that you cannot trust or rely on such [a] person...At the very beginning of my political career, it was very difficult for me to choose the people who would comprise my team...Now, when I look back, and with all the experience, I think it would be much easier for me to do that...*

Of all the women I interviewed, Edith Cresson and Benazir Bhutto seemed to be particularly and strongly conscious of the power of the media. Cresson urged that a newcomer to politics have members of her team who know how to work with journalists:

> *I will advise her to try to form around her a very serious protection made of people who know well the media and who are ready to spend a lot of time with the journalists to explain what she does or what she wants to do, to get surrounded by a certain number of women, and I will advise her not to work constantly, but also to polish the image she wants to give of herself, and to polish it by frequent encounters with political journalists.*

Cresson issued the following assessment and warning:

> *...the game is not what people may think it is at first. And there is also a very big distortion of democracy which is amplified by television through the constant speeches given, not by politicians, but by the ones who comment on politicians; and the true power is, in fact, in the hands of these people. Someone who is in politics or someone who achieves something thinks that he*

has to fight against his political opponents, but in fact he has to fight against professional people who do not have to question themselves, who do not take any risks, who are never penalized, who therefore get what is the closest to absolute power.

Benazir Bhutto offered a somewhat similar analysis:

In fact, I think that we are on the threshold of a whole new world; the previous world had been [an] industrial age...But now we are on the basis of the information age, when images from one part of the world can so quickly and rapidly be transported to another part of the world. Ninety percent of the people believe what they see, so it's going to be information and the people who are in information who are going to be the real leaders of power and influence the shape of society.

She continued:

The media follows stories which interest it; not all stories are considered interesting, and usually those stories are considered interesting which are scandalous or which are not good...So in the past, while we taught our children--at least I as a child when I was growing up was taught about heroes and historical figures or even contemporary figures who would inspire one forward-- today there...seems to be a [reversal] of that rule, when an attempt is made to scrutinize and analyze to such an extent that one is not looking for the good qualities in a person, that's not news, goody goody is not news. But scandal is.

Ninety percent of the people are not reported. It's only 10 percent of the people who are reported so...90 percent view the remaining 10 percent. And we very much depend on it, on the media people, and that's why I see a shift of power towards those who are in the world of journalism, television, media and the entertainment the world of journalism,

However powerful it may be, the media is only one ingredient in the complex mix that must be dealt with by a leader. Corazon Aquino spoke of the need to hear out the views of all of the institutions and persons who are a part of a particular situation:

> *As president of a democracy, you have to contend not only with the legislature, and also the power of the judiciary, but we have these other sectors like, well, the environmentalist and other organizations...which you would have to contend with, and it's not as if you can just dismiss their concerns. I mean you really have to talk with them, to have a dialogue with them and find out how their perceived concerns can be addressed, and how both of you could be working together.*

After all the dialogue, Maria Liberia-Peters pointed out, comes the moment when a leader does what she's there for:

> *One advantage of consensus is that you can get a broader participation. But you have to know when the moment has been reached to say well, o.k., now I have to assume my responsibility. Because if you don't know, if you lose the momentum of assuming your responsibility, then you know, everything can be lost. Even sometimes when assuming the responsibility, you know that you are going to face a very difficult situation. I have had difficult situations of general strikes in the community where you go on talking with all the various interest groups in the community, you talk to the business world, you talk to the unions, you talk to the church groups, the women's groups, to all kinds of groups, and listen, this is what has to happen, and do you all realize for the benefit of the country, etc., etc., etc. But what comes out is that everybody realizes what has to happen, but when it comes down to unpopular measures, everybody lets you feel it's your responsibility. So then you have to assume your responsibility, come what may. So consensus, yes. But know when to assume your responsibility and take the decision that you feel you have to take.*

Hopefully, decisions are made in the context of some overall sense of direction. Benazir Bhutto put it like this:

I believe the most important thing is not to lose the perspective of where one is heading. To me the most important aspect of my own government, my first term and second, has been economic management.

She cautioned:

One must be flexible to survive in politics, not rigid, not dogmatic. Yet one must not abandon one's principles, so I would say that flexibility within a framework of one's beliefs and values [is basic].

Leadership may also involve finding new, innovative ways to communicate. Mary Robinson, when elected president of Ireland, faced the problem of holding an office that did not initiate policy or advocate new laws.

I've had to change the style and method of communication because the office of President of Ireland is not an executive, policy-making, or legislative-initiating office, and so I have to use the language of symbols, and think of lateral ways of communicating, and of encouraging trends in society without being directly involved in policy making. It's very interesting.

Robinson further explained her search for the "language of symbols:"

...in the inaugural address, I was trying to envisage the various ways in which I might seek to address an influence. And I remember that I said that I would wish to play a humanitarian role on behalf of the Irish people, because this is a small democracy with its own past history, which can give it an empathy and a closeness linked to developing countries. But in saying that I would like to play a humanitarian role, I had no idea, I had really no idea. I remember saying to myself, what could I do, as a non-executive president?

In fact, it has been possible to play that role in practice, for example, visiting Somalia and being general rapporteur of an inter-

regional human rights meeting in Salzburg last January, and in other, smaller ways. But I remember agonizing over how specifically it would happen, and I think it has been true in a lot of other areas. I wanted to link with the extended Irish family around the world; how do you link? You start, apparently, as I learned, with a very modest emblem, a light here in the window of my residence. And by placing that light physically in the window, where it can be seen from the public road, going through the park, and then referring to it--there will always be a light in the window [of the presidential residence for the people of the Irish Diaspora]--I have somehow focused on a symbol that has traveled all around the world. And when I go to Australia, when I go to New Zealand, the Irish community there knows about that light. So, it's very interesting to recognize the power and potency and communication that there can be through symbols, through language, that touches on values, rather than specifics, of immediate policy.

Finally, in leadership, there is always room for humor--and room for silence.

Maria Liberia-Peters: *I started out in 1962 as an early childhood educator. O.K. You do it [govern] with psychology and keep meeting, there is basically no difference in the behavior of a four-, five-, six-year old or a forty-, fifty-, or sixty-year old. Basically no difference. And I keep telling them that in the meeting of the Council of Ministers. The behavior of grownups.*

Q: Still need to pat them on the head, give them cookies and milk.

Liberia-Peters: *No difference.*

Corazon Aquino: *What...I learned was not to give unsolicited advice-- just keep quiet.*

Chapter IX: Reflections on Women's Leadership

Let us go back for a moment. What are the reasons articulated for having women leaders?

Simple and basic: women have different points of view, values, experiences, priorities, interests, and conditions of life. Theirs are not necessarily better, more noble, more important, but they are theirs.

Any issue carries different prisms, depending upon one's personal life. Cuts for kindergartens may mean something different for men than for women. A man may rely upon child care, but just not know it in the same way that a woman might.

If a man takes care of the household finances, he may be aware of and concerned about the capital gains tax and its impact. If a woman works in a low-wage job, she may focus more clearly on workplace problems.

A man can understand and empathize with the woman who tells of her fear to walk outside at night, but he needs to experience the threat and may not ever be able to do so. During law school, a professor of mine related a story of how Supreme Court justices, dealing with an issue of personal security, were unable to understand how a woman felt during a purse snatching and mugging. Only the one woman then on the Supreme Court understood.

Men and women can walk in one another's shoes only partially. The rest is either imagined or not considered at all.

So women must be able to represent themselves.

None of us escapes our background, sex, class, race.

This is of, course, true for the women leaders in this book.

Despite their similarities, they are not all alike. They hold different religious beliefs, different political beliefs, and different orientations towards their still-unique roles as woman leaders. While they are the largest simultaneous group of modern women presidents and prime ministers the world has seen to date, most of them have not functioned in an environment where they were surrounded and supported by many other women.

According to Drude Dahlerup, a European political scientist, three conditions are crucial for women leaders if they are to strongly support (assuming they wish to do so) the kind of feminist agenda that would be relevant in any country, namely, an agenda which ensures women's personal safety and security, provides the ability to plan and control childbirth, equalizes access to government and free market resources, and can change political and legal rules to give women true equality with men.

The first of Dahlerup's three conditions is that there must be a large number of women inside political institutions. Second, there must be well-organized, strong, active women's organizations to both support and criticize women (and men) politicians, and to act as experts in assisting on issues of importance. Third, there must be continuing sources of "outside" energy to continue to challenge any "Establishment" with new and more flinty visions. The latter two conditions are those that also help put more women into political institutions, condition number one.

More than one of these leaders came to power not in some ordered, evolutionary fashion connected with the conditions Dahlerup proposes, but before the "natural time" when one would expect such leaders to emerge. They came as anomalies to women's development, like wild flowers growing because of rare genetic mutation. Because of lack of a full supporting structure, the advances they can make for women may come in flickers--perhaps, for example, appointing other women to cabinet posts or judgeships, or to posts where their appointees can in turn appoint other women down the line.

To do even this much may require overcoming not only external forces, but internal resistances as well. A woman leader may, paradoxically, carry some of the same prejudices and stereotypes put upon her gender by others. Or she may strongly believe that it is up to the individual--female or male--to make a way in the world, independent, self-responsible, not looking to government to in any way assist or even out a playing field. Religious beliefs may affect her attitude towards reproductive freedom, which will in turn affect major issues like her country's population demands. A woman leader may sense that her mandate is severely limited, and that it is far too risky to extend herself into new territory or to take on the agenda that really represents her own unique perspective. Her party or her advisers may be strongly against her doing so. And once in office, it is a rare leader who does not want to maintain and enlarge a power base. Ignoring more radical women who are making demands may be one way of doing so.

Of course the external constraints are endless. In countries like the United States, where huge amounts of money are legally poured into electoral races to maintain the power of all kinds of special interests, financial hurdles may keep a woman from challenging an incumbent to begin with. The power of money and the power of incumbency are such that, although voters decry those currently in elected office, they generally vote them back in at a ratio of about 9:1 in the U.S. This in a system where key leadership and committee chair positions are largely male territories.

How individuals get elected in a particular nation can substantially lessen or increase opportunities for women. Almost all countries in the United Nations that call themselves democracies enjoy some form of proportional representation in voting--exceptions being the United States, Canada, and Great Britain. Proportional voting puts lists of candidates in front of the voters by parties. It is quickly obvious if a party list includes many, if any, women. A clear picture speeds the ability to demand quotas or other forms of demonstrable representation. Proportional voting also gives voters a wider choice of political views and parties, and, although it creates less stable governments and leads to more elections, it does open the gates for parties that have small but active constituents (such as the women's party in Iceland, or various Green parties).

When the head of the party that wins an election automatically becomes the prime minister, it is easier for a woman to become head of government. In this kind of system, unlike that in the United States, voters do not choose a chief executive directly. Instead they elect their representatives to parliament, and the leader of the party with the most representatives becomes prime minister. Those who put themselves forth to head a party are known to other party members through party meetings, actions on the floor, and other kinds of close interaction. In the much more diffuse U.S. system of naming a president, where parties count for less and less, and candidates must try to mobilize the electorate in state after state, the top leader who finally emerges is now likely to be the end product of television ads and a handful of "presidential debates."

What are the other factors that keep women out? Depending on the nation involved, the answer may involve cultural norms, religious beliefs, economic demands, educational opportunities, and a host of other factors that are part of a country's history, apart from the explicit mechanics of its electoral process. The first step for women in seeking fuller representation will be to analyze their own specific barriers to greater power. As can be seen from some of the country histories which appear later in this book, what has counted for women historically is to organize, organize, and then organize some more.

Various studies have indicated that, to make a difference, women must reach a "critical mass" in political institutions. The number necessary for critical mass has been found to vary. The United Nations Division for the Advancement of Women did studies in 1987, 1990, and 1994 which found that a 30% representation was the number necessary. Not to make a revolution, but to make a difference. However, revolutions are made one step at a time. Critical to a revolution for women will be the media, as Edith Cresson and Benazir Bhutto noted in their interviews. If the print media, talk shows, and other outlets do not cover women's "political" activities, broadly defined, it will be up to women to demand that they do so.

Whatever the limitations of today's media coverage, it has the ability to spread images, like pollen, around the world. CNN, *USA Today*, and other outlets all carry pictures of women leaders, and these pictures help remove, pebble by pebble, the stone wall which surrounds the definition of who women are and what they can accomplish. Vive la femme.

Chapter X: Biographies

Ten years have passed since the biographies on the fifteen women leaders were written. These brief sketches of their backgrounds, time in office, and, when applicable, what they have engaged in afterwards have been revised for 2007 in this current edition. Many more women have been elected president or prime minister since the initial fifteen leaders were interviewed. Four of them--Kim Campbell, Prime Minister of Canada, Jenny Shipley, Prime Minister of New Zealand, Vaira Vike-Freiberga, President of Latvia, and Ellen Johnson Sirleaf, President of Liberia—were also gracious enough to allow me to interview them, the transcripts of which are found in Chapter XII. Those four new biographies are included here as well.

Corazon Aquino – President, The Philippines (1986-92)

Manila--where I flew to meet former president Corazon Aquino--was troubled with brownouts, traffic jams, and pickpockets. Security guards and metal detectors were at the ready. Jeepneys with names like BABY and LOVE BOY carried passengers up and down the streets. The headlines of the <u>Manila Star</u> read: "More Terrorist Bombings Warned, Ramos Not Considering Martial Law".

President Fidel Ramos is the person Aquino favored as her successor. He took her side in the days of People Power, when thousands of Filipinos came into the streets to support her. When I met with Aquino at her office in Quezon City, on a hot and humid day, she was poised and gracious; she became especially animated when talking about the women's development projects that are now her special interest. Religious images in her office testified to her devout Catholicism.

...not being president anymore, I do not have the kind of re-sources necessary in order to organize everywhere. But...I...go to the affluent women first because I have to tap them and their personal resources...I feel since they have been blessed, then they're the ones who really should be prepared to make...extra sacrifices in order to reach out for those who have less in life.

--Corazon Aquino

Corazon Cojuangco Aquino, president of the Philippines from 1986-92, was born in Tarlac Province, Luzon, on January 25, 1933. Her powerful landowning family--one of the fifty or sixty important families of her country--was politically active: her father was a congressman, both grandfathers were senators.

A devout Catholic, Aquino was educated at parochial schools in Manila and the United States. She graduated from Mount St. Vincent College in New York City and returned to the Philippines to attend law school at Far Eastern University. In 1954, however, she made a decision that was to have more consequences than she or anyone could have imagined: she left law school after her first year to marry Benigno Aquino, Jr., a successful young journalist who would soon leave journalism for politics to become one of his country's martyrs.

Like Corazon, Benigno "Ninoy" Aquino came from a wealthy landowning family involved in sugar plantations; however, an article that he authored for *Foreign Affairs* magazine in 1968 showed his awareness of his country's problems: "Here is a land in which a few are spectacularly rich while the masses remain abjectly poor...a land consecrated to democracy but run by an entrenched plutocracy... honeycombed with graft." Ferdinand Marcos had come to power in 1965; in 1972 he was to declare martial law and throw Ninoy Aquino into prison for more than seven years.

Corazon "Cory" Aquino has defined the period of her husband's imprisonment as the pivotal crisis in her life. A shy person who had previously devoted herself to a private existence raising their five children, she became her husband's link with the outside world, receiving weekly tutoring from him as he tried to remain politically involved from behind prison walls. Eventually Ninoy was allowed to go to the U.S. for medical treatment. The family settled in Newton, Massachusetts, from 1980-83, where Ninoy worked as a research fellow at Harvard University and MIT. However, when Marcos declared elections for 1984, Benigno Aquino decided to return home. His plane had barely touched down at Manila Airport on August 21, 1983, when he was assassinated. Word was telephoned to his family, still in the U.S.

Aquino returned to the Philippines to lead processions to her husband's lying-in-state and to his grave. She began working for anti-Marcos candidates, fifty-six of whom gained seats in the National Assembly in October of 1985. Although not seen as a political leader immediately upon her return, Aquino eventually was recognized by anti-Marcos politicians as someone who could mobilize the electorate. A "Cory for President" movement began; she asked for, and received, a million signatures in support of her candidacy within a month. A forty-five-day election campaign started, with her opponent, Marcos, sometimes declaring that "a woman's place is in the bedroom." When Marcos eventually tried to steal the election, the people of Manila came into the streets by the hundreds of thousands; two of Marcos's key military leaders revolted. Marcos was forced to fly into exile. Corazon Aquino became her country's president.

Aquino saw her mandate as a continuation of her husband's attempt to restore democracy to the Philippines. She called for a new constitution which set more limits on presidential power; she abided by that constitution when she left office after one six-year term. Her presidency was troubled by continual attempted military revolts; seven separate attempts resulted in more than one hundred fifty deaths. When Aquino made her first official visit to the Philippine Military Academy, she reminded those present: "This revolution began with a bullet shot by a soldier into the head of my husband."

In her interview for this book, Aquino spoke of her efforts to initiate military reform: "Well, first the military found it extremely difficult to accept a woman commander-in-chief. And certainly it was also difficult for me...I was, in fact, very directly responsible for putting in...reforms in...selecting the colonels who would become the generals. Before my time, the process was very subjective...the criteria...had not been quantified."

Aquino also concerned herself with the appointment of women to high positions. She tapped a number of them to head departments or commissions, and appointed three women (of fifteen justices) to the Supreme Court. In the later years of her administration, Cory Aquino focused her attention on assisting the development of non-governmental organizations (NGOs) and cooperatives. She once told a Filipina journalist: "Government cannot do it alone. This is the reason I want to be more involved in the NGOs."

After leaving office, Aquino retired from politics, but continued her work with NGOs. She is a chairperson of the Benigno S. Aquino Jr. Foundation, which links NGOs to raise the quality of life for Filipinos. Aquino is also a co-president of the Forum of Democratic Leaders in the Asia-Pacific, which promotes democratic solidarity in the region.

On August 21, 2003--the 20th anniversary of Ninoy's death--she launched the People Power People Movement to identify outstanding organizations. Aquino wrote: "My current goal is to expand the concept of People Power, with which I hope to be forever associated. People Power shouldn't be a mere political tool. It can be used to create jobs, deliver social services, improve the lives of all our people."[1]

Sirimavo Bandaranaike – Prime Minister, Sri Lanka (1960-65; 1970-77; 1994-2000; d. 2000)

Sirimavo Bandaranaike's hobby is growing roses, and some of these beautiful flowers were visible when I visited her home in November of 1993 to interview her. In the periods of her prime ministerships, she told me, she got little time to garden, little personal time at all.

"Mrs. Banda," as she is known in Sri Lanka, has dark eyes, a skin of light tan, and her hair severely pulled back in a bun. A number of male

aides stood by during our interview, somewhat on guard, ready to assist her as needed. During the course of the visit, she showed me photographs of her husband, Solomon, and of members of the Gandhi family, with whom they were friends.

Q. How do you think that men and women differ as leaders?

Well, probably women deal with things a little more humanely. Men are tough and impatient.

--Sirimavo Bandaranaike

In 1960, Sirimavo Bandaranaike of Sri Lanka (then Ceylon) became the world's first elected woman prime minister.

Born on April 17, 1916 into a well-off and politically-involved family with five children, Sirimavo Ratwatte described her upbringing when she was interviewed for this book.

> *I was brought up in my maternal grandfather's home by my parents and grandparents, who belonged to the landed gentry... We were a very closely knit family...We are a Buddhist family and followed Buddhist philosophy.*

For her schooling, Bandaranaike was sent to a Catholic convent school in Colombo, where she remained until age eighteen. Six years later, her parents arranged for her marriage to an Oxford-educated lawyer-politician who also came from a wealthy landowning family. Her new father-in-law had once been a chief aide to the British governor of Ceylon.

By the time of Ceylon's near-complete independence from Britain in 1948 (Ceylon still had a governor-general tie to Britain's Crown), Sirimavo Bandaranaike was raising her children--there were eventually three--and was active in the Ceylon Women's Association (*Lanka Mahila Samiti*). Its aim was "to ameliorate rural conditions and improve the social and economic life of the people, particularly in the rural areas" of Ceylon. Family planning and women's development became two of her concerns.

Bandaranaike's husband Solomon, meanwhile, had been elected to the new House of Representatives and had served as minister of health and local government in the cabinet of D.D. Senanayake, Ceylon's first prime minister after independence. A socialist and strong nationalist, Solomon Bandaranaike eventually, in 1956, became prime minister himself. Part of his program involved replacing English with Sinhalese as the national language, and making Buddhism the national religion. These proposals, opposed by Ceylon's Tamil-speaking Hindu minority, set off riots. Eventually a state of emergency was declared. In September of 1959, Solomon Bandaranaike was assassinated.

His grieving widow was asked to campaign on behalf of his party, the Sri Lanka Freedom Party (SLFP). In May 1960 she became its leader. In July, the SLFP won 75 of 151 seats in the House of Representatives. "Mrs. Banda", as party leader, was appointed prime minister, serving in that capacity until 1965.

Sirimavo Bandaranaike did not serve briefly and then retire into private life. Despite an initial reluctance to play a political role, in time she became a professional politician, sometimes in and sometimes out of office. A leftist-nationalist like her husband, her politics often challenged the Cold War policies of the United States and were in turn challenged by ultra-leftists within Ceylon. During her second term as prime minister, from 1970-1977, Ceylon became the Socialist Republic of Sri Lanka, severing all remaining political ties to Britain.

Bandaranaike's bid for the presidency in 1986 was unsuccessful, but she won a seat in the National Assembly in 1989 and headed the opposition. In August 1994, her daughter--Chandrika Bandaranaike Kumaratunga--became the new prime minister. In November, Kumaratunga was elected as Sri Lanka's first woman president, and, at the age of 78, Sirimavo Bandaranaike was appointed to her third and final term as prime minister.

She filled the office for six years, resigning in August of 2000. Two months later, on October 10, 2000, Sirimavo Bandaranaike suffered a fatal heart attack on her way home from voting in the general elections.

Benazir Bhutto – Prime Minister, Pakistan (1988-90; 1993-96; d. 2007)

In a dazzlingly bright blue dress with black dots, and with her usual Muslim head scarf over her dark hair, Benazir Bhutto made a bit of a grand entrance as she appeared in the luxurious living room of her home to greet me. She sat down on a beige sofa and interacted tenderly with her shy, very young daughter. A sealed package of Susan B. Anthony coins which I had brought as a gift was opened by Bhutto's security staff--a small sign of the safety measures surrounding her.

Bhutto is dignified, eloquent, and charismatic. She speaks English with touches of an Oxbridge accent, thanks to her several years in Britain. She is a fiery public speaker who can animate large crowds of admirers.

> *I was extremely idealistic as a child, I still am idealistic to a great extent. But I found that in life everything is not up front as we would wish it to be and that some of us are too simple. I think I was a very simple, naive person, and the knocks of life have taught me that life is not always fair, it is not always just, but even if it is not fair, and even if it is not just, it is important to go on working for what you believe in.*
> *--Benazir Bhutto*

Benazir Bhutto's political life has been a hard journey in a harsh land. Pakistan's military has governed her country for half of the years since independence from Britain in 1947. The parliamentary government in Pakistan masks the power of the generals, who stand ready to intervene in affairs. They hanged Bhutto's father in 1979 – a pivotal event in her life.

Benazir Bhutto had just returned from several years of study abroad, in 1977, when the army surrounded her family's house and took her father, the prime minister, away to jail. Zulfikar Bhutto had two sons and two daughters; Benazir was his particular favorite. From prison, he asked her to carry on his work.

She was born in Karachi on June 21, 1953, to Zulfikar's second wife, Nusrat. The Muslim family was "feudals"--one of the important landowning families of Pakistan, sometimes called "the twenty-two." Educated by Catholic nuns at a convent school in her early years – as were several of the other leaders in this book, regardless of family religious background--Benazir Bhutto was sent abroad for her post-secondary education.

She graduated from Harvard (cum laude) in 1973 with a degree in government; her father insisted that she continue on to Oxford, which he had attended. There she became the first foreign woman to be elected president of the Oxford Union, the university's famous debating society; her father had also headed it. She has called her years in England her happiest. By 1977, it was time to return home to begin a career in diplomacy.

Instead, Bhutto found herself placed under house arrest or jailed, time after time for years, as she protested her father's incarceration and the rule of the military. Hers were not country club jails. At times she was in solitary confinement, suffering from extremes of heat and cold; poison was deliberately left in her cell as a temptation to suicide. At one point she was told that she might have uterine cancer, and subjected to an operation whose results were never made known to her. Pressure from abroad, and a dangerous ear infection, finally led to her being allowed to leave Pakistan for London in January of 1984. From there she continued to protest conditions at home, focusing her efforts on the forty thousand political prisoners incarcerated there.

Bhutto's opportunity to return to Pakistan came in April, 1986. General Mohammed Zia ul-Haq, the martial law ruler, felt secure enough to allow political parties to operate once again. Huge crowds greeted Bhutto's return, and she campaigned for two years to build up her Pakistan People's Party, calling herself the "sister" of her people.

In 1987, she agreed to an arranged marriage with Asif Zardari, a businessman of similar social background. She felt that marriage was a necessity for political reasons, and this marriage turned out to be a fulfilling one. The couple have three children.

In the summer of 1988, General Zia was mysteriously killed in an airplane crash. Bhutto and her mother (a member of parliament) led their party to victory in autumn elections. In December of 1988, Bhutto again walked in her father's footsteps by becoming prime minister of Pakistan. She was the first woman to lead a modern Muslim state. Despite her previous hardships, the obstacles had only just begun.

To be able to freely govern, Bhutto agreed not to reduce Pakistan's military budget nor interfere in Afghan policy, which supported the Afghanistan guerrilla movement. The agreements reduced monies available for the social programs that she had promised and since her party did not hold a majority in either house of parliament, little significant legislation was passed. Bhutto was able to remove restrictions on the press, trade unions, and student organizations, and to free women who had been imprisoned under Pakistan's Hudood ordinances. But the ordinances – permitting women to be lashed or stoned for adultery (or for rape called adultery) – remained in place. On August 6, 1990, Pakistani President Ghulam Ishaq Khan exercised his constitutional prerogative and dismissed Bhutto as prime minister.

However, she remained in the National Assembly as leader of the opposition. In October of 1993, after three years of government crises and disputed elections, she was named prime minister for a second time. Major distractions were to include disputes with her mother and a brother returned from exile over the latter's political role in a country where males are dominant over women. Bhutto's brother was later killed in a police encounter.

In 1996, Benazir Bhutto's government was again dismissed, amid allegations of corruption. Her husband was jailed, and Bhutto went into self-imposed exile with her children and mother. None of the corruption charges were ever maintained; she continued to denounce them as politically motivated, citing a precedent of similar charges being leveled at "every civilian prime minister [in Pakistan] since 1950."[2]

While in exile, Bhutto reached out to a former political opponent and fellow former exiled prime minister, Nawaz Sharif. As of mid-August 2007, the Supreme Court allowed Sharif to return to Pakistan, enabling him to contest presidential elections scheduled for the end of that year. Bhutto continued negotiations for a power-sharing deal, which incorporated a plan for transition to democracy, with General Pervez Musharraf, who seized control during the 1999 coup. The proposed deal was initiated to quell the growing unrest during Musharraf's presidency, and included Musharraf stepping down from his military position.[3]

Bhutto returned to Pakistan in order to run in the elections that were to take place in late 2007 and early 2008. While campaigning in the run-up to the parliamentary elections, she narrowly avoided death from an attack by a suicide bomber. Following the attack she was placed under house arrest by President Musharraf. After being taken off house arrest she continued her campaign. On December 27, 2007, Bhutto was standing and waving to supporters from the sunroof of her bullet-proof vehicle when gunment opened fire. Her vehicle was also targeted with explosives, killing over 20 people. Critically wounded, she was rushed to a nearby hospital but died after undergoing surgery. Benazir Bhutto was the first modern woman to gain political power in a Muslim country.

In 2008, Benazir Bhutto's husband was elected President of Pakistan.

Gro Harlem Brundtland – Prime Minister, Norway (1981; 1986-89; 1990-96)

Norway's prime minister, a native of Oslo, impresses one immediately as a take-charge person with a precise, analytical mind. Her name has come up as possible top Secretary-General of the United Nations.

A pragmatist as well as an idealist, Bruntland can cap wages or devalue currency when necessary, but she is a strong defender of Norway's highly developed "safety net." As she has said, if you are born strong, with parents who give you the best, you have an even stronger responsibility for the people who didn't get the same start." [4]

The prime minister skis and sails. The story is often told of how, when her husband accidentally fell from their sailboat during a sail, and could not climb back on board, Gro Harlem Brundtland was able to bring him and their boat home through rough water after two hours of struggle.

> *It's very difficult to evaluate a leader in a very short-term perspective because to be a leader you must be able to have a long-term perspective. You must be able to carry changes which take many years. And this is why you can really see whether it has been a good leadership after some years have passed.*

> *--Gro Harlem Brundtland*

Gro Harlem Brundtland, a medical doctor, was Norway's prime minister on three separate occasions during the 1980s and 1990s-- each subsequent time for a longer period. She is a dominant presence in her country and has an international reputation for her work on the environment and with the World Health Organization.

Brundtland was born in a suburb of Oslo on April 20, 1939, one of four children. Her father was a physician who would hold cabinet posts in Labor governments, and both parents were political activists. Brundtland herself was involved in Labor activities by age seven, when she joined an affiliated youth group.

In 1960, while attending medical school at Oslo University, Gro Harlem married Arne Brundtland, a political science student; they began a family of four children. The mid-1960s found both parents studying at Harvard, where Gro Brundtland earned a master's degree in public health in 1965 focusing on environmental studies.

Back in Norway, Brundtland held several government posts administering health care services. As she pointed out in her interview, it was her strong feelings about abortion rights for women that brought her to public attention when the issue was debated in Norway in the 1970s.

Being appointed Norway's minister of the environment in 1974 further increased her public recognition. The following year she was elected deputy leader of the Labor party. In 1979, she resigned from her environmental post to enter the Storting (Parliament) and to work at building up her party. In February of 1981, after a Labor prime minister resigned, she was chosen by her party's central committee to be party head and hence her country's new prime minister, at age 41.

Her first term was short-lived--Labor lost elections in October and the Conservative party formed the next government. Brundtland remained in the Storting, and in 1983 she was asked to chair the United Nations World Commission on Environment and Development. The commission held hearings on environmental problems in several countries around the world and issued the influential report *Our Common Future* in 1987.

Of all world leaders, probably very few can match Brundtland's grasp of the serious long-term implications of current environmental trends. She is equally concerned with justice for the Third World and advocates much greater financial assistance to poorer nations, in part so that they can by-pass the "dirty" phases of development by using newer, cleaner technologies. As she said in an interview with the *UNESCO Courier* in 1990: "...the developing world will need increasing amounts of energy to provide for its economic and social development. This means that energy will have to be saved in the industrially developed countries...We must aim for a type of economic growth which uses less energy and [fewer] natural resources. And this can only be done by agreement. There must be sufficient information and pressure from public opinion so that nations will get together and take decisions on this issue."

Brundtland came back into the prime ministership for three years when the Conservatives lost voting strength in 1986. Commentators like to note that she then formed the world's first "gender-balanced cabinet," with eight women ministers and nine men. In her third period as head of government (1990-1996), she matched this with nine women of nineteen ministers.

Dr. Brundtland has said that political feminism starts in political parties, because "in a political party the ideals of equality and how things should be are a part of the process itself. You discuss what a society should be."[5]

In 1998, Dr. Brundtland was nominated for the position of Director-General of the World Health Organization. As Director-General, Dr. Brundtland used her political experience and medical background to raise public health on the international political agenda and to establish a link between the health of a population and sustainable development initiatives. "There's no way to make a difference in health without getting issues before those who are going to make political decisions."[6] She made significant progress toward eradicating polio, and won accolades for effectively organizing the global fight against SARS, for which she was recognized by *Scientific American* as their 2003 Policy Leader of the Year.[7] She announced that she would not run for re-election in 2003, citing her age. "I realized I would be 69 if I completed another term... it's a bit too late in life to have that kind of total burden and responsibility."[8]

After stepping down from her WHO post, Dr. Brundtland continued her international involvement in a number of capacities. She served on the United Nations Secretary-General's High-Level Panel on Threats, Challenges, and Change, whose members were asked to address common security problems and challenges facings UN member states.

In 2004, she was named a Health Policy Forum Fellow at Harvard's Malcolm Wiener Center for Social Policy, and in the same year was recognized by the *Financial Times* as the fourth most influential European of the past quarter-century--behind Pope John Paul II, Mikhail Gorbachev, and Margaret Thatcher. In 2006, Dr. Brundtland was a member of the Panel of Eminent Persons for the United Nation's

Conference on Trade and Development, which examined ways to enhance UNCTAD's development role and impact. Most recently, she was selected by Secretary General Ban Ki-moon as one of three United Nations Special Envoys on Climate Change.

Kim Campbell – Prime Minister, Canada (1993)

I met Kim (as she is known by one and all) first at an airport lounge. Her first comment was, "Why didn't you interview me for the video documentary?" I had to explain, red-faced, that my criteria was 9 months as prime minister. I quickly added that she would most certainly be asked to join the Council, which she did, becoming Chair of the Council at an important juncture for the organization.

Kim has become a wonderful friend. I suspect she conveys that feeling to many people. Since we've met, I've stayed at her homes in Boston, Los Angeles, Madrid, and Paris, attended incredible concerts by her husband Hershey Felder, shopped together, and always stayed in contact.

Kim is warm, generous, and always willing to give credit and acknowledgement to others. She is the ultimate connector of people with the philosophy that the more people she introduces, the better everyone will be. I've been an eager and admiring spectator to Kim in her post prime ministership.

Not all leaders take their political capital and use it fruitfully on the world's stage. Kim has done so quite purposefully. Her strong interest in equity and women's equality energized her to take the roles of Chair of the Council, President of the International Women's Forum, and Secretary General of the Club of Madrid, along with boards and advisory councils. Kim is also an accomplished painter and musician and the best imaginable host of dinner parties.

Avril Phaedra Douglas Campbell, who is more commonly known as Kim Campbell, was born in Port Alberni, British Columbia, on March 10, 1947. Her mother left the family when Kim was 12, leaving Kim and her older sister Alix to be raised by their father, George Thomas Campbell. Campbell attributes her mother with teaching her that women could do anything. In an interview with the author, Campbell tells how "as a teenager, my goal was to be the first woman Secretary General of the UN."

After finishing high school, Campbell attended the University of British Columbia, receiving her BA in Political Science. At the London School of Economics, she studied towards a doctorate in Soviet government, but married her husband Nathan Divinsky before completing the degree. After marrying in 1972, Campbell lectured at the University of British Columbia and at Vancouver Community College. She then returned to her own studies, receiving a Bachelor of Laws degree in 1983 from the University of British Columbia. She went on to practice law in Vancouver for the next three years.

In 1983, Campbell, then divorced from Divinsky, made an unsuccess-ful bid as candidate of the British Columbia Social Credit Party for a seat in the British Columbia Legislative Assembly. Three years later, however, she was elected to the representative body.

Interested in pursing higher office, Campbell resigned from the legislature to run in the 1988 federal election. She won and immedi-ately joined the Cabinet--becoming the Minister of State for Indian and Northern Development. A year later she was appointed Canada's first female Minister of Justice and Attorney-General where she served for three years until she was named Minister of National Defense. This extensive experience in multiple portfolios elevated Campbell within party leadership and when Prime Minister Brian Mulroney announced his retirement, Campbell successfully defeated her competitors to become the leader of the Progressive Conservative Party and was sworn into office as Prime Minister on June 25, 1993. She, Margaret Thatcher, and Angela Merkel are the only three women leaders to participate in G8 Summits.

Within months, however, elections were called. With rising unem-ployment and more general discontent with the direction the country seemed to be heading, the general population voted the Conservative Party out of office, thus ending Campbell's term as prime minister.

In an interview with the author, she addressed the issue of her shortened term, explaining that although she did not serve for an extended period of time, barriers were broken. Due to her push for women's issues to be heard within the government, great change was brought. She convened the first ever national summit on Women, Law and the Administration of Justice when she was Minister of Justice--an effort which launched a broad range of gender sensitive legal reforms.

In 1996, Kim Campbell was appointed by the Liberal government to be Consul General to Los Angeles, a post she held until 2000. After her career in public office, Campbell served as a Fellow at the center for Public Leadership at the Kennedy School of Government at Harvard and then taught as a Visiting Professor of Practice at the school. Among her courses was, "Gender and Power." She served as chair of the Council of Women World Leaders from 1999 to 2003 and then as president of the International Women's Forum until 2005. In 2002 she was a founding member of the Club of Madrid, an invitation-only organization of former heads of state and government that works to strengthen democracy worldwide and served as its secretary general from January 2004 to December 2006. She remains an active member and governor of the organization.

Violeta Chamorro – President, Nicaragua (1990-97)

In a hot Managua, a gracious Violeta Chamorro meets with me in a room whose furnishings include photographs of world leaders, well-crafted cowhide chairs, large potted plants, and a life-size picture of her martyred husband. A security inspection had included the removal of a small pocketknife from my purse.

We are served water glasses wrapped in white linen; in return for my gift of a book of national park photographs, the President makes me a present of a carved gourd. She wears a green-and-black two-piece dress and prominent dangling earrings; her eyes are brown and her grey hair is stylishly cut.

We're working together, have extended our hands to Nicara-
guans, are working for reconciliation, are working for peace, are
working to bring back all the Nicaraguans who...left this country
in the exodus.

--Violeta Chamorro

Violeta Barrios de Chamorro, elected to a six-year term as president of
Nicaragua in 1990, inherited a divided nation. Her predecessor,
Daniel Ortega, won the first internationally monitored, corruption-free
elections that Nicaragua had held in decades, in 1984. But as Ortega's government continued to be opposed by the United States--
which funded a fighting force (the Contras) against it for nearly a
decade--war-weary voters looked to Chamorro to bring peace, an end
to the draft, and U.S. aid for their ruined economy.

Chamorro is one of seven children, and was born into a wealthy
landowning family on October 18, 1929, in Rivas. She still owns a
"very small piece" of the cattle ranch where she led a happy childhood,
swimming in Lake Nicaragua and horseback riding with her father.
Eventually her family sent her to the U.S. to attend Our Lady of the
Lake Catholic School for Girls in San Antonio, Texas. She continued
on to Blackstone College, in Virginia, but left within a year when her
father died in 1948.

Back in Nicaragua, she was soon introduced to Pedro Joaquín Chamorro. The Chamorros, like the Barrios family, came from the country's wealthy landowning class; they had been active in Nicaraguan
politics for generations. Pedro Chamorro began opposing a series of
Somoza dictators while still a law student: his activities in the 1940s
led to his being exiled, as were his parents, publishers of the newspaper *La Prensa*. The family was able to return to Nicaragua and re-
open their paper by 1948.

Pedro and Violeta were married in 1950; they started a family of four
children (a fifth child died). Pedro Chamorro, an extremely courageous man, used his pen and his organizing abilities against the

Somozas for thirty years. His wife raised their children and took meals to prison when her husband was jailed several times for his activities. When Pedro Chamorro was gunned down by assassins in 1978, his wife became *La Prensa*'s publisher.

Pedro Chamorro's death so outraged Nicaragua's business and professional classes that a historical turning point was reached. Peasant guerrillas, students, and urban revolutionaries who had physically battled the Somozas for years now had new allies. In the summer of 1979, the last of the Somozas fled abroad, only to be assassinated in Paraguay. Nicaragua had had a successful revolutionary insurrection.

Unity was to be short-lived. The Sandinista Liberation Front, the dominant political force in the new revolutionary government, had different ideas for Nicaragua than did others who had joined in the anti-Somoza effort. The Sandinistas seized extensive Somoza properties, instituted land reform, and began major health and literacy campaigns. Remnants of Somoza's police and military forces fled to the border with Honduras and were soon receiving money and arms from the U.S. By the early 1980s, Nicaragua once again had fighting in its rural areas. Casualties soon mounted into many thousands.

Reflecting the divided state of their country, Violeta Chamorro's four adult children split evenly over Nicaragua's future. Two (Claudia and Carlos) actively supported Sandinista policies; two others (Pedro and Cristiana) were actively opposed. Cristiana's husband--Antonio Lacayo--became Chamorro's chief campaign strategist and presidential adviser. Chamorro was often outspokenly anti-Sandinista, but kept her family together, speaking of her respect and love for all of her children, and of her desire to unify her people and move ahead. This capacity for caring beyond politics--illustrated by Chamorro's table at family dinners--is still an important civic model in Nicaragua.

When she took office, Chamorro ended the draft and greatly reduced the size of the Sandinista army. But some of her policies--notably, retaining Humberto Ortega, Daniel's brother, as army chief--alienated former political allies who had supported her presidential run. She traveled to the United States in May of 1991 to ask for at least ten years of financial aid. But substantial help for Nicaragua was not forthcoming. Chamorro ended her interview by commenting: "Some abroad do not understand what we are trying to do here, some do understand."

In 1996, Chamorro published her autobiography, "Dreams of the Heart: The Autobiography of President Violeta Barrios de Chamorro of Nicaragua."

After her term, Violeta Chamorro declined to run for election again, citing a lack of political unity. She has retired from politics to her home in Managua.

Mary Eugenia Charles – Prime Minister, Dominica (1980-95; d.2005)

Eugenia Charles was a lawyer who didn't stand on ceremony. The first woman prime minister in the Caribbean once greeted a delegation of foreign conservationists wearing a house dress and low shoes, her head wrapped in a towel. She had just finished washing her hair in a waterfall behind her house.

The island that Charles governed, between Guadeloupe and Martinique, is known for its black volcanic beaches and rugged rainforest terrain. The extremely rare sisserou parrot--red, dark green, and violet--lives only here. Dominica is reached by six-seater airplane from more developed islands of the Caribbean; landing on its small airstrip made some of my fellow-passengers nervous.

I was taken to Charles's small office in Roseau, the capital, by Harvey Royer, a cameraman whom she knows and who, in turn, seemed to know everyone on Dominica. Chickens and goats poked around the parking lot. The prime minister speaks in a lilting West Indian voice; her manner is approachable, down-to-earth, forthcoming. She loves hanging plants, and requested some macramé hangers when asked what small gift I could bring her as a thank you for our interview.

To me equality is the important thing. I don't want preferences, I don't want to be preferred as a woman. But I want to be permitted that I am a human being who has the capacity to do what I have to do, and it doesn't matter whether I was born a man or woman. The work will be done that way.

--Eugenia Charles

Eugenia Charles is usually described as one of five children of a "well-to-do" family of Dominica--her three brothers were doctors, her sister was a nun. In her interview for this book, Charles stressed her father's self-made roots:

People always describe me now as a daughter of a millionaire, my father was so rich. He wasn't. He worked very hard for what he had...he had only primary school education. So did my mother. But my father and mother really continued to educate themselves by their reading...as a child, I took it for granted. But looking back I realize how they were always reading.

Her father's belief that "education was the answer to everything" is reflected in Charles's own education. Born on May 15, 1919, she first attended Catholic schools on Dominica and Grenada. When college time arrived, she set off for University College of the University of Toronto (1942-1946), receiving a bachelor's degree in law. From there she went to England to study at the Inner Temple, Inns of Court; she was called to the English bar in 1947, and enrolled for additional study at the London School of Economics. She then became the only woman lawyer practicing on Dominica.

An effort by the governing Dominica Labour Party to limit dissent with a sedition act, in 1968, brought Charles actively into politics, and eventually led to the formation of her political party, the Dominica Freedom Party (DFP). In 1975, Charles, as its leader, became government opposition leader.

Dominica achieved its independence from Britain three years later, in

1978. Charles had warned that the country might not be ready for its new status. After a series of crises, the DFP won a very large electoral victory in the summer of 1980, and Charles became prime minister. The highly competent Charles held the position until 1995. According to journalist Myfanwy van de Veld, the DFP "traditionally appealed to business and plantocracy interests, but becoming Prime Minister Miss Charles broadened that appeal considerably and she was later seen very much as a 'leader of the people.'"

Strongly anti-Communist, Charles encouraged the U.S. invasion of Grenada to quell a Cuban-backed military coup. She became known as the 'Iron Lady of the Caribbean' for her "steely determination to put her country on the path to stability and prosperity and for her outspoken stance on controversial issues."[9] During her term in office, Eugenia Charles spearheaded extensive government reform. In response to corruption, she even ordered the 200-member defense force to disband and hand over its arms to the police.

Dominica faced problems of poverty and underdevelopment. The year before Charles took office the island was devastated by Hurricane David; Charles supervised its reconstruction, rebuilding roads and restoring power. In the 1980s, Charles was able to obtain millions of dollars from the U.S. to build up Dominica's weak infrastructure. She initiated reforms in education, health care, and economic development, cut inflation from 30% to 4%, and halved the island's trade deficit. Charles was not interested in the wrong kinds of development for her small, unspoiled island. She would not allow foreign businesses to open casinos or night clubs, fearing that they would attract criminal elements. Although she increased tourism, she did so cautiously, and was mindful of its environmental impacts, telling writer Anthony Weller: "I won't have any package tours coming here and barging around. I've seen what mass tourism has done to other islands. It doesn't help the people financially or otherwise, and it ruins the place." Dominica's motto (in Creole) was "*Après Bondie, c'est la Ter*"--After God, the Earth.

Eugenia Charles was knighted by Queen Elizabeth II in 1991. She said she had never met anyone she wanted to marry, and lived with her father until his 1983 death at 107. After retiring from government in 1995, "she became involved in President Jimmy Carter's election monitoring organization and undertook speaking engagements, largely in the US."[10] Charles died in Martinique on August 30, 2005, at the age of 86, while being treated for a broken hip.

Tansu Çiller – Prime Minister, Turkey (1993-96)

Tansu Çiller--interviewed in Ankara in June of 1994--paid tribute to her husband's ability to be the mate of a woman in politics. She said that Ozer Çiller--a businessman and engineer with a master's degree in computer science--"has his own preferences...his own personality, but, despite everything, he stood up...beautifully. And now in a country like Turkey, people are talking more about this kind of thing more than ever."

Çiller is a lively woman who smiles frequently. She said that she was "learning to have fun" at her job, despite "all the adversities"--which have included sexist chants by her opponents: "Tansu mutfaga"-- "Tansu back to the kitchen."

> *I'm hoping more women will participate...*
>
> *The reason for that is not that I am a woman only....when you take the women and the younger population, they're almost 75 to 80 percent of the population in my country, and therefore we need more women and young people...to have a fairer... representation of the population...*
>
> *--Tansu Çiller*

Tansu Çiller became prime minister of Turkey, the world's only secular Muslim state, in June of 1993. She thus became the third woman to govern a modern Islamic nation, with Benazir Bhutto (Pakistan) and Khaleda Zia (Bangladesh) as her predecessors.

Turkey differs from other Muslim (and even some Western) countries in having a long historical tradition of women in the professions, dating back to the early twentieth century. Such women -- often practicing law or medicine -- were born into Turkey's wealthier class, and lead lives very different from those of the mass of Turkish women. Çiller, age forty-seven at the time of her appointment, was an important part of a continuing unique tradition.

Born in Istanbul, she is the daughter of a well-to-do provincial governor. She married early, after high school, and has two sons. Her husband, Ozer, took her family surname of Çiller. Tansu Çiller attended American-run Roberts College in Istanbul, and then pursued further education in the United States. She earned a Ph.D. in economics at the University of Connecticut and did additional postgraduate work at Yale.

After her return from the U.S. in 1974, Çiller began teaching economics at Istanbul's Bosporus University. She moved from academia to politics in 1991, when she became Turkey's economics minister, appointed by Süleyman Demirel, her predecessor as prime minister. She had earlier served as one of his advisers.

In the summer of 1993, Demirel's party, True Path, saw Çiller as someone who could bring a fresh image of youth, vigor, and change to the office of party head (and, in consequence, of prime minister). Demirel was quoted as saying that Çiller's selection by True Path "shows that Turkey is a part of the Western world, that Turkey is a civilized country."[11] According to *Lear's* magazine, Istanbul's teens break-danced at Çiller's victory celebration, chanting "Down with the fossils."[12]

When she came into the prime ministership, Çiller announced an attack on bureaucracy and on bribery. She also planned to privatize some Turkish state-run enterprises. In her interview, Çiller commented that money from privatization could build "a lot of schools, a lot of hospitals."

However, Çiller faced severe economic problems, as well as the issue of Kurdish separatism. She proposed to the Turkish parliament that

Kurdish-language schools and radio broadcasts be legalized. The press reported visits from Turkish military officers warning her not to be soft on Turkish terrorists. In the spring and summer of 1994, such terrorists were setting off bombs in Istanbul, and human rights groups were denouncing Turkey's human rights record. Muslim fundamentalists--and their Welfare Party--were being viewed by some as a long-range threat to Turkey's secular politics and legal system.

The latter part of Tansu Çiller's time in office was characterized by internal politics. In 1995, a number of accusations of corruption were made against Çiller, but she continued to govern after receiving a vote of confidence. The next year, Çiller formed two coalition governments, first with Mesut Yilmaz, the leader of a rival conservative party, and then – after Yilmaz was censured by Parliament--with the Welfare Party. Under the second coalition, Çiller served as deputy prime minister, and was widely expected to be reinstated as prime minister in 1997. However, the leader of the Welfare Party, Necmettin Erbakan, resigned in an attempt to force an early election, preventing Çiller from being reinstated.

She continued to lead the True Path Party until 2002, when the party garnered 9.55% of the vote in the general elections – just under the 10% required to enter Parliament. Tansu Çiller then retired from politics.

Edith Cresson – Prime Minister, France (1991-92)

"One of the most obvious characteristics of the bourgeoisie is the boredom it produces." This line from Edith Cresson's autobiography would have been well understood by French writer Simone de Beauvoir, a fellow rebel against middle class ennui and female restriction.

Edith Cresson's life has certainly not been dull. The elegant woman I interviewed--who was wearing a blonde suit and sitting in front of white shelves of objects d'art--has been pelted with tomatoes by French farmers who were resentful of her reforms of their protected markets.

According to biographer Olga Opfell, while she was involved in promoting French trade, Cresson "rode a French motor scooter to work to prove that French models were as good as...popular Japanese ones." The former prime minister likes to swim and bicycle.

> *Even if [a man] does not succeed in accomplishing anything, it does not matter, because he asserts a certain number of things, or he presents himself as a leader in a way which...corresponds to tradition. People expect of a woman results, and quick ones, if possible.*
>
> *--Edith Cresson*

Edith Cresson had already handled difficult assignments for President Francois Mitterrand when he appointed her France's first woman prime minister in May of 1991, making her potentially one of the most powerful women in Europe.

From 1981-84 she served as France's Minister of Agriculture, absorbing tough comments from French farmers unaccustomed to a woman in that post. Later she became Minister of Industrial Restructuring and External Trade, at a time when the iron and steel industry was undergoing change: "It was very hard...I used to go to Lorraine every month to speak to the factory workers and the unions to try to make the transition easier."[13]

Cresson was born on January 27, 1934, in a fashionable suburb of Paris. Her parents, Gabriel and Jacqueline Campion, were well-off bourgeoisie who had two sons as well. Cresson's father worked for the French government. The family hired an English nanny for their daughter, and she is bilingual in French and English.

Cresson's early life was shaped by conditions in France during World War II. Her father was working for the French embassy in Belgrade, Yugoslavia, when France fell to the Nazis. When the embassy was closed, he settled his family in Thonon-les-Bains, on Lake Geneva, and then returned to Paris. Edith Cresson was enrolled in a convent boarding school, Sacre Coeur.

She witnessed the fates of the French Jews and other persons under the Nazi-controlled French government ("...in the mountains, where I was sent on holiday and to be better nourished, the head of the house where I lived was deported and died in Mauthausen"[14]). The distinction that Cresson likes to make between those who look respectable and those who are truly admirable came to her early as she saw "the conforming middle class, and, on the other hand, people whom I knew to be in the Resistance"[15]

When she was seventeen, Cresson was admitted to one of France's prestigious schools--the Haute École Commerciale (HEC)--where she earned a business degree. In December of 1959, she married Jacques Cresson, an auto executive with Peugeot. The couple has two daughters. Edith Cresson later returned to HEC to earn her doctorate in demography. Her thesis was based on interviews with Breton farm women.

Cresson's career in politics began when she became a campaign worker in one of Mitterrand's early presidential campaigns in 1965. He lost, but ran again in 1974. Cresson joined his Socialist Party, and was asked to run for the National Assembly from Châtellerault, a conservative town in Vienne. She was expected to lose, and did, but was appointed to a party post. Soon after, she began to win elections and appointments.

In 1977, she was elected mayor of the city of Thure; in 1979, to the European Parliament; in 1981, to the National Assembly. In 1983, she even became mayor of Châtellerault, where she had lost her first race. Meanwhile, Mitterrand won the French presidency in 1981, and asked his prime minister to name Cresson to the agriculture portfolio. She continued on to other portfolios, including that of Minister of European Affairs.

After she was appointed prime minister, however, it was unclear that France was ready for her, or she ready for France. Always very frank, Cresson did not change her style when she became head of government. Some topics of absolutely no significance on which she had once given her opinions to the press drew attention and denigration.

She was satirized on a French television show as a cat, "Amabotte," nuzzling the boots of Mitterrand. Her experience, seriousness, and intelligence were overlooked as her popularity dropped in the polls. The Socialists began to see her as a liability, and in April of 1992 she resigned as prime minister. While initially silent about her treatment by the media and her party, Cresson later shared with a woman journalist her strong feelings of anger about this treatment. In 1995, Cresson was appointed to the European Commission, where she was in charge of Education, Research and Development, and Human Resources. She and several other Commissioners resigned four years later due to corruption allegations, including accusations of favoritism leveled at Cresson. She has retired from politics.

Vigdís Finnbogadóttir – President, Iceland (1980-96)

The residence of Iceland's president is on a low promontory, outside Reykjavik, facing the sea. Green grounds and no obvious signs of security arrangements greeted us--rather, a friendly, warm house-keeper, who invited us in to sign a guest book, "look around," and listen to her recitation of some Icelandic poetry--Iceland's people are proud of their literary heritage, as is their head of state.

"President Vigdís" is an articulate, attractive woman with short, blondish hair and dark blue eyes. Dressed in a white wool suit, she answered my questions in her fine library, and showed me some photo albums of her meetings with other world leaders. Iceland's small population means that the president knew even the cabdriver who delivered us to her residence--but, as she colorfully said, the importance of a country "is not counted by hats." Iceland, she believes, has mes-sages for the world.

> *I think that the growing number of women as heads of state is due to the work women have done themselves to promote wom-en, to prove to the world that women are in no way inferior to men when it comes to having important posts. It has been a*

great struggle to prove that, and to know that half of the world doesn't know that yet.

--Vigdís Finnbogadóttir

Vigdís Finnbogadóttir, elected president of Iceland in 1980, commented, "They chose me because I'm a woman and in spite of my being a woman." The former theatre director and television teacher was the world's first elected woman president.

Finnbogadóttir was Iceland's fourth head of state after the country became independent from Denmark in 1944. Iceland's presidents serve as cultural ambassadors and symbols of national unity. The president does not introduce legislation, and Finnbogadóttir did not even belong to a political party. The Icelandic constitution requires that the president sign into law all bills passed by the parliament (Althing). Although no president had ever refused a signature, Finnbogadóttir came close.

In 1985, the Icelandic Women's Liberation Movement called a nationwide strike of women in Iceland, asking them to boycott their jobs or housework to protest unequal wages for women, as well as other forms of discrimination. (According to a *New York Times* story on October 25, 1985, "groups of men crowded into hotels in the early morning, after their wives refused to cook breakfast for them. Most of Iceland's telephone switchboards were left unstaffed.") Women flight attendants for Icelandic Air wanted to join in the boycott, but the Althing passed a bill forbidding it. Finnbogadóttir resisted signing this bill, but ultimately was argued into doing so. (The flight attendants joined the boycott anyway.)

Iceland's president was born in Reykjavik, the capital, on April 15, 1930. Her parents were professionals. Her father was an engineer and a professor at the University of Iceland; her mother, a nurse, was for many years chair of the Icelandic Nurse's Association.

Finnbogadóttir began her college studies at home, but soon went abroad to study French language and literature at the University of

Grenoble and at the Sorbonne. She also studied theatre history in Denmark and Sweden before returning to Iceland to work in English literature and in education.

She began a career teaching French at two of Iceland's junior colleges and then became an instructor in French drama at the University of Iceland. At this time she also became a teacher on the state television network, giving French lessons and speaking on drama. In 1972, her deep interest in theatre led to her appointment as director of the Reykjavik Theatre Company. She knows Iceland's playwrights well, and wishes that their works were more frequently translated.

In 1980, Finnbogadóttir was heavily lobbied to run for president by people who felt that the time for a woman head of state had arrived. Divorced and a single mother (she adopted a daughter, Astridur, when she was forty-one) she found these features of her personal life no handicap in her campaign: "I think people liked it that I had the eccentricity to adopt a child as a single woman."[16]

Women in Iceland keep their maiden names when they marry. The president's last name derives from her father's first name, Finnbogi, and has no connection to her early marriage. She is known in Iceland as President Vigdís.

Highly cultured and very conversant with Icelandic history, in interviews Finnbogadóttir declines to discuss the sensitive political subjects which are not considered to be part of her presidential arena. But like President Mary Robinson of Ireland--another "nonpolitical" head of state--she is well aware of the significance of her position. As she told *Scandinavian Review* the week after her first inauguration:

> *I'm convinced that the fact of a woman winning the presidential election here will help women in my country, as well as women in other countries. I can already see that from the many letters I've received from women all over the world. They've taken note of my election and they think that it's exciting and encouraging...It's time women stood together. We can't wait another 20*

years. It's wrong to wait too long and think that things will change tomorrow. We have to change them today.

Finnbogadóttir was re-elected to the presidency four consecutive times. After finishing her last term in 1996, she stayed active in public life. She received several awards for her work promoting Nordic culture and heritage; in 2001, the University of Iceland named its foreign language institute in her honor.

Finnbogadóttir also remained a frequent figure on the international level. She was a founding Chair of the Council of Women World Leaders in 1997. Then, in 1998, she was appointed as a UNESCO Goodwill Ambassador for Languages. Two years later, Finnbogadóttir was also named as a member of the Eminent Persons group supporting the United Nations World Conference against Racism, Racial Discrimination, Xenophobia and Related Intolerance. She currently serves as a UNESCO Goodwill Ambassador for the Promotion of linguistic diversity, women's right and education.

NEW Ellen Johnson Sirleaf – President, Republic of Liberia (2006-)

Regal, determined, untiring — a few of the first words that came to mind when President Ellen Johnson Sirleaf walked into the room for our interview on October 17th, 2006. She would never have to <u>say</u> she was a leader. You just knew it.

Most people would have been exhausted from the 18 hour flight from Africa--a flight that had been delayed en route for 24 hours. Other than her request for a glass of mineral water, the President was eager to speak about women's leadership. She clearly took personal pride in her country's women--the market women, in particular. She wanted to brag, not about her own efforts, but about theirs.

She was comfortable with the topic, the purpose of the questions, and the fluidity of her answers. She knew her message and she gave her answers with freshness and energy. We were sitting in a funky mansion in a room filled with Victorian lace, an Elvis guitar, pictures of world leaders, candles, mismatched furniture, and a canopy bed—none of it fazed her. She became quickly "at home" in her responses and drew from a depth of experience and wisdom and with a charm that made me both comfortable and fully aware that I was meeting with a unique leader among leaders.

> *They criticize me; I criticize them. That's what democracy is all about. But when you've been through it and you've competed as a woman to reach a leadership position, you lose any fear of being different; because you're so self-confident of what you do, you've achieved it on the basis of effort.*

> *--Ellen Johnson Sirleaf*

Ellen Johnson Sirleaf, inaugurated President of Liberia on January 16, 2006, was born in Monrovia, Liberia, on October, 29, 1938. Two of her grandparents were indigenous Liberians and another was a German who married a rural market women. Johnson Sirleaf grew up with very deep ties and connections to Liberia Therefore, her aspirations to make it a great nation come as no surprise.

After completing her high school studies in Liberia, Johnson Sirleaf attended Madison Business College in Madison, Wisconsin. She received her degree in Accounting in 1964 and earned a second degree in Economics from the University of Colorado in 1970. Pursuing advanced studies, Johnson Sirleaf received a Master's of Public Administration degree from Harvard University in 1971.

She then returned to Liberia, intent on serving and improving her country, and immediately entered politics. Johnson Sirleaf became the Assistant Minister of Finance in the William Tolbert administration. However, in 1980, Tolbert was overthrown and subsequently killed by a military coup led by Samuel Doe. Knowing she had to flee, Johnson Sirleaf went into exile in Nairobi, Kenya. Her strong academic background in economics and accounting landed her a job as the Vice President of the African Regional Office of Citibank.

In 1985, she returned to Liberia to continue her journey to bring freedom and democracy to Liberia. While campaigning for Senate, she spoke out against Doe and his military regime, and was sentenced to ten years in prison. During a TIME magazine interview, Johnson Sirleaf said these years were her toughest moments. She explained how she was in prison "with about 12 other so-called rebels, all of whom were killed. At that point, I felt a bit of fear, I must admit." She was eventually freed and moved to Washington, DC, where she returned to banking as Vice President and Executive Board member of the HSCB Equator Bank.

Back in Liberia, civil unrest erupted once again and in September of 1990, Samuel Doe was killed by a member of Charles Taylor's political party. With the crisis escalating rapidly, Johnson Sirleaf opted to stay abroad and worked from 1992 until 1997 as the Director of the UN Development Program Regional Bureau for Africa.

By 1997, the situation in Liberia reached greater stability and Johnson Sirleaf campaigned in the open elections, placing second to Charles Taylor out of a field of fourteen candidates. The elections were declared free and fair by international observers. However, a new civil war began in 1999 that involved two separate rebel groups and the sitting Taylor government.

When Charles Taylor stepped down in August of 2003 as part of a peace agreement, Johnson Sirleaf became active in the transitional government. With elections scheduled for 2005, she took over the Unity Party and again decided to run for president. Based on a platform of economic development and an end to corruption and civil war, Johnson Sirleaf won enough votes to initiate a runoff vote against her opponent, former soccer-star George Weah. In November, the National Elections Commission declared Johnson Sirleaf the president-elect of Liberia, winning with a margin of almost 20% of the vote. All independent, international, regional, and domestic observers declared the vote to be free, fair, and transparent. She was sworn in as President on January 16, 2006 and U.S. Secretary of State Condoleezza Rice along with U.S. First Lady Laura Bush were among the list of distinguished guests that attended Johnson Sirleaf's inauguration.

Currently in her second year in office, Johnson Sirleaf's government has made great strides towards rebuilding her war-torn country. Years of civil war and unrest have left Liberia in need of great repair. Many issues ranging from domestic policy to women's rights had been neglected and ignored for years. Even though the people were hungry for change and a new Liberia, she still faced opposition and criticism from people who doubted she was up to the job. With the strength of her vision and her governance, Johnson Sirleaf's developing legacy as Liberia's "Iron Lady" is a watershed moment for women's global leadership. Echoing this achievement, Liberia and Johnson Sirelaf will host the 2009 International Colloquium on Women's Empower-ment and Leadership, inviting many women leaders from around the world. From the start she said she would like to serve only one term which in Liberia is a term of six years. Johnson Sirleaf has said, "I think that's enough to make the changes and put Liberia on an irreversible course toward peace, reconciliation, democracy, and development."

Maria Liberia-Peters – Prime Minister, The Netherlands Antilles (1984-86; 1988-94)

The office of the prime minister of the Netherlands Antilles was located in a Dutch Colonial-style building on the waterfront in Willenstad--a colorful city painted in Caribbean pastels. One reminder of Maria Liberia-Peters' former profession is children's drawings on a wall. Framed photos speak of her interest in photography.

The former prime minister's ethos is that of a dedicated public servant; she is clear, intelligent, and likable, noted for keeping people informed and playing fair. It seemed not inappropriate that, while I was in her hometown, the Caribbean Association for Feminist Research and Action sponsored a poetry reading to celebrate the publication of Creation Fire an anthology of Caribbean women's poetry.

> *I've realized that you cannot reach your goal without power. So it's not a nasty word, it's an important word. But you must know what you want to do with that power. Serve mankind,*

serve for humanity, and then, yes, give me all the power in the world.

--Maria Liberia-Peters

Maria Liberia-Peters, the first woman prime minister of the Netherlands Antilles, is a popular leader known for her abilities to convince and build consensus.

The former kindergarten teacher was born Maria Peters on May 20, 1941, in Willenstad, Curaçao, Netherlands Antilles. Her husband, Niels, is a civil servant. The couple adopted two young children, now teenagers, through the Roman Catholic Archdiocese of New York.

The former prime minister speaks four languages (Dutch, English, Spanish, and Papiamento--the latter a mixture of the first three plus Portuguese, seasoned with Arawak and African additions). Liberia-Peters was educated in Europe.

> *I did my teacher's degree in Holland. I worked for five years [starting in 1962] in early childhood education, and then went back for training in pedagogy and became a teacher in training college here. And then I said farewell to teaching...I expect some day I will be back in the classroom.*

As she explained further, her position as a teacher made her aware of the social needs of students and their families. She organized parents' groups for political and social action, and joined a political party (the NVP – National People's Party). After she was approached to run for office, she won a seat on the Curaçao Island Council in 1975. From 1975 to 1980, that body named her to an executive council which met regularly with Queen Beatrix's representative.[17]

In 1982, Liberia-Peters was elected to the Staten (legislature) of the Netherlands Antilles, and also became minister of economic affairs in a coalition government that collapsed in June of 1984. In September, she was asked to form a new coalition government; she took office as prime minister that month. Her first period as prime minister lasted until 1986, when political events intervened to make her, instead, leader of the opposition. She came back into the premiership in the spring of 1988.

The 1980s brought difficult economic times to the Netherlands Antilles, a country of five islands (Curaçao, Bonaire, Sint Maarten, Saba, and Sint Eustatius) north of Venezuela. The economy had traditionally been heavily dependent upon two oil refineries that refined Venezuelan oil. Exxon's refinery closed in 1984. The Netherlands Antilles was able to keep the Shell refinery operating by taking it over on advantageous terms and leasing it to a Venezuelan oil company, PDVSA.

During these and other economic difficulties, which included high unemployment, Liberia-Peters told the *New York Times:*

> *What I really hope is that I will be successful in at least setting out the lines for the future, for a new future, so that the people of the Netherlands Antilles can say "O.K., we're going through a difficult situation, but nevertheless this is where it's going to lead...there is light..." It's a situation you have to handle very carefully, so that my people don't panic. As the Spanish people say, I have to keep away la desesperación – the desperation.*[18]

Under Liberia-Peters, the islands sought a diversified economy partially grounded in different forms of tourism; Bonaire is known as a scuba divers' paradise.

The burdens of office did not prevent Liberia-Peters from having fun. Her self-confidence as a leader was demonstrated when she declined to watch the annual Carnival parade from the prime minister's traditional place in a reviewing stand, and instead danced in the parade (as she had for seven years), wearing pink and green lamé. She told a journalist that she had "struggled" with the decision, but "knew she would not feel happy as a spectator...standing at the side." Although some people felt her dancing was not appropriate, the prime minister said, "In the first place I'm Maria, and in the second place I'm prime minister. So I'm going."[19] In the spring of 1994, the National People's Party lost elections, so Liberia-Peters moved into a role she had played before, leader of the opposition.

While Maria Liberia-Peters is no longer occupying an elected political office, she remains active in her political party on an as needed basis. In particular, she has been involved in recent parliamentary elections, increasing voter turn-out, and the referendum in which the residents of Curaçao opted for autonomy within the Kingdom. This referendum altered the composition of the Kingdom of the Netherlands by terminating the existence of the Netherlands Antilles as a political entity and granting autonomy to the independent island states of Curaçao and Sint Maarten within the Kingdom of the Netherlands.

Kazimiera Prunskiene – Prime Minister, Lithuania (1990-91)

Vilnius, in January of 1994, reminded me of parts of Russia. There were wide boulevards, and hard-to-spot shops containing limited, imported consumer goods. Some of the vegetables for sale had come from too-near Chernobyl, I was told, so that many people refused to buy them. Residents had shrugs for their difficult conditions.

Kazimiera Prunskiene, Lithuania's former prime minister, very generously invited me to dine with her at a local restaurant, subsequent to our interview, and even played chauffeur, driving a small old car. A charming woman with reddish hair and a collection of stories, Prunskiene has written a book about her experiences, Cost of Freedom.

> *I think that a very important feature [of a leader] would be... experience in state matters. It's very difficult to imagine a person coming to politics, to the state level, by chance--the person who has no earlier, no previous experience as a leader, even on a lesser level.*
>
> *--Kazimiera Prunskiene*

Kazimiera Prunskiene was prime minister of Lithuania during nine critical months in which her Baltic country sought to establish its independence from the Soviet Union.

She was born on February 26, 1943, in the village of Vasiuliskiai; World War II-Lithuania was at that time occupied by the Germans.

As she stated in her interview, Prunskiene was bereft of her father as a child of one; her mother raised three children alone. Despite whatever challenges these circumstances presented to the family, Prunskiene was able to achieve a high level of education. She received a degree from the University of Vilnius in 1965 in economics where she stayed on to teach. In the 1980s, she received a doctorate in her field. Her personal life included becoming the mother of three children. She eventually divorced, and remarried later in 1989. She joined the Lithuanian Communist Party in 1980.

Lithuania has had a difficult history. In the 1920s, its first president, A. Smetona, became dictatorial. In 1940, the USSR annexed the country; then the Germans invaded; in 1944, the USSR re-invaded and annexed Lithuania once again. The 1980s brought the new and influential ideas of perestroika (restructuring) put forth by Soviet President Mikhail Gorbachev.

Prunskiene became a founding member of Sajudis (the Lithuanian Restructuring Movement); it was to become the main pro-independence group in Lithuania. However, independence came only in stages and with much struggle.

By 1989, Prunskiene filled several roles as a minister in the Soviet-controlled Lithuanian government, an elected member of the USSR Supreme Soviet, and an active member of Sajudis. In these forums she was, according to biographer Olga Opfell, "energetic," "forceful," and "a skilled debater."

President Gorbachev, despite his restructuring doctrines, wanted to keep Lithuania within the orbit of the USSR. But huge street demonstrations occurred in Vilnius, and in March of 1990, the Lithuanian parliament (Supreme Council) voted for independence. Six days later, it appointed Prunskiene to be prime minister.

Prunskiene seems, at first, to have underestimated the possible reaction of her "dear friend" Gorbachev to Lithuania's declaration of independence. After an embargo of oil, gas, and raw materials was declared by Moscow against her country, in mid-April she set off on travels to the U.S. and several European capitals, asking for their intervention on behalf of negotiations with Moscow. She finally met with Gorbachev for talks on May 17, but his offer of independence in two years was not accepted.

Moscow's boycott damaged the Lithuanian economy. Prunskiene was able to end it after two and a half months by getting the Supreme Council to agree to suspend independence while negotiations were active with the USSR. She also urged controversial free-market economic reforms within Lithuania. Conflict continued during all of 1990; one focus was the issue of Lithuanian "draft evaders" from the Soviet army: the Supreme Council had decided they had no obligation to serve.

In January 1991, events moved towards a new state of crisis. Prunskiene met again in Moscow with President Gorbachev, but did not receive assurances that the Soviet army would not be used against Lithuania. On the same day, she learned that a set of her economic policies had been rejected by her parliament at home. Prunskiene resigned as prime minister. Nine months later, Boris Yeltsin came to power in Moscow, and the USSR recognized the independence of the three Baltic republics.

Prunskiene served as a member of parliament in 1991 and 1992. She then returned to the private sector, first drawing upon her background in economics to start a consulting company and then teaching at a university. In 1996, Prunskiene re-entered the public sector when she was elected to parliament, where she was a member of committees on economics, European affairs, and social affairs and labor. In 2004, and again in 2006, she was appointed the Minister of Agriculture and Forestry.

Mary Robinson – President, Ireland (1990-97)

A light which the president of Ireland keeps burning at all hours on the second floor of the presidential mansion is her chosen signal to Irish people living abroad that they have a tie to their homeland and are remembered there. Even today, Ireland's citizens actively compete in a lottery to migrate to the United States – because of a lack of jobs for them at home.

"Caring" is one of the first words that comes to mind to describe President Robinson; one feels her deep sincerity as a humanitarian idealist. She concluded her official interview by commending the work of Irish author Roddy Doyle, saying that hers was "a complete book family." Then she invited us for refreshments, and a look at her "favorite room," leading the way in a red-and-green plaid suit and black stockings.

> *You move politics along by being able to inject a sense of vision about certain values. Take, for example, relations on this island. If it's possible to project the values of pluralism, of respect for difference, of accommodating and finding space for difference, that should influence the policies of a political framework for peace and reconciliation.*
>
> *--Mary Robinson*

When Mary Robinson started her campaign to become president of Ireland, the odds against her were considered to be 100-to-1. She was an intellectual activist whose views were often at odds with those of Ireland's conservative, Catholic-dominated culture. The "leading candidates" were men, sponsored by Ireland's two largest parties. The presidency had become something of a sinecure for retiring male politicians, whereas she was known as a woman reformer.

Mary Robinson won. She declared her 1990 victory "a great, great day for Irish women," and said, "The women of Ireland, instead of rocking the cradle, rocked the system."

How did she win? Three factors seem primary: her particular qualities as a human being; her campaign's hard work--she extended the traditional campaign season by many weeks, and traveled all over Ireland in her campaign bus; and a bit of luck: the voting system was complicated and rather unusual, giving Robinson the votes of the person third in line to add to her own second-place totals. Ireland now seems proud that it elected Mary Robinson; reports on her activities glowed with enthusiasm, and even her defeated main opponent spoke approvingly of her job performance.

Robinson comes from a well-off Catholic family from County Mayo. She was born in Ballina, on May 21, 1944; both of her parents were physicians, although her mother stopped practicing medicine to raise five children. Robinson's four brothers and she all attended Trinity College, Dublin, a predominantly Protestant institution. Robinson received a B.A. in French and then a law degree, compiling such an outstanding academic record that she was given a scholarship to Harvard to do graduate work in law. She has said that the year of study at Harvard--in 1968--was particularly important to her development, largely because there was so much questioning of social institutions going on there, and in the United States generally, at that time.

When she returned to Ireland, Robinson (at twenty-five) became the youngest law professor in the history of Trinity College. She also entered the upper house of the Irish parliament, running as a Labour candidate. She served there for twenty years, continually challenging Ireland's severe prohibitions against divorce, abortion, homosexuality, and even the sale of contraceptives (in 1985, legislation finally passed in Ireland allowing the purchase of contraceptives without a doctor's prescription). In 1991, the year after she was elected president, Robinson received word that some of her former legal work had resulted in the biggest equal-pay settlement for women in the country's history.

She had her own view of feminism. Married to a former Trinity College classmate, Nicholas Robinson (a Protestant), and the mother of three children, she insists that true feminism allows each woman to go her own way: "We've gone beyond the stage of simply wanting more women in particular positions...It's much deeper than that and much more fundamental." She once asked a journalist: "If feminists don't value the work of the women who stay at home, how is society going to value it?"

Robinson found her presidency particularly interesting because it was a restricted position: Ireland's president does not initiate legislation and cannot give a speech or leave the country without permission from the prime minister. But Robinson looked for "symbolic" ways to assert her values of tolerance, pluralism, and human concern. She did this through the places she chose to visit, both inside and outside of Ireland, and through the groups she invited to the presidential residence in Phoenix Park. She traveled to Northern Ireland to meet with an IRA leader in the interest of peace-seeking; she traveled to Somalia and published her private travel diary to raise funds for relief; at Christmas time in 1992, she welcomed thirty-four representatives of Ireland's gay and lesbian organizations to a special reception at her residence.

She has spoken frequently of the challenging language of "symbols":

> *What I've learned is the importance of symbols – as long as they are grounded in values. This office works on two levels. One is the level of values above politics, for example, offering the hand of friendship to the two communities in Northern Ireland. The other is below the political: meeting small groups concerned with community self-development. Unless I'm in touch at that level, I won't know the symbols. It's important to listen...a phrase you use is appropriate only when you've been listening – in touch with the small print of people's lives.*

In 1997, Robinson was appointed the United Nations High Commissioner for Human Rights; she resigned from the presidency four months early to begin serving in this position. During her five-year tenure, Robinson was known to have incensed governments around the world through her outspoken criticism of their human rights records. She also personally visited areas of civil conflict, including Sierra Leone, Chechnya and the former Yugoslavia. After the attacks of September 11th, 2001 in the United States, Robinson voiced concern for the plight of Afghan civilians, and warned the Chinese government "not to use the war against terrorism as a pretext to suppress ethnic minority groups." In 2004, Robinson received Amnesty International's "Ambassador of Conscience" award for her work with human rights.

Today, Robinson is the Executive Director of Realizing Rights: Ethical Globalization Initiative, which integrates human rights concerns with the globalization process, and supports capacity building in good governance in developing countries. She is also a professor of international affairs at Columbia University; one of the founding members of the Council of Women World Leaders and the current chair of the Council; Vice President of the Club of Madrid, and a member of the newly-formed council *The Elders*, launched in 2007 and comprised of an international group of former heads of state, Nobel laureates, leading entrepreneurs, and philanthropists who are expected to tackle an array of global problems.

Jenny Shipley – Prime Minister, New Zealand (1997-99)

Jenny, as she is known universally, has the manner of a woman who reflects the hardy, common-sense, no-nonsense approach that one imagines of pioneer women. She is straight-forward, speaks her mind, and tells you exactly what she thinks and where she stands. Confidence and competence are at her beck and call. Whenever she gives a keynote speech, people always want a copy of it. She reasons issues through to their logical conclusion and persuades with that logic and her own conviction.

Jenny is a strong supporter of the Council of Women World Leaders and sees the value of the collective voice of women. She is always a source of solid advice and has on more than one occasion given me clear and compelling direction for the benefit of the Council.

In December 1997, having gained progressive prominence in her party throughout the prior decade, Jenny Shipley became New Zealand's first female Prime Minister as leader of the National Party, a position she held until December 1999.

Born Jennifer Mary Robson in Gore, New Zealand in 1952, Jenny Shipley was educated in Wellington and Blenheim before graduating from Christchurch Teachers College in 1971. After teaching primary school for several years, she married Central Canterbury farmer Burton Shipley, and they settled together on his family farm near Ashburton. In her new hometown, Shipley continued her commitment to public service through a developing interest in local government and by serving in several educational and child care organizations. This includes the Plunket Society, which aims "to ensure that New Zealand children are among the healthiest in the world." In 1987, she eventually won a seat as the National Party candidate for the Ashburton electorate (voting district).

In the Parliament, she first gained the position of Opposition Spokesperson on Social Welfare and later became the Minister of Social Welfare and of Women's Affair when party control shifted in the 43rd Parliament. Under the leadership of Prime Minister Bolger, Shipley then assumed the position of Minister of Health and attempted to reform the public health system through the introduction of an internal market.

Having gained power and prominence in the National Party, she was able to garner the necessary support to replace him when she became increasingly frustrated with his cautious pace of reform. She was chosen as Prime Minister in December 1997, gaining leadership of the then unstable Coalition Government. Even when the Coalition broke down in August 1998, Prime Minister Shipley retained her position as Prime Minister. Upon her appointment as Prime Minister, Shipley joined the Council of Women World Leaders in 1997.

Jenny Shipley was the first New Zealand Prime Minister to attend the gay and lesbian Hero Parade as a leader of the National Party. She further demonstrated her support by reaching out to the gay and lesbian community in New Zealand through working towards voting and party expansion for a more inclusive and representative National Party.

Although she hosted the Asia-Pacific Economic Cooperation (APEC) annual forum that attracted top international leaders to discuss trade and economic issues in September 1999, policy developments advanced by the National Government failed to gain New Zealand voters' support. In the November 1999 election, the Labour Party, led by Helen Clark, defeated the National Party. Shipley retained her seat in the Parliament and remained Leader of the Opposition until late 2001 when she retired from elected public service.

In 2007, she joined the financial services firm Sentinel. She sits on the boards of Richina Pacific, Momentum, and China's third largest bank, as well as chairing the construction company MainZeal. She also works on business development in China. Jenny and her husband, Burton Shipley, have two children, Anna and Ben. Her interests include gardening, music, walking, and water sports.

Hanna Suchocka – Prime Minister, Poland (1992-93)

While she was prime minister of Poland, Hanna Suchocka was said by the press to have presented an image of calm and control, even though aides knew the burdens of office could drive her into tears. The woman I met was hospitable and very honestly responsive, exercising disagreement where necessary and also sharing stories of her travels in the United States – where she disliked skyscrapers, but enjoyed Nevada.

She has remained single, a practicing Catholic who refuses photo-opportunities inside churches; the former prime minister supports abortion only under extremely limited conditions (such as a threat to the mother's life).

> *I had to look for balance between seven political parties. For me it was not important [if] there were men or women...the parties*

were so different that for me it was problem number one...the problem of man and woman was (in) the second place, it was background.

--Hanna Suchocka

Hanna Suchocka was born into a Poland that had only lately come under the dominance of Moscow. Her life parallels the emergence of an independent Poland – with Suchocka, a popular prime minister, presiding over a recent phase of free market reforms.

Suchocka was born on April 3, 1946, in Pleszew, in western Poland. She came from a highly cultured family with politics in its background --one of her grandmothers was a government minister as far back as 1919. Suchocka speaks several languages and plays the piano; she has said that music, poetry, history, and the Catholic religion were important in her home. Her parents ran a pharmacy that had been founded by a grandfather who also lectured on pharmaceutical botany at the University of Poznán. They hoped she would continue the family tradition in pharmacy, but Suchocka chose to study law, as did her younger sister, Elzbieta.

After Hanna Suchocka finished law studies at the University of Poznán, in 1968, she was given a teaching position there for one year. Her contract was not renewed after she refused to join the requisite political party. Instead, she joined another smaller party and pursued more education. In 1975, she obtained a doctoral degree in constitutional law from her alma mater; she later on became a university lecturer.

In 1980, Suchocka became a member of the Communist parliament. It was the year that Solidarity--the trade union movement that was to become a national drive for democratic freedoms--was born in Poland. The country came under martial law in December of 1981 as the government struck back at Solidarity and forced it underground. Lech Walesa and other leaders were interned. Suchocka refused to vote for punitive measures against Solidarity, and upon the expiration of her term in 1984, she left parliament.

Poland changed after President Mikhail Gorbachev introduced reforms in the Soviet Union in the late 1980s. Political agreements in Poland led to elections in June of 1989, which were won by Solidarity-backed candidates: Suchocka was one of them. She joined the Democratic Union party, which was headed by Tadeusz Mazowiecki, the new prime minister. In 1990, Mazowiecki and Lech Walesa both ran for president of Poland, with Walesa the victor. In 1991, Suchocka was elected to a four-year term in the lower house of parliament (the Sejm).

Legislating in the Sejm was difficult because of the multitude of parties represented there – nearly thirty parties in 1992. The voting system was later changed to require that a party win at least five percent of an election in order to be represented. Coalition governing was inevitable, with skill required to put coalitions together. President Walesa went through three prime ministers before Suchocka's name was presented to him. She became his fourth prime minister in 1992.

Suchocka was a strong believer in the free market. Reforms in Poland produced one of the highest levels of economic growth in all of Europe, but also caused high unemployment and great hardship for pensioners, farmers, and public sector employees, including teachers and nurses. An unemployment rate of more than fifteen percent in August of 1993 led to Suchocka's party being rebuffed at the polls in September of that year, despite her personal popularity. Voters turned back to the Communist Left, as had occurred in Lithuania--in effect, asking for a slowdown in reform policy. Suchocka has said that governing is "a bit like mushrooms after the rain. Solve one problem and the next day, two, four, eight spring up."

Suchocka served as Minister of Justice and Attorney General from 1997 to 1999. In 2001, she was appointed to be the Ambassador of Poland to the Holy See.

Lady Margaret Thatcher – Prime Minister, U.K. (1979-90)

I met with Lady Margaret Thatcher at her office in an elegant section of

London. A policeman was on guard at the front steps; a small statue of Sir Winston Churchill graced the office mantelpiece. Lady Thatcher wore a two-piece blue dress which set off flashing blue eyes; her quick mind and debater's skill were evident during the interview. Afterwards, she graciously invited me to tea.

During my questioning, the former prime minister shared memories of growing up in which her father's influence, particularly, played a dominant role: "We were taught to read the papers and discuss the issues of the day...We only rarely went to a film, and it had to be a good film...Not necessarily a terribly learned one--for example, we did go to see Fred Astaire and Ginger Rogers because [the] dancing was just exquisite--but...you were expected to make your own entertainment...We weren't allowed [children's newspapers] full of the comic strips. Those were not permitted in the house."

There's no point in getting too sensitive if you're in politics. What you've got to discern is that what you're doing can be justified by principle, by argument, and to put it across. That's the important thing.

--Lady Margaret Thatcher

Margaret Thatcher – the first woman to become head of a modern European government – also became Britain's longest-serving prime minister in the twentieth century. Other women leaders are invariably compared to her.

Both her family background and college politics shaped Thatcher's intense interest in government and governing. She was born in Grantham in Lincolnshire on October 13, 1925, the second daughter of a small-town grocer, Alfred Roberts, and his wife Beatrice. Her father, a Methodist lay preacher, was very active in his community and served in a variety of civic positions, including those of alderman and mayor. According to Olga Opfell, at the time when her father was a part-time justice of the peace, "Margaret often accompanied him to the courthouse, where she was so fascinated by the unfolding legal dramas that she thought she had erred in choosing a future in science." But a family friend told her to get a chemistry degree before she studied law. She did.

Alfred Roberts believed in giving his daughters a good education, something that had been denied to him. Margaret was the academic daughter, doing well in school and absorbing her adored father's advice and values – thrift, hard work, independence and success. At seventeen, she entered Somerville College, Oxford, where she joined and became president of the Oxford Union Conservative Association. After her graduation, she became a research chemist for a plastics firm – but also began to plan her political future.

Staying involved with the Conservative Party, she became a candidate for Parliament, but lost her first two races (in 1950 and 1951). Nonetheless her political activities led to her meeting Denis Thatcher, a businessman. The couple married in December, 1951 and Margaret gave birth to twins, a daughter and a son, in October, 1953. By then she was studying law, and she was called to the bar the next year. Her specialties became tax and patent law.

In 1959, Thatcher made her third race for a seat in Parliament, and she won. Her maiden speech was impressive, and her hard work, energy, and command of statistics were noticed by Conservative leaders, who had few women in their party. She was made "shadow minister" for several portfolios, following the British custom in which the party out of power creates a mirror cabinet of the party in office.

When the Conservatives did come to power, in 1970, Thatcher was made secretary of education. Her first post quickly became controversial when she canceled the free milk allowance for schoolchildren, in line with Conservative intent to reduce government spending.

The Conservatives lost general elections in 1974, and Thatcher decided to enter the battle to choose a new party leader. She won, in February 1975, having outpolled several other candidates. With Conservative victories in 1979, she became prime minister for the first time; she won her second term in 1983, and her third in 1987.

Many of Thatcher's goals in office were similar to those of President Ronald Regan in the United States: reducing government spending and regulation; lowering taxes for business and the better-off; curbing the power of labor unions (whose membership dropped from 50% to 35% of the labor force during Thatcher's three terms). She also moved to privatize many of Britain's publicly owned industries. Thatcher's friendships with Reagan and Soviet President Mikhail Gorbachev enabled her to play a role in ending the Cold War.

A different war consolidated her power during her first term as prime minister. Patriotic Britain rose behind Thatcher as she fought the brief 1982 Falkland Islands War against Argentina. Michael Genovese has written that "the Falkland victory proved to be the seminal event in Thatcher's years in power. She was now seen as _the_ leader of Britain..."

But Thatcher's period of prime ministership ended when she was challenged from within for leadership of the Conservative Party. Economic problems, foreign policy issues (including her positions against European integration), and an unpopular poll tax which Thatcher championed (adopted, but since abandoned), resulted in a change of party leadership in November of 1990.

Lady Thatcher briefly remained in Parliament after stepping down as prime minister, but soon became a member of the House of Lords, after her elevation to the peerage by Queen Elizabeth II. The position gave her platform from which to speak out on international issues, as she did in the conflict in Bosnia. She wrote two volumes of memoirs as well as a book on international politics. Due to health problems, she retired from a career as a much-sought after public speaker in 2002. But she continued to head the Thatcher Foundation, which is dedicated to helping emerging private businesses in Eastern Europe.

Vaira Vike-Freiberga – President, Latvia (1999-2007)

I've known President Freiberga and her ambassador for some time now. We have met yearly at the World Economic Forum Annual Meet-

ing in Davos, Switzerland. Her chief of staff, ambassador, and other senior advisors are youthful and worldly. What fasicinates me is that the President is able to lead a democracy precisely because she did not live in Latvia in her full adulthood. Similarly, a senior staff of a president would be generally middle-aged. But those who have lived in Latvia during Communist times were immersed in the conditions of those times--unlike these young people and unlike the President with her previous longtime residence in Canada.

President Freiberga is a formal woman in many ways with regal bearing and yet has a dry and piercing wit that emerges unexpectedly, sotto voce. She is also quite disarming. My birthday is March 8th, International Women's Day, which she remembered and for which she gave me a lovely gift.

Vaira Vike-Freiberga was born on December 1, 1937 in Riga, Latvia. She and her parents were World War II refugees to Germany after fleeing the Red Army in 1944. While living in refugee camps in Germany, she suffered several traumatic incidents, including losing a 6-month old sister to pneumonia. Through the UN refugee agencies, she and her family were able to move to Casablanca to do technical work. In 1954, when Vike was 16, they moved to Toronto where they settled with many other Latvians. In Toronto, Vike married a fellow Latvian exile named Imants Freiberga, a future professor of computer science. Vike-Freiberga studied psychology and Latvian Identity at the University of Toronto where she received her BA and MA. She went on to earn her PhD in psychology from McGill University in Montreal, specializing in the relationship between thought and language. She worked as a professor of psychology from 1965 until 1998, when she was asked to become the head of the new Latvian Institute in Riga. The Latvian Institute was established to raise the profile of Latvia and Latvians abroad.

A year after returning to her home country, Vike-Freiberga was chosen as President of Latvia on June 17, 1999, making her not only the first women president of Latvia but also the first women president in Eastern Europe. In Latvia, the president is elected by the *Saeima* (parliament). She was chosen over several better-known candidates by a tight three-vote majority. Originally not a candidate, Vike-Freiberga was chosen as the compromise candidate after a failure to elect a president after the first round of voting required the *Saeima* to choose a highly-respected person not affiliated with any of the political parties in the parliament. She was then re-elected as President on June 20, 2003 for another four-year term by an 88 to 6 margin.

As President, Vike-Freiberga focused primarily on gaining Latvian membership to the EU and NATO; she achieved both goals, on March 29, 2004 and May 1, 2004, respectively. She was particularly active in foreign policy and was known for her outspoken criticism of Russia. Domestically, Vike-Freiberga was successful in stabilizing the econ-omy and cracking down on corruption. To help aid the Westernizing process, she also relaxed the language laws (prior to, Latvian was the only official language allowed in schools, public affairs and many aspects of private business) to meet EU standards of multi-lingual acceptance. She has earned the reputation of lobbying foreign heads of state "with the iron capitalist will of Margaret Thatcher and the refugee-made-good vigor of Madeleine Albright." (Rafael Behr, 2000) Vike-Freiberga left office in July of 2007. She and her husband have since founded VVF Consulting and in December 2007, Vike-Freiberga was appointed Vice President of the Reflection Group established by the EU to debate the EU economic model and to fight global warming.

Vike-Freiberga is the author of eight books, over 160 book chapters and articles in English, French, and Latvian, and over 250 scholarly papers, speeches and allocutions. Aside from Latvian, she is fluent in French, English, Spanish and German. She has been recipient of several honors and distinctions, including, but not limited to: the Anna Abele Prize in Latvian Philology (1979), the Marcel-Vincent Prize and Medal for distinguished work in the Social Sciences from Associa-tion Canadienne Francais pour L'avancement des Sciences (1992), and the Pierre Chauveau Medal for Distinguished Work in Humanities from the Royal Society of Canada (1995). Vike-Freiberga also previ-ously held the position of President in the Canadian Psychological Association, the Social Federation of Canada, and the Association for the advancement of Baltic States (USA). She is currently a member of the Council of Women World Leaders.

She has two grown children: a son, Karlis, currently living in Latvia, and a daughter, Indra, currently working in the Latvian Development Agency.

Khaleda Zia – Prime Minister, Bangladesh (1991-96; 2001-2006)

Prime Minister Zia has been described as rather shy. But she believes that her self-effacing style is welcoming to her people because it contrasts with the style of past military dictators. A kind of dignity characterized her presence when I interviewed her in her nicely appointed office, complete with a computer. She wore a white and black sari with a traditional head scarf.

> *I can tell you that whenever there is a woman leader at the helm of affairs, they face it with courage and determination... women work with patience and they need cooperation.*
>
> *--Khaleda Zia*

East Bengal became East Pakistan which then became Bangladesh. The shy wife of a military officer became the widow of a president, then a party leader and prime minister of her largely Islamic nation.

Khaleda Zia was raised as one of five children, the daughter of a businessman and his social worker wife. Born on August 15, 1945, she grew up in East Bengal and attended primary and secondary schools there. At age 15, she married a captain in the Pakistani army, Ziaur Rahman, and the couple had two sons.

Pakistan's turbulent politics – which featured military takeovers, engineered elections, and the successful seperation of East Pakistan from West Pakistan (to become Bangladesh, in 1971)--frequently affected the life of Ziaur Rahman. However, he advanced in his military career, and by 1975 was military chief of staff. One coup and one assassination later, Zia was given several portfolios in a martial law administration. He eventually was elected president of Bangladesh and founded the Bangladesh Nationalist Party (BNP).

On May 30, 1981 President Zia and two aides were shot while asleep in a military guest house, victims of a disgruntled general.

In March of 1982, H. M. Ershad seized control of Bangladesh in yet another military coup. Martial law was declared once more, and political parties were declared abolished. Nevertheless, the BNP continued to exist, and Khaleda Zia entered politics as BNP's vice chair, and then as the party chair in 1984.

From 1984 until 1990, when Ershad finally resigned, Khaleda Zia was involved in constant protest efforts to end martial law and restore free elections, and was placed under house arrest. Ershad was ultimately forced out and arrested. Fair elections in February of 1991 were won by the BNP, and Khaleda Zia became prime minister in March. Later that same year, a national referendum endorsed a new parliamentary form of government for Bangladesh.

After taking office, Khaleda Zia gave top priority to population control, mass literacy, compulsory primary education, the alleviation of poverty, and rural electrification. Bangladesh is one of the poorest nations in the world, with female literacy rates under thirty percent. Under Zia's rule, population rates dropped and the country was cited as an example of how family planning programs could be made to work even in the world's most impoverished nations.

Although Zia was re-elected in 1996, the government was soon dissolved in response to a boycott by opposition parties. However, she remained politically active, and in 2001, Zia was elected to her third term in office as prime minister.

During this term, she cracked down on Islamic insurgency and promoted development initiatives to help women and children. In an interview with *Time* magazine, Zia remarked that, "Girls' education is very important. If we want to progress as a country, if we want to remove poverty, if we have to spread awareness of family planning and bring down population growth, we have to educate them, give them equal rights. Women have to prove that they are no less than men."

In 2006, Forbes magazine ranked Zia 33rd on its list of the world's 100 most powerful women.

Chapter XI: Geography and Gender

While geography may not drastically change over the course of a decade, issues of gender certainly can. The status of women in the countries of the original 15 leaders have been updated as necessary and the four additional countries of Canada, Latvia, Liberia, and New Zealand are included in this chapter as well.

Bangladesh

In Bangladesh, women are subordinate, second-class citizens by virtue of historical and religious tradition. Sons are valued as the sex that provides for parents in old age; girls have traditionally been less educated and have even been fed less food--a deprivation reflected in the fact that women are less than half the population of Bangladesh. Because a woman must customarily bring a dowry to her husband's family when she marries, and takes her capacity to labor there, a saying in the country is that spending money on a girl child means "planting trees for other people's gardens."

Bangladesh, with its large population of approximately 142 million, is an overwhelmingly agricultural society. Women's rural labor has been needed to help families survive. Women still hold only a small fraction of wage-earning jobs in the country; the garment industry is one area where they are concentrated.

Given Bangladesh's great poverty and its anti-female traditions, it is interesting that the country has recently had about the same percentage of women in the legislature as the U.S. Congress--around 15%. Bangladesh has reserved some parliamentary seats for women only. However, the number is so small (thirty of over three hundred seats) that "women's seats" have served as a token to enable parties to avoid having more women candidates on regular party slates. Much press reporting has been generated by the fact that two major parties are led by women--one of them Prime Minister Zia and the other Sheikh Hasina--who are antagonistic to one another.

A political scientist has written that "one of the liabilities of [women's] entry into public life remains the threat of character assassination by whisper and innuendo that is damaging to the honor of the women concerned. Women leaders conform publicly to the tradition of purdah, albeit symbolically and nationally, by covering their heads with their saris. Some degree of accommodation to the customs and values prescribed by religious-cultural traditions is necessary, for the national constituency remains conservative and imbued with patriarchal values."

In a country where literacy rates are low for both men and women-- but significantly lower for women--the government is trying to develop its educational resources. The government in 1991 made universal primary education mandatory, but warned that it could not fully implement the law promptly. Pilot programs have been started, and in 1993 the government created a Division of Primary Education, separate from the Ministry of Education, to report directly to the Prime Minister's office. As of 2006, primary school enrollment for both girls and boys was above 90%, and secondary school enrollment was about 50%, with slightly higher percentages of girls attending than boys. The Government had made special efforts to improve female literacy rates through policy measures that included provision of free education for girls at secondary school levels, food-for-education, and allocating a 60% quota for female primary school teachers.

Bangladesh is one of the nations proving that efforts to limit population growth can work even in the poorest countries (life expectancy for both sexes is about fifty-five). Average family size has fallen from seven children in 1970 to approximately four in 2003. The government is attempting to work with NGOs (nongovernmental organizations) to achieve educational and other reforms.

Bangladesh has been said to have a "nascent" women's movement, built on a variety of women's organizations: "It is on issues concerning violence and oppression...that women's groups have responded with the most vigor." In Bangladesh, women are still flogged, stoned, burned, and disfigured by acid for giving "moral offense." A Cruelty to Women law has been on the books since 1983, but enforcement is weak, especially in rural areas where most people live.

As in other Muslim countries, an Islamic fundamentalist party is active in Bangladesh, and seeks to confine women to traditional ways of life. Hundreds of men came into the streets of Dhaka in the summer of 1994 to advocate death for a feminist author who outspokenly advocates female liberation, including sexual liberation, akin to that enjoyed by many women in the West. Bangladesh is also often considered the birthplace of modern microfinance, since Nobel Laureate Mohammad Yunus initiated his Grameen Bank at the University of Chittagong and its surrounding villages. Since the creation of the bank the majority of loan recipients have been women.

Canada

The United States' neighbor to the North reached several key benchmarks in women's rights and political participation in the early 20th century, but Canada has since outpaced the U.S. in various measures of equality. Women in Canada were granted the right to vote in 1917 and were able to stand for election beginning in 1920. In recent decades, this nation has instituted policies promoting wage equality, accessibility of government-provided childcare, paid maternity leave, eliminating violence against women, and access to safe abortion.

From June 25th until November 4th, 1993, Kim Campbell served as the first and only female Prime Minister of Canada. After the unpopular Prime Minister Brian Mulroney stepped down from his position, the Progressive Conservative Party elected Campbell to take his place. The majority of her term was dominated by the fall's election, and her party lost their majority government. Currently, 21% of seats in the

House of Commons, 33% of seats in the Senate, and 23% of ministerial positions are held by women. Additionally, Her Excellency Mihaëlle Jean is the current Governor General, the monarchy's representative in government, and is the first person of Afro-Caribbean heritage. She is the third woman, and the second immigrant to hold this position.

Although geographically a large country, Canada has a population of just over 32 million people. The population density of three people per square kilometer is among the lowest in the world. Canada is also one of the wealthiest countries in the world, ranking 17th out of 229 countries as measured by per capita gross domestic product estimates from 2006. Women comprise 47% of the total labor force, with 60% of women working in comparison to 72% of men. With regards to the gender wage gap, Canada is ranked 28th internationally, with women earning 71% of men's wages for similar work.

Canada also has a history of an organized and visible women's movement. Developed primarily in the 1970s and 1980s, organizations promoting women's rights, most notably the National Action Committee on the Status of Women, have been working to improve women's political influence and legislative success. The demands of a party-structured parliamentary system and a burgeoning movement of conservative groups have posed several of the greatest challenges to advancing women's equality through the political system.

Dominica

Dominica is one of the least developed of the Caribbean islands, with a small population of about ninety thousand. Approximately 80% of its people are Roman Catholics. In 2007, life expectancy at birth was more than 78 years for women and about 72 years for men. The literacy rate for both sexes is equal, at about 94%.

Dominica's economy has traditionally been heavily dependent upon its banana crop, which is sent to Great Britain. A land reform program was put into effect after independence in 1978 and received wide support: large estates were acquired by the government, divided, and tenure granted to former workers. In 1989, there were about thirteen thousand female workers in a total island labor force of some thirty thousand. General unemployment was high in 1991--approximately 15%. Less than 10% of the work force is unionized.

Dominica's prime minister, Dame Eugenia Charles, was the first woman in the Caribbean to hold such office, and be active in regional institutions. Under her leadership, "Dominica has become favored as a recipient of international aid." UN figures for 1987 showed women as nearly 13% of the country's parliament (House of Assembly), which has thirty members. As mentioned in chapter seven of this book, women have in some recent years held more than 20% of ministerial-level government positions. In the civil service, salaries are attached to a position and gender is irrelevant. However, there are no laws requiring equal pay for equal work in the private sector.

Problems for women in Dominica have included inheritance law (in 1993, a woman could not inherit property to sell if her husband died without a will, although she could live on the property) and sexual harassment, which is unregulated by law. The Welfare Department assists battered women, but in 1993 there was no long-term residence shelter available for them. Women's groups in Dominica have called for more programs for pregnant teens and teenage mothers. (In 1992 the age of consent for sexual relations was raised from fourteen to sixteen.) Women's rights groups have also sought legislation to govern domestic violence and sexual harassment. As of 2007, neither have been criminalized.

France

Simone de Beauvoir, France's well-known writer, stated that work is a *first* condition of independence; she also declared that "la liberté de la femme commence au ventre" (women's freedom starts in the belly).

Women are doing quite well on these scores today in France: approximately 48% of French women work, and abortion was legalized by the French National Assembly in December of 1974. Access to abortion has become greater and greater, with state funding available in 1982. Contraceptives became widely and freely available in France in the late sixties.

Jane Jenson and Mariette Sineau have written about this country of sixty million people: "Since the late nineteenth century France has had one of the highest rates of female labor-force participation and until recently one of the smallest gaps between women's and men's wages [around 30 to 35% in 1991, but up to around 50% in 2006]. It is, however, a country where the vision of wives as totally subordinate to husbands was not modified in the Napoleonic Code [which treated wives as, essentially, minors] until the middle of the twentieth century and where everyday language celebrates the difference between women and men."

Attitudes dictating the role of women as culture bearers, as highly significant presences within the home, date back into the nineteenth century, and make it prestigious for women not to work. The *femme au foyer* has been seen as a teacher of civilized values and an arranger of important functions in a culture that values the domestic circle and a high quality of daily living.

An ironic effect of the granting of suffrage to French women in 1944 was their emergence as conservative voters. Only in the 1980s did French women appear in a new role, as more liberal voters than men, and as equally frequent casters of ballots. A study found that "the factor most able to produce such a change [was] active participation in the labor force. Women in paid employment were much more likely than other women to participate in elections and vote for the Left, especially the Socialists."

However, women remain few in elected office, especially at high levels. In 2006, only 12% of parliamentarians and 18% of ministerial positions were women. According to Jenson and Sineau, French political parties "continue to be clubbish and oligarchic institutions that are closed to women..." The Socialist Party has had statutes stipulating women's quotas for governing bodies inside the party, and for some candidacies (not the national legislature), but the quota system "has not been respected inside the party organization, nor has much effort been made to elect women to the National Assembly." Jenson and Sineau also maintain that "the largest and most visible wings of the contemporary women's movement in France have never focused on the feminization of elected institutions." A study showed that "male politicians have an image of women politicians as constituting a tiny minority. Teased about being different, women politicians are reduced to their sex and considered inferior because of it."

In 2007, Ségolène Royal, the female Socialist Party candidate for the presidency, lost to Nicolas Sarkozy by approximately 2.2 million votes. Ms. Royal was largely supported by urban lower and middle-class voters, students, and the left-leaning regional departments. Her candidacy was the closest a woman has come to winning the presidency in the French Republic. Although Royal was unsuccessful in her bid for the top office, Sarkozy's election still garnered a political win for women--for the first time in French history, the cabinet included almost as many women as men with seven of the 15 ministers appointed being women, including high-profile portfolios such as Justice, Finance, and Interior ministries.

Iceland

Many of the things that women need to live decently are provided by Iceland's extensive social welfare system: "There is a comprehensive system of social security, including old-age pensions, family allowances, maternity grants, widow's pensions... Pensions and health insurance now apply to the whole population. Accident insurance applies to all wage and salary earners and self-employed persons..." Icelandic law even mandates adequate public day-care "as part of the extensive 'law of the child' passed by the Althing [parliament] in 1992." Prior to the 1992 law, one town (Akureyri) influenced by women's activism wrote into its budget that all single parents not able to get their children into the town's day-care centers were to receive money instead, "for three, six, or nine months."

Iceland is a small country of approximately 260,000 people, some 100,000 of whom live in the capital city of Reykjavik. An extraordinary event in Iceland's history was the October 24, 1975 Women's Strike--in which 90-95% of all Icelandic women refused to work for a day in order to demonstrate the force of women's labor and to protest inequalities. In Reykjavik, according to police statistics, twenty-five thousand women attended a rally. The success of the effort has been attributed to "effective and comprehensive organization," involving almost all of Iceland's women's organizations, and an executive committee where all of the country's political parties and Iceland's largest labor unions were represented.

Social changes had occurred in Iceland in years prior to the Women's Strike. In 1964, only 28% of married women over age sixteen held full- or part-time jobs. The numbers went up until, by 1980, they were as high as 65% in the capital city. Today, 71% of women participate in the labor force. Women's educational level also rose: in 1970, only 15% of those graduating from the University of Iceland were women; by 1980 women were 41%. In 2006, 79% of women were enrolled in institutions of higher education, in comparison to only 44% of men.

In 1970, the feminist revival which had begun to affect the United States and Europe came to Iceland in the form of the Redstocking movement--initiated by women who had few ties to older women's organizations in the country. The Redstocking women had a varied agenda: they wanted free abortions, more money for day-care centers, equal pay, and more power for women in political parties and labor unions. They were able to have some influence because of a leftist government (1971-74) which sympathized with their concerns. Also, although there were only three women in Iceland's parliament at the time, one of the three women (Svava Jakobsdóttir) became their spokeswoman. They thus complied with Gloria Steinem's injunction to "surround the goal" by having activists both inside and outside of government.

The number of women in the Althing was to be tiny for many years. Between 1971 and 1983, for example, only three women were members, despite the fact that women's suffrage dated back to 1915. However, Iceland uses a proportional system of voting, and the introduction of women's lists in the early 1980s began to produce gains, first at the municipal level and then in parliament. In 2006, 33% of parliament and 27% of ministerial positions were held by women. Women's List is currently an active feminist political party. Since the 1990s, not only was a woman president of Iceland, but women were also Chief Justice of the Supreme Court and Speaker of the Althing (the latter more of a ceremonial post than in most other nations).

Icelandic women do not have "abortion on demand," but a law (of 1975) permitting doctors to decide on the sufficiency of grounds for abortions is very liberally construed.

Issues prioritized by the Women's List in Iceland include equal pay for equal work, domestic violence and rape. There is overall a difference of 40% in earnings for women and men, and complaints have been that police and the courts are not sensitive to issues of violence against women. One improvement reported in 1993 was that the Reykjavik City Hospital emergency ward "now has an all-female staff to care for rape victims."

Ireland

Ireland--traditionally one of Europe's most conservative countries for women--is still a country of challenge. Irish women labored hard, even went to prison, to get the vote in 1922. However, they still must go abroad (usually to Britain) to get an abortion. According to the Irish Family Planning Association, between January 1980 and December 2004, at least 117,673 women traveled to Britain for abortion services. There are no available statistics to account for the number of women who travel to other countries for abortion services. Women also live in a culture where divorce remained constitutionally forbidden until the Family Law (Divorce) Act of 1996. Major battles were waged in this 95% Catholic country to make contraceptives widely available in the 1980s.

During her campaign for the presidency of Ireland, Mary Robinson made a remark which was supposed to have been, but turned out not to be, politically suicidal. She said: "...the whole patriarchal male-dominated presence of the [Catholic] church is probably the worst aspect of all the establishment forces that have sought to do down women over the years." Ireland and Catholicism have been virtual synonyms; however, new forces are today on the scene. Ireland's participation in the European Economic Community creates legal obligations for the country, and these ties have affected the issues of abortion and homosexual rights in Ireland. The European Court of Human Rights ruled in 1988, for example, that Ireland had to decriminalize homosexuality.

In 1992, Ireland's voters declared in a national referendum that women have a right to abortion *information*--a position opposed by the Catholic Church. The voters, also, voted down a right to abortion on narrow grounds--an outcome welcomed by some feminists because the grounds were so limited. These women felt that other routes-- legal ones--to wider abortion rights are to be pursued.

Ireland is a small country with a population of just over four million people; traditionally agricultural, it is now nearly 60% urban. Nearly 50% of Ireland's women play traditional roles as wives and/or mothers and do not have wage-paying jobs; Ireland has fewer women in the labor force than any other European Community country. Complicating the situation for women who would like to work is the absence of social services.

When they do hold jobs, a human rights report found that women "are discriminated against in the areas of equal pay and promotion to senior positions in both the public and private sectors." In 2006, the average hourly wage for women was 70% of what men received.

In 1990, the government established the Second Commission on the Status of Women to "promote greater equality for women in all facets of Irish life," including training and education, employment opportunities, and legal rights. At the time the Commission was established, women did not have automatic joint ownership of the family home. There is a quasi-official Council for the Status of Women, representing over one hundred national women's organizations, that works on women's issues.

As might be expected, there are low numbers of women in high elected national office in Ireland. However, in addition to having its first woman president, the country, in October of 1993, saw the first woman elected leader of a national political party--Mary Harney of the Progressive Democrats. Ms. Harney is currently the Minister of Health and in 1997, Ireland elected its second female President, Mary McAleese who is the current Head of State. In 2006, women made up 13% of seats in parliament and 21% of positions in ministries.

Latvia

Much of the history of Latvia can be characterized by foreign occupation. Following World War I, full independence was proclaimed on November 18, 1918, followed by a War of Independence. On the brink of the Second World War, Latvia was forced to accept a pact of mutual assistance with the Soviet Union that allowed the Soviet Army to station troops in Latvia, even though most of the Baltic Germans had left Latvia by 1939. Allegations of pact violations led to Soviet occupation of the country and formal annexation into the USSR by August 1940.

Beginning in 1989, the process towards the Restoration of Independence of the Republic of Latvia began with a resolution by the Supreme Court of the USSR that declared that the occupation was not in accordance with law and not the will of the Soviet people. Latvian independence was won on August 21, 1991. Since this time, Latvia has focused on rejoining Europe by becoming a member state of NATO and the European Union. These two goals were achieved in 2004. As a parliamentary representative democratic republic, Latvia has one of the highest GDP growth rates in Europe, though still has one of the lower standards of living on the continent. While Latvia's population historically has been comprised of a multitude of ethnicities, demographic trends in the 20th century have shifted towards a majority-minority composition with 60% of the 2.3 million people being Latvian and about 30% being Russian.

Women officially received the right to vote in 1918, but because of historical circumstances and changing systems of governance, more widespread political participation by women is most significant in the past two decades. In addition to President Vike-Freiberga, there are currently 21 women, including the Speaker, in the 100-member parliament and 4 women in the 18-member cabinet of ministers. From the 2006 World Economic Forum's *Gender Gap Report*, Latvia ranks 42nd out of 115 surveyed countries for women's representation in parliament, 23rd for women in ministerial positions, and 10th for number of years with a female head of state.

Violence against women, sexual harassment, and trafficking in women are substantial problems for the country. Existing legislation seems to contain gaps in the criminal code, such as criminalizing rape but not acknowledging incidences of spousal rape. Additionally, law enforcement against domestic violence, harassment, employment discrimination, and pay equity has been relatively ineffective. In the labor market, women experience discrimination in both hiring and pay, particularly in the emerging private sector. On average, women make 63% of men's salaries for comparable work. Women are also trafficked or otherwise work in the informal sector such as sex work. Latvia is primarily a source and transit point for trafficked persons, with the main countries of destination being Germany, Spain, Great Britain, Italy, Switzerland, Sweden, and Norway. According to the U.S. Department of State report, women, including well-educated women, homeless teens, and minors graduating from orphanage boarding schools, are among those most at-risk of being trafficked. The National Action Plan to Combat Trafficking in Persons was adopted in March of 2004, but a lack of resources and competing budget priorities have limited its ability to provide direct assistance to trafficked persons.

While still facing many gender disparities in certain sectors, Latvia has achieved gender parity in education where primary schooling is free, compulsory, and universal through the 9th grade and free through the 12th grade. Access to healthcare is universal, thus also achieving gender equity.

Liberia

Freed slaves from the United States began to settle the country now called Liberia in 1822. By 1847, the Americo-Liberians had established a republic for former slaves wishing to return to their native continent. In the mid-twentieth century, President William Tubman worked diligently to encourage foreign investment in Liberia and bridge the social, economic, and political gaps between the original inhabitants of the region and the descendents of the settlers.

Following a substantial period of democracy and stability, Samuel Doe led a military coup in 1980, instigating nearly a decade of authoritarian rule. In 1989, Charles Taylor launched a rebellion against Doe's regime that sparked a civil war. Doe was eventually killed and the 1997 elections brought Charles Taylor to power, though much of the internal conflict continued. In 2003, a peace agreement led to the end of the civil war and Taylor was exiled to Nigeria. After two years of interim government rule, Ellen Johnson Sirleaf won a multiparty election to become the first female president of Liberia and in Africa. As the first leader after more than two decades of political instability and violent conflict, Johnson Sirleaf has the great responsibility of leading massive reconstruction and revitalization in a republic of approximately 3.5 million citizens.

As is frequently the case within the context of a country in conflict, women were one specific set of victims in Liberia during the 14-year civil conflict. While the transitional government generally respected the human rights of its citizens, problems persisted in particular geographical areas. Reports from both the new government in Liberia and the annual Country Report on Human Rights Practices released by the U.S. Department of State recount cases of discrimination and violence (particularly sexual violence) against women, female genital cutting, neglect and abuse of children, and trafficking in persons. Recent legislative measures have strengthened the existing rape laws.

Incidences of poverty, unemployment, and illiteracy remain wide-spread and continue to act as obstacles to women in the post-conflict reconstruction phase. Due to the destroyed infrastructure, many adolescent girls and women were displaced, preventing them from attaining any formal education or pursuing a livelihood in their traditional responsibilities of food production and distribution.

Liberian women do have the legal right to inherit land and property, receive equal pay, and own their own businesses. Women's profes-sional groups have emerged over the last year to advocate for their needs and raise public awareness regarding government corruption, the economy, and security issues. The women working in the exten-sive network of markets throughout the country played a significant role in the election of President Johnson Sirleaf. In coordinating their support of Johnson Sirleaf's candidacy, the market women demon-strated their power and influence within Liberian society. In 2007, the United Nations Mission in Liberia (UNMIL) received the first all-female peacekeeping unit, consisting of 100 Indian policewomen, to help rebuild the Liberian National Police force and possibly reduce the incidences of sexual exploitation and abuses reported by UN peace-keepers.

Lithuania

A major problem for women in Lithuania in recent years has been the economic struggle to survive. In 2004, 21% of citizens lived under the poverty threshold (defined as 60% of their country's median income). The transition to a free-market economy has been difficult.

Lithuania is a country of approximately 3.5 million people, with substantial ethnic minorities of Russians, Poles, and others. Most ethnic Lithuanians are Roman Catholics by belief or by family background. Under the new 1992 constitution, citizens are granted the right to "old-age and disability pensions, as well as to social assistance in the event of unemployment, sickness, widowhood..."   A comprehensive state-funded health care system was introduced when Lithuania was still under Soviet domination; since independence, private medical practice has been legalized. Life expectancy for women was sixty-eight in 2006, which is ten years higher than that of men, but nearly ten years lower than the average life expectancy for women in the early '90s when the country first became independent. Although there have been set-backs in women's health indicators, women do enjoy maternity and day-care benefits.

Lithuania's work force is employed in a number of different areas, including industrial production (food processing, light industry, machine building) and agriculture. In 2006, 52% of women were participants in the labor force. Unemployment has recently been low by most standards, but underemployment is a serious problem. An interesting footnote to Lithuania's labor situation is a shortage of trained lawyers--of either sex.

According to the 2006 World Economic Forum *Gender Gap Report*, women make 59% of what men make for similar work.   They are also under-represented in government "for cultural and historical reasons":

in 1993, only ten members of the 141-member parliament (Seimas) were women, and there were no female ministers in the cabinet. By 2006, 22% of parliamentary seats and 15% of civil service positions were held by women, so the situation for women in government is improving. One political party--the Lithuanian Green Party--was chaired by a woman, Irena Ignataviciene. Lithuania has two Chernobyl-type reactors, worrisome to some, and the issue of environmental pollution has been on the agenda since the late 1980s.

A growing number of organizations that promote women's rights are active in Lithuania, but "public awareness of women's issues is still at a rudimentary stage..." One problem for women is spousal abuse associated with alcoholism.

The Netherlands Antilles

The Netherlands Antilles has been called--to the annoyance of some-- a "rich developing country." Despite hard times since the 1980s, the Netherlands-affiliated, five-island nation has reached a level of income well above that of other Caribbean countries. For example, UNDP shows the Netherlands Antilles as having a per capita GDP of approximately $12,550 in 2004, while Dominica, by way of comparison, is shown at $5,643. A well-developed union movement in the Netherlands Antilles has helped keep wages high. Economic conditions vary substantially from island to island.

The country has a population of approximately 223,000. In 2002, there was still substantial unemployment at around 17%. In earlier years, money from oil refining and shipping had produced wealth to support government services. The oil refined in the Netherlands Antilles is imported; the country lacks natural resources and does not even have much arable land. Food is imported also.

An educational system similar to that in the Netherlands has produced a high adult literacy rate in the country, about 96% for both sexes. The political and religious circumstances of each of the five islands vary. Political parties are indigenous to each island, and three of the islands are mostly Roman Catholic, while two are mostly Protestant. Life expectancy (2006) is about comparable to that in the U.S., seventy-eight years for women and seventy-four for men.

Work outside the home is seen as "normal" and "nothing new" for women in the country. Women work in the public sector, in the usual "women's professions" (such as teaching and nursing) and, though less frequently, as businesswomen, attorneys, or other professionals. Because women *do* work outside the home, one of their greatest needs is the sharing of housework and childrearing duties. Since 1995, labor laws have been changed to improve the status of women workers, such as the Old Age Insurance Act which made it possible for women to collect their own pensions separate from those of their husbands.

Issues of violence against women are also on the country's feminist agenda. In January of 2002, a law was finally passed against marital rape, but there is still no specific law against domestic violence and very few shelters for battered women exist on any of the five islands (in 2002 there was only one, on the island of Sint Maarten). Women who need to escape from abusive men sometimes go to the Netherlands.

Interestingly, although abortion is not legal in the Netherlands Antilles, it is "not an issue." Women "know where to go," according to a women's activist.[1]

In March 2006, Emily Saïdy de Jongh-Elhage became Prime Minister of the Netherlands Antilles. Jongh-Elhage is the leader of the Party for the Restructured Antilles, a political party that was formed in the aftermath of the constitutional referendums held in 1993 in which a majority of citizens voted against the dissolution of the Netherlands Antilles. Since then, the party has steadily increased its political following, winning the prime ministership first in 2002 and again in 2006.

The Netherlands Antilles is to be disbanded on December 15th, 2008 to form two associated states of Curaçao and Sint Maarten, while Bonaire, Saba, and Sint Eustatius will become a direct part of the Netherlands as special municipalities. It is unknown whether certain policies such as prostitution and same-sex marriage will become legal on these islands.

New Zealand

Located southeast of Australia within the islands of the South Pacific Ocean, New Zealand is believed to have been originally settled by Polynesians between 1000 and 1300. The descendents of these settlers established a distinct way of life and became known as the Maori. Evidence of Europeans visiting the land dates back to the mid-1600s but European settlement did not substantially commence until the early 19th century, with a primary focus on establishing trading stations and carrying out Christian missionary work. A series of armed conflicts over land ensued between the Maori people and the European settlers throughout the middle of the 19th century. With European settlers in dominant control of the land, New Zealand became a colony of the United Kingdom in its own right in 1841. The volatile combination of these conflicts, disease, and loss of land precipitated a fall in the Maori population, from a high of around 86,000 in the 18th century to just over 40,000 by the end of the 1890s. At the turn of the twentieth century, New Zealand decided against joining the Commonwealth of Australia and gained its independence from the British as a separate *dominion* in 1907.

Throughout the history of conflict over territorial claims, women have played a vital role in the creation of New Zealand as a nation. Granted the right to vote in 1893, women have been full and active participants in the political realm. Ranked 11th out of the 115 countries in the World Economic Forum's 2006 Gender Gap Index on women's political empowerment, New Zealand currently has 39 women in the 121-seat Parliament, seven women on the executive council (comprising 25% of the 28 ministers), and women serving as prime minister, speaker of the house, and chief justice of the Supreme Court. Prime Minister Helen Clark has directed New Zealand ever since 1999 following Jenny Shipley who governed from 1997 until 1999.

With regards to economic equality, however, New Zealand has not performed as well. Participation of women in the paid workforce has grown from under 30% in 1959 to over 60% currently. Average hourly earnings of women range in estimates from between 63% of men's earnings, according to the World Economic Forum, to 87% of men's wages, according to the New Zealand Department of Labour. The Pay and Employment Equity Unit was established in 2004 to implement a plan of action that includes an equitable job evaluation tool, administering an annual fund to projects that support equitable pay, and providing ongoing training and support. In addition to specific units within individual ministries, New Zealand has a Ministry of Women's Affairs, tasked with providing policy recommendations to improve the status of women, recommend qualified women nominees for state sector boards, and manage international obligations in relation to the status of women under the UN Convention for the Elimination of Discrimination Against Women.

In New Zealand, violence against women affects individuals from all socioeconomic and ethnic groups. Although Maori women and children comprise only ten percent of the total population, they constituted over half of the individuals who utilized the National Collective of Independent Women Refugees. It indicates that this population may be at an increased risk of violence within families. Through a government task force for Action on Violence within Families, the government has supported women's shelters, rape crisis centers, sexual abuse counseling, family violence networks, and violence prevention services.

The country has taken a strong stance against the trafficking of persons; while there have been no confirmed cases of internationally trafficked persons since 2001, incidents of migrant workers, mail-order brides, and those committed to arranged marriages are at a higher risk of losing their autonomy and becoming victims of trafficking.

General indicators on quality of life for women are high, with average life expectancy at close to 82 years (6 years longer than males) and gender parity in literacy at 99%.

Nicaragua

As has been typical for women in Central and South America, Nicaraguan women, prior to the revolution of 1979, were part of a gender division that "ties women to their home and family in a subservient position, while men...occupy positions of leadership in all spheres, particularly the public political one." This division has been traditionally discussed in relation to the concepts of *marianismo* and *machismo*--the first requiring women to be humble and virtuous (like the Virgin Mary) and the latter expressing male self-assertion, autonomy, and dominance.

Under a series of Somoza-family dictators, social conditions in Nicaragua were so repressive and impoverishing that "mass poverty caused family disintegration. Men without work...frequently abandoned their families, going off to search for jobs. Women found themselves alone, with responsibility for home and children." In 1963, for example, census figures showed 25% of the households in Managua, the capital, to be headed by women. Because they had no choice, "larger numbers of women in Nicaragua came to participate in the labor force than in other Latin American countries where repression was less acute." Statistics from the OAS (Organization of American States) in 1979 "showed Nicaragua leading the rest of Central America in the percentage of females in the total work force." In 2006, only 36% of women were in the labor force, as opposed to 86% of men.

In the 1960s, Nicaragua began to slowly move towards revolution. One researcher has compared the involvement of women in guerrilla movements in five countries. She found that "women took part in every phase of the Revolution to overthrow Somoza and made up 30% of the FSLN (Sandinista National Liberation Front) guerrilla membership at the time of the final offensive," in 1979. Women took part in strikes and demonstrations, hid combatants and weaponry in "safe houses," and, towards the end, led major military offensives. The new revolutionary government "supported the women's movement and recognized the need to address and respond to women's issues." AMNLAE, a new women's organization aligned with the government, was founded, and was named for the first woman (Luisa Amanda Espinoza) who died fighting Somoza's National Guard.

Under the new government, "alimony and child support became newly legislated rights. Common-law marriages, the most typical kind, and 'illegitimate' children, the majority of all children, were now recognized." Laws such as the "Law of Nurturing" assigned equal responsibility for childrearing to men and women both. However, abortion rights were not one of the rights given to women--the subject is too sensitive in Catholic Nicaragua, even though unsafe abortions have been a main cause of maternal deaths. In 2006, the abortion law was made even more strict, imposing 30-year jail sentences for women who terminate their pregnancies—even if the procedure was done to save the woman's life. Backed and campaigned for by the Catholic church, the law was supported by all the major political parties.

In the 1990s, the situation for women in Nicaragua was shaped by the extreme poverty caused by a decade of U.S.-funded war. The well-documented gains in literacy and public health conditions achieved by the Sandinista government were eroded. Diseases like cholera were on the rise, infant mortality was increasing, and diarrhea became the most common cause of death among Nicaraguan children. Government spending on health and other social services has been cut, partly at the behest of international lenders, and nongovernmental organizations are struggling to maintain health and family planning services with private contributions. Unemployment and underemployment are commonly assessed to run as high as 50 to 70%. Many of Nicaragua's approximately 5.5 million people are seriously malnourished.

In 1987, parliamentary seats in the national legislature were about 13 % held by women. According to the U.S. State Department, in 1993 women "occupied some senior positions in government, the trade union movement, and social organizations, but were underrepresented in management positions in the private sector and formed the majority of workers in the traditionally low-paid educational, textile, and health service sectors."

Women's groups independent of AMNLAE have strengthened in Nicaragua. An organizer for La Malinche, one such group, stated: "We won't set up clinics...We target patriarchy more than the government. Above all we don't ask anyone's permission to be feminists." In 1992 some groups joined together to form the National Feminist Committee (CNF).

As of 2006, literacy rates for men and women in Nicaragua were around 77%, and there was approximate gender parity in enrollment in primary and secondary school (at 87% and 43% respectively for both men and women). Women's participation in government has also been increasing, with 21% of parliamentary seats and 14% of ministerial positions occupied by women. There are still major challenges for women's equality in this country. There have been both gains and losses in recent years.

Norway

Norway--a country of 4.6 million people with egalitarian traditions-- impresses an observer on many fronts. Not only does it have a parliament (the Storting) that is more than one-third women (with women also one-third of municipal councils and equally or even more frequent on county councils), but its highly developed social welfare benefits include national health insurance (abortions are paid for as part of health services); extensive paid parental leave (42 weeks at 100% wage compensation or 52 weeks at 80% wage compensation with 9 weeks explicitly reserved for the mother and 4 weeks explicitly reserved for the father); legally mandated worker vacations of twenty-

172

five or thirty-one days per year (the latter for workers over sixty); and a legal work week of 37.5 hours. Norway's women began coming into the labor force in large numbers in the 1970s and currently, more than 70% of women work.

Historically, Norway has had many "firsts" for women. It was, for example, the first country in the world to allow daughters to inherit legally with sons, in 1854. For the first three years after World War II, the work of women in the house was counted as part of the country's Gross National Product, until Norway was forced to give up this practice in order to comply with international labor standards. Women obtained the national vote in 1907, second in Europe after Finland (1906).

Some women's organizations in Norway date back into the nineteenth or early twentieth century; political parties and trade unions have had women's branches (Norway is heavily unionized, with membership about 60% of the work force). In recent years three major parties have been simultaneously headed by women. The National Machinery for Gender Equality is also well-developed, complete with specific committees within the Parliament and of state secretaries from various ministries, the politically-independent Centre for Gender Equality, and the politically-independent Gender Equality Ombud to enforce the Gender Equality Act.

In 2007, there were 61 women in the 169-seat parliament (36%), six of the 19 Supreme Court justices were female, nine of the 19 government ministries were headed by women, and over 27% of the country's judges were women. As noted in chapter seven of this book, however, several years of effort were needed in order to raise the number of women in elected office in Norway to present levels. Agitation for more women on party candidate lists began at the municipal level in 1967. Write-in provisions of electoral laws allowed the scratch-out of men's names and the writing-in of women's names. These electoral provisions were changed at some points by political parties when women appeared to be gaining too many seats. Year by year, however, inroads were made.

One researcher found that "the most effective, overarching strategy developed by Norwegian women activists" to promote change was "the building of a strong coalition" between older and newer women's organizations: "After the mid-1970s, the establishment women and the new feminists created a tightly knit network of committees which worked on getting party nominations of female candidates and their placement in top positions on election ballots. Moreover, a concerted effort was made to develop policies catering to women's interests and to gain acceptance of such policies by political parties." [1,2]

Norway adopted its Gender Equality Act in 1978 as a practical instrument for creating de facto gender equality. Founded in the Nordic philosophy that equality extends beyond equal opportunity, the Act makes an active effort to promote the status of women. Part of the Gender Equality Act is the Equal Status Act that promotes "equal pay for work of equal value." According to one researcher, "the bill has not resolved the ominous wage differences between the sexes, despite the longevity of this important issue"; typically, women work in lower-paid and substantially sex-segregated fields. [3] Norwegian women have not been able to influence the business world as they have the political, nor have union groups always been on their side. In 1981, the ESA was amended by parliament in an important way: to provide that government-appointed public committees, boards, and councils have a 40% women representation.

Since women hold many jobs in the public sector in Norway (70% of state employees are women), cuts in public services caused by difficult economic times can affect women's jobs disproportionately, and also disrupt the "safety net" which strengthens their lives.

Norway is a country where crime against women is not widespread; the crime of marital rape is recognized in the law; access to abortion in the first twelve weeks of pregnancy has been a "civil right" since 1978; and a government-funded network of shelters for battered women that consists of over 50 shelters and five crisis hotlines have been provided since 2007.

Pakistan

The situation for many women (and children) in Pakistan today is so deleterious to their welfare as to be almost unbelievable to a 21st century observer. In the 2006 World Economic Forum's annual *Global Gender Gap Report*, Pakistan was ranked overall 112 out 115 countries surveyed. While acquiring low rankings in economic participation and opportunity, educational attainment, and health and survival rankings, Pakistan did achieve a top-third ranking (35 out 115) in political empowerment.

Primary education is not de facto compulsory in this country of 157 million people, despite a 1962 law that was to have begun the process of mandatory primary education. Local laws do not mandate free public education with most schools charging tuition and fees for books, supplies, and uniforms. Although the government has adopted laws to protect child laborers, enforcement is weak. According to the Human Rights Commission of Pakistan (HRCP), there were approximately 10 million child laborers in 2006 and there are "unofficial estimates" that "one-third of Pakistan's total labor force of thirty-three million is made up of workers under the age 18." The Employment of Children Act of 1991 set seven hours as the maximum workday for children under fourteen and prohibited work in factories, mines, and other hazardous locations. A study found that approximately a million children are engaged in the cottage industry of weaving carpets, which are a Pakistani export; these children had either never been to school or had dropped out. Absent mandatory primary education, Pakistan's relatively high illiteracy rate of 25% (male) and 45% (female) is not surprising.

In Pakistan, boys still seem to be preferred and thus receive family resources, including calories. Women are discriminated against in every area of life--despite their agricultural labor alongside men's in a country that is three-quarters rural--and they do not have equal legal rights. In 1992, the country's Supreme Court invalidated the requirement that a husband give written notice of a divorce to a local council. A husband can simply say (or deny) that he has divorced his wife. In one situation in 1993, a lower court sentenced an "adulteress" to be stoned to death, and her second husband flogged one hundred lashes, when her first husband denied he had divorced her. Fortunately, the couple was able to produce evidence that they believed themselves married. They were acquitted on appeal.

During the martial law regime of General Mohammed Zia ul-Haq, laws called the Hudood ordinances were passed regarding adultery, fornication, rape, and prostitution. Under the ordinances, four witnesses must testify that a woman has been raped--otherwise, her behavior may be considered adultery or fornication, punishable by stoning to death or flogging. A woman's testimony in court carries half the legal weight of a man's. The Hudood ordinances have not been seriously challenged by any government since they were created.

In 1991, a Shariat bill was passed which called for "bringing all aspects of government and society in Pakistan into conformity with the tenets of Islam." On December 4, 1992, the *Toronto Star* reported that all women on state-run television had been ordered to wear Muslim head scarves; radio stations had been ordered to drop hundreds of songs regarded as socially or religiously inappropriate; and Pakistan's penal code had been altered to make execution mandatory for anyone who "directly or indirectly defiles the sacred name of the Holy Prophet."

According to the *Star*, "militant mullahs have always been a voice in the corridors of power in Islamabad." One consequence: in 1985, religious minorities lost the right to vote in the same manner as Sunni Muslims; minorities vote from separate rolls for a limited number of "reserved seats" in parliament.

Women, too, have had a history of "reserved seats." These seats were dropped in 1990 but were reinstated later. In October 2005, indirect elections for reserved minority and women's seats occurred, and international observers found that all of the participating political parties engaged in intimidation, coercion, and vote-buying. Nevertheless, significant increases have been made in women's political participation. While only 2 women (Benazir Bhutto and Nusrat Bhutto) sat in the National Assembly in 1991, by 2006, the 342-

member National Assembly contained 73 women-over 20% of the seats. This number exceeds the 60 reserved seats. Additionally, five women serve in the Cabinet. Women received the vote in 1947, when India and Pakistan became independent from Britain.

There are professional women, working particularly in the fields of teaching, medical services and the law, in Pakistan. In Karachi, there are a substantial number of women judges in the civil courts. Women's organizations exist throughout the country, but are concentrated in urban centers.

Pakistan's population is rising at a rapid rate (2.03%), with the fertility rate at over 4.5 births per woman. Family planning services are limited with only 28% of married women using contraception methods. These are opposed by Islamic fundamentalist scholars and village clergy. Pakistan appears on a list of UN countries that spent more for the military than for health and education combined in both 1960 and 1986, a statistic that isn't improving: Pakistan's military costs amount to 4.5% of GDP while public spending on the health and education systems are at 0.7% and 1.8% of GDP, respectively.

Domestic violence is widespread in the country but is considered a private matter; marital rape is not a crime under Pakistani law, and "rape of another man's wife is a common method of seeking revenge in rural and tribal areas." Domestic disagreements can result in death and disfigurement through burning or acid. While the Punjab Assembly passed a resolution against acid attacks, the sale of such substances is not controlled. According to the HRCP, one out of every two women has been the victim of violence and another study found that as many as 90% of married women have been abused by their husbands. Underreporting is a problem due to the stigma of divorce, economic dependence on relatives, and importance of maintaining the family reputation.

In the 1990s, an organization called WAR (War Against Rape) took on the issue, and found in studying sixty rape cases in Lahore that members of police forces were substantially implicated. Women in police custody in Pakistan faced sexual and physical abuse.

In January of 1994, international press photographs showed
Prime Minister Bhutto opening Pakistan's first police station staffed
exclusively by women.

The Philippines

The Philippines, a basically agricultural country of eighty-three
million, has had educated women and active women's organizations
since the first decades of the twentieth century. It was because of
both that a remarkably determined fight for the suffrage could end in
success in 1937. When the all-male legislature of the time established
that the right to vote would be given to women only if--in a national
plebiscite--no fewer than 300,000 women voted in its favor, women
organized so well throughout the country that they surpassed their
goal by almost 150,000 votes.

Women were also active at this time in social movements directed
against U.S. colonial rule, as a few had been active in earlier movements against Spanish colonialism. One researcher has summed up:
"...from the beginning of the [twentieth] century to the outbreak of
World War II...women in the Philippines...were launched into a new
world altogether after centuries of enforced domesticity, illiteracy, and
cruel repression under Spanish rule."

After the World War II Japanese occupation, the Philippines became
independent in 1946. Between 1946 and 1972, when Ferdinand
Marcos declared martial law, a tiny number of women were elected to
the national legislature (eighteen), to be governors (six), or to be city
mayors (two). Many more held lesser civic posts.

By the 1970s, some women had become active in radical groups
responding to the country's prevalent poverty: the social structure of
the Philippines remained, as it had since the Spaniards, rooted in a
small, wealthy, landowning class. Women became guerrilla fighters in
the New People's Army, or active with MAKIBA (Free Movement of New
Women), which held mass actions, established cottage industries, and

helped set up day care centers. Activist nuns, influenced by liberation theology, worked to assist political prisoners and the urban poor. GABRIELA, another group, protested the U.S. military bases that remained on Philippine soil, and the extensive prostitution (involving many thousands of women) that was associated with them. The corruption of the Marcos regime extended to the fact that his government promoted "sex tourism" to bring money into the economy: "The Ministry of Tourism regularly conducted sex tours for male visitors...Never before had Filipinas been so degraded."

After the 1983 assassination of Benigno Aquino, Jr., "women from all classes and persuasions worked side by side in challenging the [Marcos] dictatorship." Large women's organizations involved were GABRIELA and KABAPA (New Filipino Women's Association), the latter being a force among rural women. Many other groups came into the streets during the final days of People's Power. With the election of Corazon Aquino, women had one of their own at the top.

The Philippines today remains poor, with an undeveloped safety net, and with opposition from the Catholic Church to birth control measures. In February of 1993, for example, Cardinal Sin--an important ally of People's Power--"organized a rally in Manila, attended by 300,000 Catholics, to denounce the birth control policies of the Ramos administration, following the Secretary of Health's public promotion of prophylactics to limit the spread of AIDS." In 1993, also, poor women were "extensively victimized by international sex trafficking syndicates, which recruited them to work abroad..." Despite the 2004 Anti-Violence Against Women and their Children Act, which criminalizes physical, sexual, and psychological abuse of women and children by their spouses and partners, domestic violence and rape remain serious problems, as is the incidence of underreporting of crimes. In a 2003 survey by the NGO Social Weather Station, women cited embarrassment, lack of information, and the belief that violence was unimportant or unavoidable as the key reasons for not reporting violent actions.

Women hold a relatively average percentage of seats in the national legislature. In 2006, thirty-seven women sat in the House (out of 236 members), four women (of twenty-four) were senators, and 2 women served in the 23-member Cabinet. Currently, there are five female associate justices on the 15 member Supreme Court, three of whom were appointed by Corazon Aquino, as mentioned earlier. Many women work in public administration, with the numbers in high-level positions well above what is typical around the world. The Philippine Military Academy began admitting females in 1993.

Illiteracy in the Philippines is about 7% for both sexes. Women who participate in the labor force are approximately 70% of all women with 40% in non-agricultural paid labor, according the World Economic Forum's 2006 *Gender Gap Report.*

Poland

Feminist efforts in Poland go well back into the nineteenth century and were primarily focused on the right to an education. In 1918, came the vote and the right to be elected. In the 1920s and 1930s, women were a small fraction (between 2 and 5%) of the two houses of the national legislature.

Under the Communist regime which came to power after World War II, an ideological emphasis on sexual equality brought more women into parliament; until in the mid-1980s, women were about 23% of the Sejm (lower house). They were not, however, highly represented in the very important Communist Party major posts. Nor were there many in top positions in Solidarity when (and while) the trade union began challenging the Communist Party for control of Poland--even though women are believed to have made up half of the rank-and-file of Solidarity, just as they made up about one-half of the Polish labor force by the mid-1980s.

During its period of rule, the Communist Party urged women to enter the work force and help Poland industrialize. The country ceased being largely agricultural as people migrated to cities. Educational opportunities were expanded and "women were provided with free health care, job and wage protection during pregnancy, and sixteen weeks of maternity leave with salary...In 1971, a new law went even further by allowing a woman with a child four years old or younger a three-year unpaid leave."

In 1980, when Solidarity was formed and began to negotiate with the Communist regime, a "three-year paid maternity leave was the only provision directly concerning women. In addition, Solidarity pushed for the expansion of kindergarten and nursery facilities for working mothers...In essence, they continued the view expressed by the Communists that women are equal, but some are weaker and have a different role to perform. What the shipyard workers wanted to see was women in their traditional role as wives and mothers..."

When Solidarity was forced underground in December of 1981, active "women who avoided being interned were left with full responsibility for their families and their imprisoned partners." The government could not, however, govern Poland without the participation of the forces that Solidarity represented--disaffection was too great. Martial law was ended in July of 1983. Strikes in 1988 helped bring about major negotiations, in early 1989, for a change of regime ("not even one woman was a chief negotiator").

Political and economic restructuring have brought this country of thirty-eight million people new institutions and freedoms. However, "women and the elderly (who are predominantly women) have become increasingly vulnerable...Indeed, women are the majority of the new unemployed and have already lost their right to long-term parental leave." After falling in the 1990s, their numbers in parliament have begun to rise again--in 2006, they constituted about 20% of the Sejm, 12% of the upper house, and almost 14% in the Council of Ministers.

Women have lost the liberal abortion rights put into effect in 1956, under which abortion was more-or-less fully available and free. After three years of controversy, between 1989 and 1992, President Lech Walesa signed an anti-abortion law "with strict limits and sentences of up to two years in prison for doctors who violate the rules." The dominance of strict Catholicism throughout Polish society makes it difficult for even a more leftist government to revise the law. In 2004, the UN Human Rights Committee said in a review of Poland's civil and political rights that even women who were legally allowed abortions did not seem to be able to find hospitals willing to carry them out, likely forcing women to seek unsafe, illegal abortions. An unintended consequence of the abortion controversy was the formation of new women's organizations, and the mobilization of older ones, around the abortion issue. But these groups were not the equals in strength of the Catholic Church, conservative forces, and President Walesa himself.

In 2007, about 70% of Poland's women are in the work force. Ironically, even though rates of women's educational attainment has risen faster than men's over the past half-century and women comprise a majority of secondary school and university students, men continue to be able to find employment more easily. Women's skills seem to be less compatible with available jobs. Unemployed women have completed more education than unemployed men.

Sri Lanka

Sri Lanka, an island nation south of India, is today the home of approximately twenty million people, about two-thirds of them under thirty years of age. Most citizens--80%--live in rural areas, and, while there has been a significant movement towards the service sector (40%), a sizeable proportion of the population (34 %) still works in agriculture, including tea culture, a major export crop.

Rural workers--including women--face low wages and sometimes poor living conditions, but Sri Lanka has had social welfare policies that have produced very creditable records of health and literacy. Life expectancy for women, in 2007, was nearly seventy-seven years (it is four years fewer for men); the literacy rate according to the 2001 census was 89% for women (and higher for men: 92%). The March 1, 1994 issue of the *International Herald Tribune* reported that Sri Lanka "has the most educated workers in South Asia." Not unrelated, it also reported that the country was having "the most sustained economic growth in South Asia."

The lives of women in Sri Lanka are affected by the civil war (in which women have taken part as fighters) between the government and Tamil rebels. According to the U.S. State Department, in 1991-93 one of the prisoners held by the "Tamil Tigers" was Thiagarajah Sel-vanithy, a poet and women's activist. Also affecting women's lives are the particular cultures of the ethnic or religious groups to which they belong. Sri Lanka is approximately 69% Buddhist, 7.5% Muslim, 7% Hindu, 6% Christian, and 10% unspecified. While "Sri Lankan women have equal rights under national civil and criminal law," matters related to "marriage, divorce, child custody, and inheritance," for example, "are subject at the local level to the customary law of each particular ethnic or religious group," including, for Muslims, Islamic law.

While there are "no de jure impediments to women's participation in politics or government...the social mores of some communities have the effect of limiting women's participation in activities outside the home." While there are women at senior levels of government service, only eleven (out of 225) members of parliament were women in 2006 (identical to the percentage in 1993), three women in the executive cabinet, and two women serving on the Supreme Court. Women have been able to vote since 1931.

Like nearly all societies today, Sri Lanka has many women profes-sionals, and more coming up. In the early 1980s, nearly one-half of university students in medical, dental, and veterinary courses were women. Articles on women's problems have appeared in newspapers in all three major languages--Sinhala, Tamil, and English--since about 1975. In the booming garment industry, where 200,000 work, the vast majority are young women.

Domestic violence and sexual assault are reported to be "common" in Sri Lanka, but are often not reported for cultural and social reasons. Women's organizations have taken up these issues, including increasing sensitization of police and the judiciary. While the law prohibits domestic violence, it is "not strictly enforced" by the government, according to the 2006 U.S. State Department report.

Turkey

Turkey is a surprising and paradoxical country where women are concerned. On the one hand, it has a strong tradition of professional working women--doctors, attorneys, and others--who derive from urban, well-off families. A far greater number of women in Turkey come from rural villages (although they may be urban migrants), may be illiterate (as are half of Turkish women), may be poor, and some-times face Turkey's widespread problem of spousal abuse.

Turkey's population (73.2 million in 2005) is growing at a faster rate than many of its European neighbors. While Turkey and France were of comparable populations through the 1990s, Turkey's women received the vote in 1934, ten years sooner than French women. If this is unexpected, so is the fact that Turkey's most progressive women's period (it could be argued) came in the 1920s and 1930s, and was greatly attributable to a man: Mustafa Kemal Atatürk. Atatürk, who led Turkey's three-year (1919-1922) war for independ-ence, believed that modern democracy depends on the participation of both sexes; he had a personal interest in women's rights.

When Turkey was established as a republic in 1923, its constitution defined the state as secular, with legal codes derived from Europe, and the state granted women full rights of citizenship. This historical period is known as the period of "state feminism." In some of the following years, Turkey had more women in parliament than it has had since.

According to the 2006 U.S. Department of State Country Report on Human Rights Practices, women continue to face some discrimination in employment and are generally underrepresented in managerial-level positions. However, they do receive equal pay for equal work in professional, business, and civil service positions. In the agriculture, retail, and restaurant sectors, many women work as unpaid family labor. Turkey has many women judges in one part of its court system, and it has large numbers of women working in career government positions (women are 29% of civil servants) but there are very few women in elected office: in 2006, 4% of parliament seats and 4% of ministerial positions were held by women. Turkey had only ten women mayors between 1950 -1980. Few women are elected to municipal councils. According to researchers, "political life continues to be dominated by parties only sometimes interested in or friendly towards women." There are women in the army who have risen to colonel positions.

Turkey is 98% Muslim. "Islamic revivalists have started a campaign to control women's sexuality and life opportunities [which] stresses their role as wives and mothers..." The conflict between Turkey's twentieth century tradition of secular government and its Islamic religionists--a conflict whose outcome is critical to the future of women--is played out in many arenas, including that of dress codes in the universities. Both "law and custom require women and men who work in the public sector or attend public universities to dress secularly..." Followers of Islam have held demonstrations and sit-ins promoting the wearing of the Islamic head scarf in universities. The issue reached the courts. Since 1982, "religious culture" must be taught in primary and secondary schools.

In 2006, the government attempted to modernize prevailing societal attitudes towards "honor killings" of women, the practice of killing female family members suspected of being unchaste, but the practice remains a widespread problem.

Turkey has abortion rights for women to the tenth week of pregnancy without the need to prove a medical justification; however, married women must obtain notarized consent from their husbands. Unlike in most countries, "the right to abortion was not granted as a result of a continual struggle by women's associations." It was, instead, granted by an outgoing military government in 1983. Military governments took over Turkey in 1960-61; 1971-73; and 1980-83.

Turkey's birthrate continues to be high, its family planning services not very successful, its "safety net" undeveloped, and its childcare centers and kindergartens few and expensive. Further educational development of its people is a concern: men are one-quarter illiterate, and a 1992 law increasing mandatory education from five years to eight will be implemented gradually throughout the country. Traditional values in rural Turkey emphasize education for sons more than for daughters. In major cities like Istanbul and Ankara, women universi scholars research and seek to address the problems of Turkey's women, as do women's organizations such as KA-MER and the Bursa Gunyuzu Women's Solidarity Cooperative. As Turkey seeks entrance to the E.U., women's rights have been placed on the political agenda with legislation being drafted to address violence against women though enforcement is still lacking.

United Kingdom of Great Britain and Northern Ireland

British women received the vote, cautiously, in two stages: in 1918, for women over thirty; in 1928, at the same (younger) age as men. As in France, the early years of women's voting showed females to be more conservative than males; in the 1980s, again as in France, the "gender gap" reversed. According to one researcher, neither of Britain's two major parties--Labour or the Conservatives--paid much attention to women party members or voters *until* the 1980s. One factor in their change was the appearance in 1980 of a new party, the Social Democratic, which pledged to achieve greater sexual equality. The Social Democrats, Liberal Democrats, and Labour all introduced some party quotas for women in the 1980s.

Britain's long tradition of democracy has produced "a highly traditional society with a centralized, secretive, and bureaucratically dominated system." Several factors have made it hard for women to gain power in government: a powerful "old boys" ("chaps") network, feeding its male members into apprenticeship pipelines; a lack of significant decision-making at a regional level, as in the United States, which would make for more positions of power; and a system without a written constitution, to help reform through law. A factor now working in favor of British women is Britain's membership in the European Economic Community, which obligates its member states to sexual equality in pay, employment, and social security provisions. The European Court of Justice, for example, directed Britain to improve its administration of the country's Equal Pay Act, on the books since 1970.

According to Joyce Gelb, "most women-oriented legislation in Britain did not come about as a result of pressure from feminists, but rather from political parties and trade unions," the two major sources of power. However, these groups continue to operate in traditional ways: "In the Labour Party, for example, the traditional industrial unions have nominating rights and, as such, a great deal of influence over the choice of parliamentary candidates. Many unions continue to support candidates that come from their ranks; these candidates typically are white men." At present only about sixty of 650 members of the House of Commons are women. Nor are women found often "in ministerial office, in the senior ranks of higher civil service, or in the higher judiciary."

It has not helped the political power of women in Great Britain that its women's movement has been extremely fragmented. There have been many localized groups with a great many projects but with widely divergent views on the relationship of women to society and to men. Activity surrounding abortion rights has been "perhaps the most sustained and widespread of all women's political participation in Britain." The country does not have "abortion on demand," but it has a 1967 Abortion Law Reform Act which has been very liberally construed by medical professionals who must decide on a woman's right to an abortion. (This law does not apply to Northern Ireland.) Women have had to defend the 1967 act against efforts to make abortion more restricted: they have successfully done so, at times with the help of the trade unions.

With respect to workforce participation, about 45% of the country's women work.

According to a 2000 report from UNIFEM, women earn 72% of their male counterparts in the manufacturing sector and 80% of male in the industry and services sector.

The 2006 *Global Gender Gap Report* from the World Economic Forum awards the United Kingdom an overall 9th place ranking out of the 115 countries, with a top rank in educational attainment, 12th for political empowerment, 37th for economic participation and opportunity, and 63rd for health and survival.

Chapter XII: Four New Women Leaders Interviewed

Since the original book was written in 1994-1995, 37 women have been elected Head of State or Government through September 2008. Unable to continue to interview all new women leaders, I felt it was important to provide a glimpse into this wonderful group of women and was privileged to interview Kim Campbell, Prime Minister, Canada (1993), Jenny Shipley, Prime Minister, New Zealand (1997 – 1999), Vaira Vike-Freiberga, President, Latvia (1999 – 2007), and Ellen Johnson Sirleaf, President, Liberia (2006–present).

Interview with Jenny Shipley – Prime Minister, New Zealand

2004

Q: What values did you learn from childhood that you brought to your leadership?

Shipley: *I was one of four girls in our family where we were taught to believe in ourselves and to lead from where we were. The leadership of ideas and the leading of people was something that was expected of us. Both my parents cultivated firmly held opinions within my sister and I through skillfully crafting our thinking, while also empowering us to sort out what we believed in ourselves. We were also encouraged to understand that leadership was the obligation of where each of us had skills and talents to share and that if we had been endowed with these gifts we should not only seek the opportunities to use them, but that we had an obligation to do so.*

Q: Where did you learn the mastery skill of communication, politics, and leadership?

Shipley: *As a child in my early years, I was described as one who talked too much at school. In my early teenage years I enjoyed speech competitions and expressing my opinion reasonably and freely in a*

189

school environment. In the latter part of my formal education those qualities began to be described as "showing significant leadership potential."

Becoming an adult and young parent, again there were many community opportunities that cried out for leadership, particularly in service development for young women with dependent children. I used my skills and indeed attended a range of workshops that further expanded those personal leadership skills at that time.

I enrolled in a number of courses and the one that stands out was the Kellogg's Rural Leadership course sponsored by the Kellogg's Foundation from the United States. The foundation identified and promoted rural leaders who may have a potential impact on the future. This was quite a defining period for me and having decided already to go into local politics, it helped me further advance my thinking as to what leadership opportunities and skills I had and where they might take me.

I had always been involved in politics. My grandfather was very closely associated with the former Prime Minister of New Zealand who was a distant relative. At his knee I heard him talk about the issues that were important to our country and he probably rather indirectly influenced my thinking. My personal interest in politics began in my late twenties.

Q: Would you describe a time you failed, returned, and recovered; a particular moment or opportunity that was pivotal to your success as a woman and as a leader?

Shipley: *I was successful in first standing in a conservative rural constituency for local government and then winning again in a select seat for central government representation. This was a conservative rural environment where a successor had been identified to the existing Member of Parliament. I decided to stand and put all my efforts in using well-established female lobbying skills.*

In terms of failing and then picking myself back up, I guess that the defeat at the end of ten years in government, just over two of which I was Prime Minister could be viewed as a failure. From my own point of view failure is only a relative thing. In this instance it was the end of one particular role, era, experience, and I went about setting myself a new series of goals to then move forward with.

I do not want to rely on the fact that I was the Prime Minister of New Zealand as the only skill or attribute I have, while it is an extraordinary privilege to lead your country, undoubtedly you acquire a range of contacts, networks, and also skills and experience that are invaluable and are not easily replicated. One's personal skills and attributes plus that experience means that a new career is not only possible, but offers great potential if you have the vision and determination to carry it out.

Q: What commonalities do you think women share in leadership?

Shipley: *While many women hold vastly different points of view, I do think women bring a further dimension into leadership roles over and above their male colleagues. Often they have the ability to be extremely decisive once having considered an issue. They are also extremely effective in terms of collaborating with others upon who they rely in order to make all decisions achievable, operational, and sustainable.*

This is a bond amongst women who have led. The journey to get to the leadership roles carry some shared experiences which are well documented. These women have felt the isolation that those leadership roles can bring. The third commonality is their absolute determination and self-belief as individuals that set them apart from others.

I remain concerned that few women are found amongst the decision-makers both within and across economies.

Q: What type of education and experience would prepare an aspiring female leader?

Shipley: *To be taken seriously in terms of leadership roles, you clearly must have demonstrated your own competence as a person.*

The elements of competence are:

a)   *Academic Qualification*

b)   *A significant and successful work experience*

c)   *Demonstration of an interest, insight, and understanding of community affairs*

d)   *Demonstration of a commitment to the voluntary sector*

e)   *For personal development: women need to seek opportunities to participate in the public speaking environment and acquire chairmanship skills*

f)   *The ability to mobilize groups in terms of setting strategies, goals, and executing them effectively, then celebrating them*

g)   *Some mothers may consider how to balance their personal aspirations and family responsibilities. This is an important personal defense mechanism and also something that will inevitably be scrutinized in detail in the public arena whether we like it or not, so anticipating the question and having a good response for your own peace of mind and for public purposes is worthwhile.*

h)   *Choose your partner well! If that is relevant they may well be your greatest supporter and you can be sure they will come in hand for future scrutiny; so anticipate this and you will find it far easier to manage and bear.*

Q: What is the most helpful advice you ever received as a leader?

Shipley: *There was a range of pieces of advice, but perhaps one that is most important is trust your instincts. In my experience outstanding leaders are willing to listen, to learn, and to absorb. In the end they must have that capacity to trust their own instincts as to how to not only move the group forward, but also use the language to craft the message in such a way to inspire others to share a dream.*

Q: In your observations what are the differences you see in men and women's leadership styles and what differences do you see in how they are treated?

Shipley: *Women have the capacity to see the whole. Men tend to focus on single issues and seem surprised when the implications of their decisions are pointed out to them in a broader context.*

There are undoubtedly significant differences as to how women are treated. People will describe women leaders who are assertive and effective as iron women, where they will describe a similar male as outstanding leaders who are clear and decisive.

Even to this day, having been Prime Minister, I often am exposed to discussions amongst men who think women are not capable; for example, of taking the 'male decisions' such as deploying troops into a war zone. Yet, the evidence based on previous women leaders makes it clear that where necessary women leaders have been capable and willing to do so.

Q: What is still required to get political, economic, and social equality for women?

Shipley: *While I believe there is an increased expectation amongst populations that their leaders will include women leaders and that leaders who are male should expect to have to promote women to senior roles in order to be credible, this is still new territory and should not be taken for granted.*

Q: How do you see change implemented in a country?

Shipley: *An enormous amount of hard work is required to deliver change. Successful change is almost always preceded by a group of inspirational leaders understanding that change is required, having a vision as to what type of change will transform the lives of people through successful execution, and change management processes that gives confidence.*

Q: A leader receives a great deal of advice from many sources. How do you sort through conflicting opinions and what process or skills do you use to make important decisions?

Shipley: *As a leader you have personal advisors you confide in, you have people from networks outside the political arena, extensive material available through research services, the internet, and other written material.*

From time to time; however, as Prime Minister you have to make decisions on behalf of your country or economy, and then carry your cabinet and country with you. In doing so you simply have to diligently and thoughtfully go through a process where you take the advice available. You then require the confidence and self-assurance to carry the decision in the public arena.

Q: Can you describe specific examples of the impact of having a women leader?

Shipley: *There are many and they include:*

a) *The public is endlessly entertained by what we wear, what we have done to our hair, and whether or not we meet the public expectations of being female.*

b) *Having got over that, the public then are immensely proud of having a woman leading the economy in both good times and bad if my experience is anything to go by.*

c) *There are instances where women will pick up the consequences of decisions and in explaining it to the public put it in language and context in such a way that people are more willing to go through the process of change. They are also willing from time to time to have women say no to them rather than say yes. Goodness knows whether that's a residual memory of one's mother doing the same thing. In my experience, decisive action by women leaders when well grounded, is strongly supported and tolerated by the public.*

d) *Unquestionably, women leaders provide a role model for women old and young within the population. There have been endless personal examples where people have come to me and said my presence as a woman leader has made them believe in themselves and that anything is possible. That in itself is a great point of personal satisfaction.*

Q: What are common qualities, traits, and differences amongst women heads of state, and/or government, and female corporate leaders?

Shipley: *Women who have achieved high-office in either the public or private sector clearly have a series of personal qualities. They have* *enjoyed an educational experience, workplace opportunities in either paid or unpaid workforce to develop their skills, and personal confidence to the point that they are prepared to take on senior levels of institutions, organizations, and politics.*

In my experience there are many qualities in common including:

a)   Being highly organized in exercising personal capability
b)   Having the ability to balance competing interests
c)   Enjoying hard work and long hours
d)   Balancing work and family responsibilities where relevant
e)   A determination to get the job done
f)   Perhaps most importantly, a vision of what is possible either for the country or the corporation.

Q: How do women gain credibility versus how men gain credibility?

Shipley: *This is a different pathway. Women are required to prove themselves over and over again, that they are not only as good as their male colleagues, but that they have extra qualities that make them worthy.*

In my experience male colleagues, if they had a half way credible occupation and had been educated at the right school, were at least half way towards their political goal. For women there are other questions that you are asked. They include whether or not you can balance the shared responsibilities you may have. If you choose to be childless that attracts its own set of critics. If you choose to have a family that attracts a highly detailed scrutiny as to whether or not such responsibilities will distract you from the public life. For a woman to be credible in the public arena they have to have demonstrated historically that they can balance a range of responsibilities, obligations, be highly effective and continue to do so in their chosen roles. It is possible.

Excerpted Interview with Kim Campbell –Prime Minister of Canada

2005 ~ Washington, DC, USA

Q: What values did you learn from your childhood that you have brought to your leadership?

Campbell: *One of the things that I learned from my childhood was the notion that girls could do anything, but that this wasn't a universally accepted proposition. My mother liked to tell my sister and me about extraordinary women, not just in Canadian history, but in world history.*

I think that I was prepared for the fact that the acceptance of women at the highest levels was not necessarily something that was going to come without a struggle. And when I was a teenager, my goal was to be the first woman Secretary-General of the UN, which is a very Canadian thing to want to be. We're very multilateral.

But I think that sense of wanting to prove that girls could do it was a very important part of who I was.

A lot of my approach to leading has been to try and communicate to people what they need to know to make intelligent choices. I think that a leader has to be a teacher; not a didactic person in speaking down to people, but from the perspective of sharing knowledge, with the faith that most people are quite capable of understanding anything if you just start at the beginning and explain it.

Q: What commonalities do you think women share in leadership, and what makes women leaders unique?

Campbell: *I think what makes women leaders unique at this stage of our history is, that most of them take on leadership positions where they often find that they are thought not really to belong. I would hope in 20 years or 50 years, when you ask the question of what makes women leaders different, the answer would be very different, because we'd be in a world where women leaders are seen to be normal,* *natural; not exotic, and that they're different because they sometimes wear pantyhose or they're different because maybe they're closer to the experience of families and children, but not necessarily, or that there is no difference.*

One of the things that most leaders, I think what makes women leaders different today, given the fact that they are a rarity, is that they take on their positions encountering a feeling by a lot of people that they don't really belong there. They know that they have to establish that they belong in positions of leadesrship. And that creates an extra level of pressure for women, because each woman's position is different.

For example, in a Muslim country, a woman has to fulfill the image people have of a Muslim woman. In a Western society, you have to still be feminine, not seen to be rejecting those kinds of stereotypes, but at the same time, going beyond those stereotypes and exercising the capacity to lead in a way that is inconsistent with that stereotype.

But it is interesting that even at those very high positions, women understand that they sometimes have to hold back. The natural strength that they want to show as leaders, because that strength isn't masculine or feminine, it's the professional requirement of the job. But if only men have been seen to do that job, that strenght is often seen as being masculine as opposed to simply being professional. And so women face that Catch-22.

In the summer of 1993, when I toured the country as Prime Minister, there were little old men who would come up to me and say, "Oh, you're going to be our Maggie Thatcher." Sometimes people idealize women and think that they're even stronger than men and more capable of standing up to the pressures to conform, or can take more unpopular positions.

It may be that women coming from the outside, coming from a marginalized view, are less vested in the power structure, and can from time to time take positions outside it in a way that people admire.

Q: As you look back on your leadership, what do you reflect upon? What do you observe about it?

Campbell: *I was very much an interactive leader. I understood that to get my legislation through, I had to build coalitions. I dealt with very controversial issues. And it came naturally to me. Now, did it come naturally to me as a woman? Women are often seen to be more naturally interactive leaders. Or was it simply an accurate reading of the power I had as a minister, whether I was a man or woman?*

I also learned that I could delegate and that was good. You have to surround yourself with very smart, able people to whom you can delegate, who report to you, so that you always know what's going on.

It was actually interesting for me that my role as a cabinet minister was a voyage of self-discovery. It gave me confidence that I could do the job if I were Prime Minister, that I tested myself and I thought, you know, I could do it.

Q: Can you describe how you see specific examples of the impact of having women as leaders?

Campbell: *It depends on the time and the place. For example, I think Margaret Thatcher had much less freedom to be an advocate for women. It's almost a generational thing. I think that if she had been seen as someone who was going to change the face of the leadership in her party by bringing in a great many more women, it would have been very difficult for her.*

When I became leader, it was a different time. But I was not able in that short period of time to do the kinds of things I would like to have done to promote more women.

But certainly when I was minister, as justice minister, I convened the first ever national symposium on women, law and the administration of justice in Canada, which... was a turning point in law reform in Canada, and in mainstreaming the concerns that women had about the justice system; about creating a dialogue and a discussion in the judiciary and in the bar, in the law schools, about what it means to give women a voice in the law.

So I think substantively, I could make a difference in mainstreaming women's issues and I always wanted to use my power to do that.

Take the issue of domestic violence. For eons, this was considered a private matter; police would not interfere. Now, certainly in my country, it's just commonplace that this is something that's contrary to the interest of society; that we don't tolerate it; that the laws are in place to fight against it.

The political pundits who watched what I did often didn't recognize it as leadership, because I didn't make the noises they were used to hearing. I didn't come out saying, "I will get my bill through by hook or by crook." If I had done that, I wouldn't have got it through by hook or by crook.

Q: What do you think about women in the military, women in combat, and also terrorism being on everyone's mind, and women's roles in terrorism?

Campbell: *I think one of the most important issues for women in the field of public policy is simply expanding people's notion of who people are. And women are so often the invisible category, the default category is male. So whether it's victims of terrorism, whether it's protagonists in struggles, we often see those actors, the people who count, as being male. Women and children are always kind of lumped together.*

I think there is a blindness there that we often forget; for example, development policy. It took eons for bodies like the World Bank and others to understand that you can't have economic development without the education of girls. Programs must engage women in the economy, because women have always been in the economy.

This notion, persists that men are making the living and the women stay home looking after the children. There is almost no culture or society in the world where that is the case. Most often, the women are in fact providing the livelihood. And it is the women primarily who support the family.

Q: How do you create time in your very busy life for reflection?

Campbell: *I think it's very difficult for people in public life to find time for reflection. A very wise Canadian public servant once used the expression tthat when you are in public life, you are living off your intellectual capital. And so finding time or the opportunity to replenish your intellectual capital can be very difficult.*

This is why I think before people go into public life, they need to try to live a life that gives them a great deal that they can live off. Not just in terms of formal education. I think reading, understanding the world's history, traveling as much as you can, and seeing the experiences of real people are very important. Politics is not an abstract exercise; it's about real flesh and blood human beings.

When you are in a leadership position, it's very important who you surround yourself with. You must surround yourself with people who have access to those who are doing the deep thinking. The American tradition of bringing academics into public service is much more common than it is in Canada.

When you are the Prime Minister of Canada or the President of the United States or President of France or whatever, you don't have time to sit and read a lot of in-depth documents, and people need to give you things in a fairly succinct way.

So you do rely a great deal on other people to determine the quality of the information on which you make decisions. And one of the luxuries of actually leaving public office, whether you do it courtesy of the voters in an election or you get term limited out, is again to have the leisure to replenish your intellectual capital. And so, even people who have a term out of office should actually welcome the opportunity to catch up on what they need to know before they head back into the fray.

Q: Do you have some final advice for young women or young men aspiring to positions of leadership?

Campbell: *Find out who you are. Find out what you love to do and do it, because if you do what you love to do, you will do it well. There are a million ways to be happy; there are a million ways to cultivate your mind. Find out what the things are that really interest you and that will lead you to stretch and grow and develop a mind that's capable of learning, of critical thinking, and able to express yourself.*

But a good education doesn't just come from an educational institution. A good education also comes from as much traveling as possible.

There are certain skills that are useful to know, basic concepts of economics. I think you should understand the constitutional structure of your country.

I also tell young people to try and find a way to earn a living so that if, heaven forbid, they should lose an election, (it does happen to the best of us) they have a way of supporting themselves.

There is no tenure in politics, and a lot of good people don't get elected and lot of dunces do get elected and, you know, I don't know which category I was in, so I won't press that question. Frankly, I think if you want to lead, you need to know what you want to lead for. You need to know what you believe. Politics isn't a popularity contest. You know, many people think, "Oh, wouldn't it be great to have people cheer you?"

It's not like that. It's actually very vicious and tough, because it's about power and nobody gives you power without a fight. But power is something that's wonderful to have, and I think goes well with women. One mustn't be afraid of saying that you want to have power, because power enables you to do very important things. Power is out there. Somebody is going to have it. It may as well be you. But you need to know what it is that you want to do with it, plus have that sense of your inner core values.

Politics is not something that you should go into without any idea of what you do when you get there.

People are going to yell at you. They are going to say things about you that you never dreamed anybody could say about you, and particularly, if you are a woman.

You have to understand that those who are close to you suffer more from the criticisms than you do, because they don't have a chance to answer back. So if you have a sense of what it is you want to do and be, and you are philosophical about the fact that you are not always going to win, you could try your hardest to win, but that it's worth the fray; then you will always be able to survive the takedowns and take advantage of the successes.

You come to realize that there are so many opportunities to do good with even the little bits of power that you have, that it all adds up, and you should never lose the opportunity to do that. And at the end of the day, when it's all over, you can look back on it with enormous satisfaction, not just because you as an individual were able to do something, but because you validated the democratic process.

And at the end of the day, that's really what it's about, to leave your stint in democratic office knowing that you haven't eroded people's sense about what democracy can be, that you have added to people's ability to have faith in democracy.

Interview with Vaira Vike-Freiberga – President of Latvia

2005 ~ Washington, DC, USA

Q: **What values that you learned as a child do you actually take with you into the leadership?**

Vike-Freiberga: *I had various cycles of very active thinking about values, and reevaluating values, and looking for a sense of purpose in life, and it seems to me that, one has to go on a quest in one's long life.*

Q: **Where do you find the time to do that kind of spiritual growth creating the uncluttered mind that allows for that kind of reflection in the busy life that you have?**

Vike-Freiberga: *I learned certain techniques of stilling the mind, of acquiring serenity and peace, peace of mind and equilibrium. I try to do a few sorts of meditation or other concentration exercises.*

Whatever the distresses of my daily life, for instance, every morning I drive to work. We arrive at a sort of plain where it's really a swamp. There are no trees. There is nothing else. To me passing through that swampy, foggy, area is a signal to me that I must close my eyes and do my daily, morning meditation to make sure that I don't forget it because I start as soon as I get up.

I'm constantly stuffing myself with information, or talking to people. So that passing through the swamp is a sacred thing.

It's making this inner silence an important element in allowing creative ideas to bubble up.

Q: **What skills are used most that you use in terms of being a leader?**

Vike-Freiberga: *I think its sincerity, frankly. To me, the skill of persuasion is important. In a democracy, particularly in a parliamentary democracy, the President does not have the kind of power that you* have in a presidential republic where executive power also rests in the same hands. In Latvia, the executive, and the Prime Minister, and the Finance Minister hold the purse strings.

I think the leadership, in the sense of ideas, of purpose, of meaning, of priorities, of self-worth, and our goals, all of those I think are aspects of being a leader, and certainly the President. They can only be achieved I think by the force of persuasion.

People will soon find out if you are just sort of waffling around and have no idea what you're talking about. I think it becomes fairly quickly apparent if you are pretending as well. When I have convinced myself that I can do it, then I can go with my whole heart and soul and argue and convince others.

I think our Constitution has a very wise provision that a President should not be younger than 40 years of age. For a woman of my age, there is a certain number of leg watching that I think simply becomes not an issue. I am protected by my wrinkles, if you would like, from much of that sort of attention.

When us girls meet together, you see, clearly there is a sense of affinity and of kinship, which these gentlemen get when they go smoking cigars in their clubs, or when they go hunting together, or as they do in Eastern Europe, they go to the sauna together.

The more women assume roles in responsibility and leadership, the more clearly we can erase all the prejudices that create either the glass ceiling or a very real one. I find that when an ambassador of a certain country presents his accreditations and I am asked to remember not to shake his hand, my feeling at that moment is frankly I wouldn't even wish to shake his hand. I have no desire of shaking the hand of a person who feels that way about women.

So that I'm just as happy to bow to him at a polite and indeed larger distance than I would normally observe. It's this sort of thing that for a woman in a leadership position can be a reminder that you may not wish to shake her hand, but she is President and you had better accept *it if you're going to serve in that country, and similarly for a woman who is bank president. If you have any prejudices against women making decisions about large sums of money, if you want to get a large loan from that bank, then you had better accept it, that this lady is going to be the one making that decision.*

Q: In your opinion do you think that women might observe things in certain situations in a country, or in a document, or something that a man might not necessarily observe because it might not be in his awareness to think, well where are the women, or is this fair to women, or is this going to have a disproportionate impact on men or on women in a way that what I call a historically out-of-power group might do?

Vike-Freiberga: *I think that's where you need very sharp analysis of the equality of the sexes to make sure that any measures are taken into society to supposedly improve, say, the standard of living, that they are not ones that continue to discriminate the disparity between the sexes.*

Q: What advice and preparation would you recommend a young woman do to become a leader, to prepare her to become a leader?

Vike-Freiberga: *Often daddy was the one who gave the girl the idea that she could be as good as anybody. I remember my daddy once saying to me, I was complaining about the boys next door not wanting to play with me and actually beating me up. He says, "Well, you have to hit them back. If they hit you, you have to hit them back." And I went out, and there they were all standing in group, boys and girls bigger than I. I just went up to each of them, in turn, and whacked them one good one, you know, piff-puff on the cheeks, and they were so stunned that it took them a while to recover.*

Interview with Ellen Johnson Sirleaf – President of Liberia

2006 ~ Washington, DC, USA

Q: I'm just wondering if you could articulate the importance of the trait of curiosity and additional traits you have identified that make for great leaders.

Johnson Sirleaf: *I think one of the greatest traits for women leaders is consistency. There are so many forces with which women have to deal. The normal forces involved and all of the other forces of development are there, and any leader faces these. But women face particular pressures because they are women. Because they bring to the task a certain dimension, or different dimension of sensitivity. Sensitivities that may conflict with what the normal decision ought to be. And being consistent in purpose and objective I think is something that a woman brings to it. A woman leader decides that – I believe the welfare of children, for example, has more priority.*

Q: You've also noted that these women really had to show or exhibit courage in a way perhaps that the men didn't, perhaps because of their life stories or in some cases they would come to power after their husband or father had been assassinated. That's the story of many of the leaders. But that the courage to step in front of the crowd, tell the difficult stories, tell the difficult truths, and having people scrutinize this woman so much, took an enormous amount of courage. I wonder if you see that in your own life experience.

Johnson Sirleaf: *Oh, absolutely. As a matter of fact, I don't think women get to top leadership positions except when they've already demonstrated courage because along the way there are so many pitfalls and obstacles that would deter you and divert you that the courage of your conviction is one of the things that sustains woman leaders and enables them to move to the top. And so that clearly, courage is one of the things that women bring to the job. Let's not forget it's an unequal world, and for women to not only achieve equality but to excel takes an extraordinary amount of being different, of being courageous, commit-*

ted, dedicated. *You might even say sometimes intensive and aggressive, and of course, as a woman pursues her goals; if it's a woman who's applying all of her talents of bringing to bear what's needed to achieve a particular goal, then she's called aggressive, of course. A man is probably called assertive. Whatever, I think it's a demonstration that a woman's commitment is strong and she has the courage of that conviction and is ready to overcome all the odds or to achieve an objective because she's – she knows exactly what she wants. And to get there, it just takes a whole lot of extra effort. To reach the top of a leadership ladder on the part of a woman just says a whole lot for what she's been through.*

Q: I would say that every one of the women leaders that I've interviewed said that the standard by which they thought they were measured was a different standard than the standard by which the men leaders were measured and that the tolerance for mistakes is less.

Johnson Sirleaf: *I think that's true, and let me tell you in my case when one has demonstrated the ability to meet all the – to overcome the odds, to meet the requirements – then, of course, in my case it was like when men were faced with saying, "Well, you know, how come she's been able to better you all and to rise above it, and oh, she's just one of the boys." All of a sudden then, you take on masculine characteristics, simply because you've been able to make it and to excel; they have to say, "Wait a minute. You know, I remain a woman. And I've achieved this even though I am."*

But that's just the way of the world not fully accepting that you could be you, that you could be a woman, that you can bring to this task what it takes as a woman and still be equal. And I think that's the fun part, because then one has to laugh and say, "I've arrived," so to speak.

Q: Well, I think also that when I talk to the women, because of their own background and upbringing, they seem to say that women also bring different people to the table than have historically been in the power seats and that therefore, they get people

who have been historically out of power more likely to get input. Has that occurred with you, and in what way?

Johnson Sirleaf: *Very much so, and in my particular case – for example, in my foreign travel, when I go around to meet groups like this, or bilateral relationship groups, or international meetings, I take with me most times a market woman, someone who's never had the opportunity to meet groups like that or to be able not only to listen and share but to have an opinion. And that's someone that no one would understand why. This is not someone of your peers; this is not some-one who's in that particular class. But I bring them because I want to give them a proper perspective, and I want people to also understand that a lack of education is not a lack of intelligence. For us, where we have large numbers of our women in the informal sector who survive and live by their wits and their ability to overcome the odds at that level, they bring us a certain kind of view... that many who don't go through their difficulties would ever understand. I think that's what a woman would bring to it. I don't think anybody who is not a woman would ever think of that dimension because normally, the crowds are normal; the ones who participate in these things are the usual people. But a woman reaches out beyond that based upon her experience, based upon her interaction, because chances are women have much more of an opportunity to interact at all levels of society than a man would. Because she's in charge of the home, and so the groups that – children groups - bring her into contact with parent/teachers association; that's a different group. Market women because you have to do the caring and buying for the home, and so only a woman can bring that to the task, I think.*

Q: Not necessarily; just the historically in-power groups.

Johnson Sirleaf: *That's right. As a matter of fact, I think because women support, women's constituency, go beyond the in-power group. That's how they get to be women leaders, because they bring a differ-ent constituency, a different kind of support; and so they reach back to that same level of a constituency that has helped to enable them to come to power, enable them to excel in their professions.*

Q: And then the corollary to that then becomes how do you win the historically in-power groups over? How do you get them to understand that this is not – you're not putting them out but you're just bringing more in?

Johnson Sirleaf: *I think one place to make sure the in-power group accepts what you do when you go beyond the normal is to establish within them your own competence, your own ability, and gain the respect from them for what you're able to bring to the task as a professional. I think that's important. Once that respect is established, then when you move beyond the norm to which they are accustomed, they then begin to question but to also say that there must be something to it; and so there's much more acceptability on their part to give it a try, to see what does this bring? What difference does this bring? And no longer do they question your motive because you've already established yourself among them, that I can play the game a normal way and I can win at that game. I can excel at that game, equal to or better than you can. So now I'm going beyond. And so that's sort of breaks the barriers a little bit; and even though there would be some reluctance and some questions, but at least it's accepted on the basis that you can do it and you know what you're doing. And what you do, you do well. So that helps.*

Q: I also have this parable – I'm actually writing a book on it *and it includes The Elephant and the Mouse* – and the parable is that if you are an elephant in a room, you feel very entitled, you feel very much that you can speak your loud voice, you very much have a vision of where you want to go, you're not really concerned about others. And if you are the elephant and the mouse is in the room, how much do you actually need to know about the mouse in the room? Conversely, if you are the mouse in the room, how much do you need to know about the elephant? Of course, you need to know everything about the elephant. So you develop quite a good skill set of figuring out what the elephant's move is, whether it's moving to the left or moving to the right, so you develop this sensitivity to the more dominant group. And my actual belief is that to be a great leader, you need to actually

have both of those sets of skills. And that perhaps men or large countries have historically had that elephant mode. Small countries know a lot about large countries. Large countries don't always know so much about small countries. Similarly, women may know a lot more about men, I think. I'm wondering if you have seen that in your own framing of issues. What do they know about us versus what we know about them?

Johnson Sirleaf: *I think so, and I think that that comes normally from the powerful, and the domination that they bring to any task tends to cloud their appreciation of some of the caveats and the pitfalls that are out there because they're just the mouse. Even in leadership roles, both men and women, too, after a while when one has accumulated a certain amount of power, you can easily miss the fact that there are little things along the way that can really, really topple you, as big as you are because you miss to see them. And I think that's a major challenge for us as women leaders that come to the leadership power with – we're part of the mouse set, so to speak, and so we appreciate what it is that power corrupts. And after awhile, an all-powerful person, even a woman, can all of a sudden miss those little things, and how do we restore that once we get there? We're always mindful that there is that little thing that we forgot that could then become – not only an irritant but will become a major deterrent to some of the bigger goals that one wants to achieve, and so I think I and other women leaders must always be mindful of that. That's why when we talk about them bringing into play the unusual, reaching beyond the power set; it is exactly because you don't want to miss the mouse. And make sure that you understand what some of their issues are and how we could go into if you have to consolidate your power in your progress. You have to continue to be inclusive.*

Q: What would you think the benefit of what a group of women leaders together like the Council – 3(7) women, heads of state and government – what could they do in your mind?

Johnson Sirleaf: *Change the world? (Laugh) No, I think collectively, identifying issues or institutions in which they want to bring their collective strength to bear can make a difference. For example, calling* *for the establishment of an agency within the U.N. system that has the full mandate and the resources to respond to the needs of women is something that women leaders around the world, if they came together and say, "This is it. This has to happen. This is what we want because it's going to make a difference. And we want the world to respond to this; we want the world leaders and world institutions to respond." I think it would happen much quicker than it would otherwise. I mean, I could be a single voice calling aid, another woman could be a single voice calling for aid, but if 35 world women say this is what we think would make a difference in the lives of the ordinary women, I think the world would listen. And there would be other such issues out there where women can bring their collective power to bear.*

Q: Certainly I know people were looking at the U.N. with the most recent Secretary-General position and saying it's time to have a woman, but the process was such that that didn't happen.

Johnson Sirleaf: *Because again, you see we'd have to plan for it. I mean, they don't just happen because you want them to happen. We'd have to – I've been working at it for years, identifying the woman who could so compete, getting the message from that woman out there, getting the profile known to everybody, doing the lobbying the way the men do. And some people have been lobbied for these positions for years. We still don't have enough special representative secretary generals who are women all over the world; and when you take a position and say why is this so – well, there are no candidates. Bring us the candidates. So all right, let's give them the candidates! Tons of them so they have no excuse anymore.*

Q: Yes, that is always a common complaint – well, we don't know any. We don't know any women candidates for whatever position. As you have led in the country for nine months, have you had people say to you that you're doing this so much differently than a man would be doing it– in other words, can you articulate some things where people are saying about you as a woman coming in as President are really doing things quite differently than men leaders have done?

Johnson Sirleaf: *Oh, I think so. In my case it's just the openness of our society, the freedoms that people now enjoy. I mean, people have said to me, wow! Sometimes there is criticism from the newspapers and everybody expects the response to be one of exercising restraint and clamping down on them. They criticize me; I criticize them. That's what democracy is all about. It comes – you know, it also comes from the self-confidence of having won the leadership. It's not like being cata-pulted or getting to that position just by happenstance. But when you've been through it and you've competed as a woman must to reach a leadership position, you lose any fear of being different; because you're so self-confident of what you do, you've achieved it on the basis of effort. And so you can afford to be different; you can afford to respond in ways that are consistent with the things you believe in without having to be reactive to what people think you ought to be.*

Q: And yet, of course, if you want to win re-election, you have to respond to – somewhat – to what people are saying. What they want, their needs.

Johnson Sirleaf: *Compromise is a way of politics. No matter how strong in your conviction, no matter how courageous in your actions, at some point compromises are necessary along the way to accommodate the views and the feelings of others without necessarily undermining in any meaningful way the things you believe and the principles for which you stand. But compromise is politics. If you're too inflexible, then of course all your good intentions could be totally disrupted or under-mined.*

Q: Interestingly, particularly with the women who were cata-pulted into power, about a third of the women leaders of the world have come to power after their husbands or fathers had been assassinated. The biggest challenge was – one of the biggest challenges, I should say – is identifying trusted advisors. While you didn't come to power that way, obviously, other women leaders have said that, too. "Who do I turn to in those moments of ultimate decision? How do I know I can trust my advisors?" Some leaders now are putting 50 percent of their cabinet women, which has been an interesting proposition. What about you?

Johnson Sirleaf: *I think in my case, the – one of the shortcomings of having been in the business for a long time and having earned the stripes the hard way is perhaps I need to listen to more advice. Because I tend to think that I can make the hard decisions, because I've done it that way. But I have to be a – I know that I have to be a bit more accommodating and that people have told me that; and I have to admit to that.*

Q: Well, this notion of, for example, 50 percent of the cabinet.

Johnson Sirleaf: *Well, I wish I could set those targets and achieve it, but I didn't approach it that way. I pushed it with setting certain criteria for cabinet, qualification and competence, no record of human right abuses, inclusiveness as much as possible to accommodate are a political thing. And then in those cases where there were women that met those three, then of course, they got a margin of preference. But what I was very clear about was to go out and identify women to hold strategic positions because I knew I couldn't carry out development agenda unless I had a woman in charge of justice, unless I had a woman in charge of finance, unless I had a woman in charge of commerce, unless I had a woman in charge of our police. And so I went for, if I can get 50 percent, they are going to be in the strategic positions that will determine that I carry out my agenda.*

Q: So you would know you had those trusted advisors around you.

Johnson Sirleaf: *That's right.*

Q: So you picked those cabinet positions very carefully?

Johnson Sirleaf: *I picked those. Very carefully. Very specifically, very strategically.*

Q: Last question. Let's go back to your childhood. What values do you think you learned in your childhood that you are now using as a leader?

Johnson Sirleaf: *That there are two things that my parents taught me that have stayed with me and have made a big difference in my life. Hard work and honesty. I remember my mother saying that the only thing that soap and water doesn't remove from you is sin. And so you can do any kind of work, and you can clean it up. And also that the one thing that lasts with you is that if people trust you. That you could be trusted, that would take you above everything else in what you do. So those two I have held onto, both I and my siblings, I think we all should remember that; and I think today, part of my own success in all the many fields in which I've worked, both at home and abroad is one thing I do stand up for, and everybody talks about it, it's just those two things. I'm called a workaholic; that comes from being brought up to work. To wash your own clothes, to clean the floors, to make your bed every morning and come back and do your chores even as you study a lesson. And the integrity that I bring to the task.*

Q: **Would your parents be surprised that you are now President of a country? What would they say?**

Johnson Sirleaf: *They would be surprised because my life has turned upside down. I think they saw in me the potential to be – my early life didn't seem to be moving in that direction. I got married right after high school, had four children before going back to college. And so at that time, I was just – apparently just on the way to being a housewife and an English teacher. So they saw the potential, but I think they would be surprised that I stayed with a goal and saw it through to final success. At the same time they would be pleased.*

Q: **As all the women of the world are pleased that you're President of Liberia. Thank you very much for your time and for the honor of us coming here to visit with you today. We, of course, wish you all the best; and the Council will help as we can. Thank you.**

Johnson Sirleaf: *I look forward to great work with the Council.*

Chapter XIII: Myths of Leadership

A man and woman are walking down the street, pushing a baby stroller. Inside is a beautiful newborn baby, dressed in stylish, matching yellow and white newborn attire. A yellow blanket is draped around the inside of the beige stroller. As the couple pauses to cross the street, another couple waiting nearby admires the baby. Before any significant conversation on parenthood, birthing, or even the newborn's eye color is discussed, the admiring couple asks the question, "Is it a boy or a girl?" Once the question is answered, they seem to know how to better relate to the baby; as if they planned to high-five a newborn boy or inquire if his birth weight is suitable for obtaining a football scholarship. Perhaps they feel it is appropriate to comment on beautiful facial features only if the baby is a girl. Whatever the case, no conversation regarding the baby takes place until the heretofore unknown gender is established. Our society places great importance on gender and its roles and, in doing so, perpetuates a system of gender schemas. We are inclined to stereotype and categorize behaviors in male or female contextual boxes, so that we know, or think we know, how to form relationships with each other.

A fascinating example of gender schemas occurred in the auditioning process of the symphony orchestra. Malcolm Gladwell talks about it in his book *Blink*; it is a well-researched phenomenon. The gender schema here, for women, was that they had a "smaller sound" when playing an instrument. When it was discovered that a bias seemed to exist in auditioning women for various symphony positions, evaluations began to be held behind screens where the player was hidden from the judges' eyes. However, the gender schema was so strong that care had to be taken to hide the shoes and mute the sound of the footsteps of the one auditioning, in order to avoid the judges making a male or female predetermination regarding the performance. Blind auditioning, as it is called, led to a substantial increase in the number of women in symphonies. Our belief structure can be so powerful that if we believe something strongly enough, we will hear it.

A fascinating exploration of how perceptions of ability are often related to men and women's behavior is the personal story of Ben Barre. A scientist by education, Ben was transgender from female to male. In his article in Science Magazine (July 2006), Barre describes the differing treatment he received when he was in a female body and when he was male. One fellow scientist commented to him that his work was much stronger than his sister's scientific work, having heard Ben make a presentation when he was female and then when he was male.

History shows us that leadership has long been considered the domain of men. We hold to an age-old theory of leadership, what I call the "Great Man Myth." This myth has held sway over our thinking for hundreds of years. It is the idea that a great and heroic leader *must* be a man. That he must be larger than life, stronger than the wind, to pull the sword out of the stone--someone who can change the weather, rule the unruly, and save the helpless female from bondage. From King Arthur to General MacArthur, men have been the historically-in-power--women the historically-out-of-power (as have other groups). Our stories, our culture, and surely our myths, have formed around our past experiences and way of life, taking on a credibility granted only by the forces of history and not by the reality of human characteristics. We have been taught that great leadership is a masculine adjective/noun combination.

Consider the following quote from John F. Kennedy, enduringly carved into a stone monument in the park at Harvard University's Kennedy School of Government:

"When, at some future date, the high court of history stands in judgment of each of us, our successes or failures will depend on the answers to four questions:

> *Were we truly men of courage?*
> *Were we truly men of judgment?*
> *Were we truly men of integrity?*
> *Were we truly men of dedication?"*

So when history judges those of us alive today, will it record as odd the idea that only men might possess courage? Cannot a woman be truly dedicated, truly human with great integrity? And what about leadership? Where in our genetic make-up is a male chromosome for courage? Or a female one for dedication? The personal qualities that comprise our human existence, the things that set us apart from insects and simple animal life are the intangible parts of our personalities, the characteristics that are a tiny part *nature* and a great deal *nurture*. We are born male and female, dark or light-skinned. We are nurtured by education, parenting, peers and our environment.

A wide variety of research exists claiming to prove that women and men are fundamentally, inescapably different. From Venus to Mars and through the pink and blue aisles of the local toy store, gender stereotyping has been used to explain everything from relationship problems to engineering skills. Rosalind Barrett, a women's studies professor at Radcliffe College, and Caryl Rivers, a journalism professor at Boston University, teamed up to author over 300 pages of evidence for how these gender difference theories "hurt male-female relationships, undermine equality in schools and the workplace, adversely affect the division of labor in the home and deprive our children of the opportunity to develop their full human potential." Their book, entitled *Same Difference: How Gender Myths are Hurting Our Relationships, Our Children, and Our Jobs,* proposes that differences are rooted in situation and power, rather than in gender. The authors write, "Put sex in the other's role, and you see a dramatic shift in behavior. And give each the same work, with the same power and prestige and the same expectations for success, and you find that men and women start to behave in ways that are increasingly similar. Situation outweighs sex." They add, "Too often, we've mistaken power behavior for gender behavior."

Our mythology about who is able to lead us influences us from a very young age. In ancient history where survival often depended largely on physical strength, leadership was conferred upon those whose skillful use of brute force made them the winner. Stories of great conquests, wars won, peoples subjugated, are rife with the illustrations of man as a powerful hero, imposing his strength and his will to create new civilizations. The world today has moved beyond the need for leaders to slay dragons and conquer Hun-like invaders. Military might is now one part physical strength and ninety-nine parts weaponry and tactical skill. Our leaders direct invasions with computers and telephones rather than swords and chariots. Courage under fire has a completely new meaning and the implications for gender changes in military leadership are evident.

Finally, we have the greatest myth of all. We know what leaders look like. This could be further from the truth but if each of us was asked to describe what a leader looked like, there would be certain common features. Most likely, first and foremost, we would see a male figure in our mind's eye. And he would be tall.

In his book *Blink*, Malcolm Gladwell has a fascinating discussion of the tallness of leaders. He describes a study of American men—16% of the population of American men is 6'2" or taller. But when the heights of Fortune 500 male CEOs are measured, 57% of these men are 6'2" or taller. Height provides a subtle advantage in our view of who has leadership capacity. Of course, there is actually no correlation between height and abilities (even in basketball).

Gladwell talks further about one of the presidents of the United States, Warren G. Harding, whom he describes as someone straight out of central casting for the role of president. He was silver-haired, a natty dresser, tall, and spoke with a sonorous voice—he just looked presidential, so people invested in his characteristics of a leader, despite a lack of evidence of his abilities. In fact, this was in contrast to his actions, which showed him to be one of the worst presidents the U.S. ever had. But he had that look.

So if you as a person do not have those physical traits, are not subtly advantaged, what do you do? You have to overcome people's mental photographs and images and prove you have the abilities, in ways that those who look the part do not.

Leaders have to be both watchers and watched, listeners and listened to. Dominant groups, those used to being in power, develop half of those skills. That is, they are used to being watched and used to being listened to. Non-dominant power groups develop more of the other skills. It is about power. The less powerful in any hierarchy of society develops their intuitive sense—they must know and watch and listen to the group in power. The reverse is not true. Great leaders ironically actually develop both capacities.

Franklin Roosevelt is a classic example of a person who was born into an elite, power group status with all that comes with that privilege in the subtle advantages he received as a white, upper class, American male. That changed when FDR became disabled. No longer a majority group member, he was in the minority in society now. His understanding and knowledge of what others went through increased dramatically (as did his understanding of how valuable his wife, Eleanor Roosevelt, was to be his eyes and ears in American life).

The women leaders in this book belie the myths of leadership-they lead-but they have these positions of power like men. They hold these titles and the authority of the positions. Not all of them are heroic, like not all men are, but the attributes and traits of leadership are not gendered. Neither baby girls nor baby boys start out with any preter-natural skills. They are learned skills that come with practice, with society's acceptance, and with recognition and encouragement and who is seen to be rightfully entitled to lead.

Even seemingly inherent personality traits like those found in the Introvert/Extrovert or Myers-Briggs tests don't doom some to the role of follower, nor guarantee leadership entitlement.

So just what are the qualities of a great leader? Passion? Wisdom? Courage? Intelligence? Confidence? Integrity? Articulate communica-tion? Are great leaders born rather than made? This book examines these questions through the interviews with those who should know best, women world leaders. Their comments and stories have shown that the qualities that make a leader successful are not gender-specific concepts, but rather personal characteristics that can be developed, nurtured, changed and improved through time and experi-ence. We see that successful leadership is quality and character that engages the people with a compelling and well-articulated vision. It is the balance of ambition and integrity coupled with competence and expertise. None of these are measurable at birth, all of these can be developed and not one is a trait found only in males. In the preceding chapters, the stories of these women who served past or present as leaders of their country, hopefully have inspired and enlightened all to understand that leadership is a skill to be learned, an art to be practiced, and a style that transcends gender completely.

Chapter XIV: Questions I Am Frequently Asked

Do women help other women or are they their own worst enemies?

The United States Secretary of State Madeleine K. Albright (1997 - 2001) has a saying: "There is a special place in hell for women who don't help other women."
In the ideal world, all women would see each other as sisters in the struggle towards equality and their complete and full place in society. The world being as it is, with individuals and their own sets of goals, self-interests, sense of competitiveness, not all women do help others.

The queen bee syndrome does exist in some. That is, the sense that "I made it and so can you. I didn't face any discrimination; I just worked hard, overcame the odds, and you should do it that way too."

What often amazes me in that syndrome is the sheer lack of comprehension about how many barriers there actually are to get to the top. It is as if the women who climbed long and hard, so normalized their situation that they didn't even see the barriers, the misperceptions, the need to perform in a far more superior capacity than their male counterparts to succeed.

Margaret Thatcher did not see it when she mentioned to me that women would probably not get into Parliament until after their children were grown, since you had to leave your district to spend four nights a week in London. It never occurred to her that this was an immediate disadvantage if women started later in their careers than men. The British Parliament is based soundly on the seniority system, so the later you start, the further behind you are. A man in his 20s who wins a seat in the House of Commons will get much further than a woman who starts in her 40s. Thatcher was completely unaware of the built-in inequity she was framing in that statement.

In truth, I am often more amazed at how much many women do to help others succeed, to be mentored, coached, and advised. I marvel at women who have little time between careers, family, their own lives and how much they are willing to spend in networking, giving informational interviews, spending time with a junior associate or speaking at a women's network meeting.

Whenever I have the urge to be critical about what women do or don't do in the revolution for change in systems, I benchmark that with how much or little men do. I often see men from historically underrepresented groups extending themselves beyond the norm to help their colleagues. They too understand that they are an embattled group that needs support beyond what the system would normally provide. And for both men and women, the ability to learn from others' experiences, go down the learning curve, share tips on overcoming subtle inequities is essential to the continued progress of change for the better.

Not one of us made it by ourselves. Others came before and help, as I say, to "hurry history." We want to keep moving forward and each individual act of our own in reaching to another in the chain will help us reach a society far more equal than it is now.

What will it take to have a woman president in the United States?

This will be a long winded response since there are many variables that inform this question.

If you are a student of government and political science, you may know that most of the women who are leading countries or who have been elected have done so in parliamentary systems. Without going into too much detail (and you can do so by reading up on electoral systems), those that elect parliaments and prime ministers don't have the same winner take all, 50% plus one vote electoral process that we have. Nor do they have the complicated electoral system we use for voting for President. Parliamentary systems may allow you to get into political partnership with others, to get elected by the representatives of the parties, etc. Women and minority groups have a fairer shot at getting into leadership because they can get into coalitions or don't have to get a majority of votes to win.

The length and cost of our electoral process discourages many from entering a race for political office. This is particularly the case for those who do not have access to a large amount of wealth, or have a large number of wealthy friends, clients and business associates. It is still true that white males in the United States hold far more higher-paying jobs or own larger business or have more connection to wealth than say a woman or an African American man.

In no country in the world does it take such a huge amount of money or time to run for the highest office in the land. In Great Britain the campaign season is limited to a six-week period imposed by the Cabinet Office during which new or controversial government initiatives cannot be communicated to the public and by a Royal Proclamation that dissolves the Parliament and requires the next election to occur with 17 working days.

In other countries, it might cost $1million dollars at most, not the $500 million it costs here. The fundamental reason that Ellen Malcolm started Emily's List was to try to overcome the built-in advantage that men had in accessing that early money one needs to show your candidacy is serious. Women don't write the large checks that men do, or have access to the PAC money in the same way. This is a serious disadvantage for women seeking the presidency.

Other countries get their Prime Ministers from many different paths in life. Poets, artists, theatre directors, doctors, lawyers, educators, social activists, business people have all become Prime Ministers of their countries. We fish from a smaller pond. In the 20th and 21st centuries our presidents have been vice presidents, governors, sometimes military men, a few Senators. For women, this really limits the possible candidates. We have never had a woman vice president. As of 2007, only twenty-nine have ever been a governor. No woman has been the chairman of the Joint Chiefs of Staff in the military or commanded a world war, and there are only sixteen women senators.

Women's career paths and the path to the presidency have not aligned well to date. The pool of ambitious, ready, well-financed women with the requisite job experience or run for the highest office has been quite small.

This small pool factor ties to what I have termed the 'power of the mirror'. It is the concept of knowing what you can be by what you see and who you see doing it. It is a major part in our own belief about what we are entitled to be or what we can imagine becoming. It is easy to imagine yourself becoming a doctor, if your mother was a doctor or a police officer if your mother was a captain in the police department.

The power of the mirror image came to me after I interviewed the President of Iceland. After she had been president for eight years, she would go around the country and meet children under 8 years of age. She noticed that the children believed that only a woman could be president and the boys were actually unsure if they could become president. They had never seen a male president and had difficulty imagining becoming one.

The United States has never had a woman president; that creates one more psychological barrier for both women and men to see women in that highest leadership role. Every time a woman takes on a new responsibility, such as secretary of state or national security advisor, we move inch by inch closer to a mirror that reflects all possibilities.

And yet 21 women have sought the presidency of the United States—prior to Hillary Clinton, there was most recently Elizabeth Dole and Carolyn Mosely Braun. Geraldine Ferraro was nominated by the Democratic Party to run for the office of vice president in 1984. Other presidential candidates in recent history include Margaret Chase Smith, Shirley Chisholm, Patsy Mink, and Patricia Schroeder.

I spoke of gender schemas before-those roles and shortcut thoughts in our mind about who can be and do what. The beliefs we hold dear to us whether they are in fact true or not. (Girls can cry, boys shouldn't).

Another gender schema belief held tightly is that men can handle crisis better than women or can deal with the evil demagogues and rogue leaders who lead some countries. We are less comfortable with the notion that a woman can be as tough and mean as her brutal counterpart might be. Could a woman handle terrorists as well as men or go to war if they must?

The answer is yes, as we have seen from Margaret Thatcher and the Falklands and from Chandrika Kumaratunga of Sri Lanka. For years, Kumaratunga had been dealing with the Tamil Tigers, a rebel terrorist group in Sri Lanka. She was wounded in a bomb attack against her in a terrorist act.

But we have fairy tale beliefs that women are kinder and gentler and can't hold up in a tough fight. A Deloitte Touche poll in 2000 found that 76% of those polled believed that a man would handle rogue nations better; 7% believed a woman could handle it better. That is a huge gap in perception. The ideal female candidate for President will perhaps have been a governor who weathered successfully a transit strike or fiscal crisis. Or perhaps a decorated female war hero (a little harder to accomplish, as women at this time are still prohibited from ground combat).

The White House Project, which I co-funded, has tracked the sentiment about acceptance of the idea of a woman for president. Great progress has been made in both men and women's willingness to consider a woman over he past decades. In 2008, more than 80% said that they would support a qualified woman for president. The trick is the word qualified because of the schemas and notions we carry inside our head about who can do the job under what circumstances. The number of acceptances goes down also when asked if the person polled thinks their neighbor would vote for a woman president (which often represents the true belief of the person being asked).

Several years ago, a TV show was created called Commander in Chief, starring Geena Davis. She was an independent, not belonging to either of the two major parties, and as Vice President became President after the (male) President died in office. Much of the plot line included the travails of the First Husband-what would HE do? Arrange the seating and flowers for the State dinners? That was too much for even this future-oriented script. Finally, the President's mother was brought in to live in the White House to do the First Lady's work. While the show was short-lived, it added incrementally to the visual image and possibilities of a woman playing the role of head of state and govern-ment in the U.S. and maybe even becoming one for real.

Will we have a woman president? Yes, most certainly at some point. The late U.S. President Gerald Ford is reputed to have said, "We will get a woman president in the following way: the woman will be elected vice president. The President will die in office and she will become president. Then we will never have another male president again!"

A Hearst/Sienna poll (Feb 2005) found those polled believe the first woman president would be a Democrat and at least as capable as a man on foreign policy. She would be stronger on health care and education but somewhat weaker as Commander in Chief of the military (these are very gendered stereotypes!). Further, the poll found some voters still couldn't picture a woman president-more than 1/5 said a woman would do a worse job than a man-others found the heightened security and terrorism issue that is the environment today, creating a hesitation on some people's part.

How the press and media cover women versus how they cover men makes a huge difference too. Barbara Lee says, "Hair and hemlines still get a lot of press coverage when it comes to women politicians." Women who run for office are often put under a microscope about their families, their personal lives, their husband's finances, their dress and demeanor. This over scrutiny also causes women to take pause before they decide to run for office.

The bar has moved, however, in how people think of a woman in dealing with foreign policy and tough dictators. This, I believe, is directly related to the recent experience of two U.S. women holding the toughest cabinet position outside of Secretary of Defense. Both Madeleine Albright and Condoleezza Rice have been U.S. Secretary of State and have shown themselves to be fully capable, handling allies and others with competence and confidence.

In 2008, we have seen Hillary Clinton create 18 million cracks in the "glass ceiling" in the Democratic primary votes. A black man, Senator Barack Obama, was voted President, another major milestone for America. Another woman, Governor Sarah Palin of Alaska, was the vice-presidential nominee of the Republican party. As I often say, "change goes from the unthinkable to the impossible to the inevitable." A woman president is the inevitable.

Yet, for women, it is still the personal over the professional - still issues relating to personal lives that can take center stage. The parties themselves, both Democratic and Republican, must step up and encourage more women leaders to run for office. The more women that run, the less they will be overscrutinized and the more "normal" it will be.

My sentiment is that the U.S. is moving forward in this arena of a woman president, but perhaps more slowly than many would have thought. Ironically, my faith in forward movement comes not from some sort of voter gender epiphanies but from money as the indicator of gender acceptance in presidential politics in the U.S.

Never before in history has a woman been seen as capable of raising the (obscene) levels of financing to create a viable campaign. Neither Elizabeth Dole nor Carolyn Mosley Braun came close to the fundraising capacity of Hillary Rodham Clinton. The parties take most seriously the candidacy of those who can raise the most money. Governor Palin injected new energy and new money into the campaing with her nomination.

That gives me a cynical kind of hope--we can hurry history.
And as far as over-scrutiny by the media, another irony here. What would actually help Clinton or Palin most would be to have at least two or three other women run for the presidency at the same time. Then they would not be the only Os in a room full of Xs and the media

and voters would actually start to separate candidates, not by their gende
but by their policies.

Women have to run--just like all of those ambitious men--Vice Presidents, Senators, Representatives, businessmen. Yet women don't.

Richard L. Fox of Union College has studied gender differences in
political ambition. His findings show not that women aren't qualified
or eligible, but that they are less likely to have seriously considered
running for any office across the board and this is whether they are
lawyers, business owners, executives, or educators.

Men are TWICE as likely to have seriously considered running for
office, or taking any steps toward seeking an office. When women do
consider an office to run for, it is at a much lower level than men's
ambition. They choose a school board instead of Congress. It is self-
image too. 58% of women rated themselves qualified or very qualified
to run for office; 72% of men rated themselves that way. Women also
often wait to be asked to run. To win the presidency of the United States
women must run!

My career seems to not have the same advantages as men.

This is not a question but more like an affirmation or concern.
Women often have the intuitive feeling that not all is equal and the
playing field is not level quite yet. They often can't put their finger on
what it is that gives them this uneasy belief but they don't want to
deny what appears to be happening as they watch men, equally or
less competent, get the better assignments, more money and quicker
promotions.

Stephen Young, Founder of Insight Education Systems and formerly
of JPMorganChase has coined the term "Microinequities" to name the
small, subtle events, or non-events that occur to women and minorities that ultimately have a large impact on their careers. Basically,
the macroinequities are over and done with in corporate America, or
the lawsuits are explicitly going after them. That is, there are no more
want ads that say "women only" or "men only." Water fountains,
hotels, buses, and the military don't exclude because of skin color or

gender anymore. There are fewer and fewer situations of outright denial of opportunity because of being a woman or African-American or other minority group. What *is* still occurring are the small things that have an impact over time. These are not necessarily so obvious, or they are seemingly so small that someone doesn't want to raise the issue for fear of seeming too sensitive, or just too much of a complainer.

Examples of microinequities:

- Who gets the office closer to the boss
- Who gets invited to go out to lunch with other team members or to play golf or go to a nightclub
- What assignment is given to whom-who gets the bigger clients, the larger research, the more important high visibility tasks
- Who gets the informal feedback and the frequency of it
- Who negotiates for a bigger raise, more executive training, sends emails or voicemails to the executives and tells more about their accomplishments

and

- Who couches statements as questions, explains with more words than ever necessary, apologizes, though none is needed
- Who speaks last at a meeting or not at all, who skips the meetings thinking they are a waste of time
- Who thinks that 'schmoozing', building networks, doing favors is all playing politics and won't do it

You get the point. These are all small, very small in some cases, actions or impressions that over time accumulate to significantly advantage or significantly disadvantage someone. It is like two small children being given an interest-bearing checking account at birth. The boy gets 4.1% interest and the girl gets 4.0% interest. In 40 years time it is a huge difference in how much they each have.

Linda Hill, the Wallace Brett Donham Professor of Business Administration at the Harvard Business School has found that if women
don't get the critical feedback, the stretch assignments, the high-
visibility projects, the mentors, and the men do, then over time there
is a performance gap between men and women.

Unfortunately, women have to be extra vigilant about these issues
that fly below the radar. Yes, you do have to pick your battles but there
will be a price to pay if you don't correct the inequities coming at you.

To be fair, some companies don't have a clue that there is a bias in
their systems. They don't realize that the performance appraisal
process may be flawed, or the succession planning method isn't open
and transparent, or that in a division the men are getting the better
assignments than the women. Often it is a matter of pointing things
out, tracking the numbers that will tell a story that can be fixed. In
one company I worked with, we looked at all of the important standing
committees of all divisions and of the central group.

Not surprisingly we found that women were over represented in the
human resources type committees and substantially underrepresented in committees that dealt with assets, income, audit and other
very important powerful groups. (The same distribution was observed
for racial and ethnic minorities.) The first step was to track it and
make those at senior levels aware that there was bias in the system,
not intentional but nevertheless prevalent.

My advice to women is that we need to remain vigilant, even hyper-
vigilant, to what occurs within the organizations we work. To keep an
eye out for both the intentional and unintentional unequal distribution of assets, resources, time, attention, favors, and assignments is
crucial. You may choose to not voice your concern about the differen-
tials but do not ignore them or take them lightly. It doesn't make you
paranoid, just thoughtful.

What is the Council of Women World Leaders and what does it do?

Mary Catherine Bateson describes how women compose their lives; she feels that, unlike men, women have more of a meandering and perhaps more meaningful life. Men, by socialization perhaps, end up in more linear careers with less flexibility to them.

I raise that point because my own career has felt composed rather than planned and what has been created was certainly nothing I could predict.

A prime example of that is the Council of Women World Leaders. This organization came out of my journey to interview the women leaders. I did not have any intentions or even any conceptual thoughts about creating an organization for women leaders at the start of my interviews. But listening to them, hearing their similar stories it seemed like it would be valuable for them to meet each other.

At the time, I did not know that there were organizations of the highest leaders of countries, but with research I found there were several that could be models for the idea of a Council. The important thing was that the leaders also liked the idea when proposed at the summit we convened in Stockholm in 1996 with the U.S.-based Center for Strategic and International Studies. The women leaders liked the possibility of meeting their peers periodically and using their power to help women and girls globally.

The Council was created in 1997 and found a home at Harvard University's Kennedy School of Government in 1997. Dean Joseph Nye Jr. was instrumental in inviting us to Harvard and his foresight allowed us to find a place to start up and get going. His great colleague, Holly Taylor Sargent, was really the woman behind the scenes that made it happen.

In 2004, the Council moved to the Aspen Institute in Washington, DC, where we enjoy an excellent relationship with the many valuable programs there. For ten years the Council has created programs, issued statements, and raised important issues about women and girls. The Council is composed of almost all of the women presidents and prime ministers, both current and former; there are now 37 as members. Most importantly we have evolved our work to include women ministers-in the United States they are cabinet-level leaders. Ministers of Defense, Justice, Health, Culture, Environment, etc. We have convened many of these ministerial groups to great advantage-it is a way to create a critical mass of women leaders to voice their position on specific topics, particularly to institutions like the World Bank, IMF, United Nations.

The Council also has a robust program of student fellows from Columbia University and the Kennedy School. These graduate students spend a summer with a woman leader or one of the men leaders from our advisory group. They hold amazing positions with presidents, prime ministers, ministers, and the students love the program.

I talk. Men don't listen-why?

Deborah Tannen has done extensive research on how men and women communicate and I recommend any of the books she has written on the subject. She has many findings but one important one is that generally women talk to enhance relationships. Men talk to enhance transactions.

This has many ramifications. Not least is that men have the upper hand because how they talk is reinforced by how we think leaders should talk. No nonsense, straight to the point, no hesitations, no questions asked or answered. This is a vicious cycle for women because leaders are often played by men in movies, television, books and they talk like men. Many leadership gurus are men, and they talk like men. So there are fewer women talking like women in these archetype roles with little reinforcing that relationship talk can also be modeled as leadership talk.

Men and women may use equal numbers of words on any day but it is all about context. Men will speak longer in meetings, for example, though perhaps are less verbal when asked their feelings about something emotional. Women will often sound tentative about an issue because they frame it in a question, though they are by no means unsure of what they are saying. The question is a device to bring others into the conversation, to be inclusive, and to communicate that you want the others' contributions and see it as meaningful. Men are less likely to frame statements into questions because they have been taught to never show doubt, to know the answers, and to reflect an image that suggests they are totally sure of themselves.

Men hear women asking questions and they wonder why she is unsure of herself and doubting what she wants to say. They may discount what the woman is saying and maybe not even hear her at all. Women think men are somewhat rude, not having too many interpersonal skills and emotional intelligence because of the straightforward, bullet point way they may talk.

Men are also comfortable acting as if they know something when in fact they don't or are not sure. Men feel competent in talking of something or feeling mastery of it when they have about 25% of the knowledge on the subject. They will have an opinion. Women feel comfortable when they have about 75% of the knowledge on the topic before they feel they are entitled to have an opinion, to speak out, or to disagree.

Women will often wait and not speak up in committee meetings until they feel very sure of what they have to say. Men will usually speak first, thereby setting the agenda or framing the issue. My recommendation is that women speak second or third in a meeting. Also, as is often the case, a woman may feel she has said something and is not heard, but when the man says the exact same thing he is acknowledged and praised. At this point, I don't take that anymore and will say, "Thank you for reaffirming what I said earlier," or better yet, I will do that for another woman. Often I now say, "That sounds just like what Mary said ten minutes ago so it appears you are agreeing with her idea." It is a small way that women can help each other combat the dynamics of male dominant speech patterns.

Men do have what is known as 'positive allusion'. They have a strong sense of themselves, far greater than their actual capacity. It is a trait I wish that more women were inclined to.

Any man on the street could see himself as CEO of a company, as a Senator, as a great sports commentator on TV, as able to attract the most beautiful movie star. Few women have that same sort of overly positive image of themselves. In fact, most women suffer from negative allusion; they don't think enough of themselves.

Anna Fels, in her new book *Necessary Dreams*, indicates that this is not a surprising state of affairs. Starting at an early age, young men and boys get a lot of positive feedback, encouragement, disproportionate attention from authority figures. Parents and family members often give boys more value. (Just think of the cultural messages in many different countries and religions about how valuable boys are versus girls). This makes boys believe they are quite good, far better than their actual abilities would take them.

In one study done by the AAUW, teachers called on boys and girls exactly 50/50 after researchers observed that teachers called on boys disproportionately more. After one month they asked the boys what it was like and the boys complained that the girls were getting all of the attention. The boys 'normal' amount of equal attention was for them around 70/30. Real equality was a take away for the boys.

I remember that when I was at the Harvard Business School getting an MBA, men would raise their hand and say "I haven't read the case, but I have an opinion!" I couldn't believe it. I wished I had that kind of *chutzpah*.

So it is not surprising that men feel like they have a rightful place in the world, to lead, to have their voices heard. This is not a bad thing by itself; it is just that women don't feel the same way and find themselves at a distinct disadvantage.

How is it possible that some countries like Pakistan or Bangladesh have women leaders when women's progress is not very great in these countries?

About a third of the women who are presidents and prime ministers have come to power after their fathers or husbands were assassinated. This was the case for Benazir Bhutto of Pakistan, both Sheikh Hasina and Khaleda Zia of Bangladesh, Corazon Aquino of the Philippines, Aung Sun Sue Kyi of Burma, Violetta Chamorro of Nicaragua, Megawati Sukarnoputri of Indonesia. The wife, daughter, or sister is imagined to be filled with the dead male heroes' ideas, values and beliefs and that she will simply carry on for him. It is also because there are high illiteracy rates in many of these countries and the family name is often what is well known to the voters. These are legacy positions and often the woman may come quite unprepared to take this high office.

In addition, women in the country get disproportionately high expectations thinking that this one woman will change their status. Realistically this can't happen as the leader is often the single woman at the top with no women in the cabinet and few women in Parliament. So even if she were interested in improving the lives of women in her country she is sharply curtailed from doing so. It also should be remembered that the legacy positions are those of a certain class, the upper class in a country; the woman is one of the country political and economic elites. She is not the average impoverished citizen.

This tradition is not limited to the developing countries. In the United States, voters often will vote for the wife of a deceased politician, especially if the husband or father has died while still in office and she is appointed to the seat. We also have seen a fair share of father-to-son political legacies. A woman may also incite strong emotions when she takes leadership. Being a woman and an advocate for change may be dangerous. Benazir Bhutto's killing was a tragic example of that.

I believe that from an early age, girls get different messages about who they should be than boys do and when they grow up those girl messages don't serve them well.

Any one of us could come up with a dozen messages we received early on from parents, teachers, other children and they are different for little girls and little boys.

Here are some examples:

Early girl message:
Don't talk loudly, too forcefully--if you can't say anything nice, don't say anything.
Early boy message:
Speak your mind forcefully, be heard, give as good as you get, have an opinion.

Early girl message:
Wait your turn, be nice and ladylike, don't push and shove, don't draw attention to yourself.
Early boy message
Interrupt and get out in front, compete to win, don't let anyone take advantage of you, get respect and don't worry if people don't like you.

Early girl message:
Don't get dirty, don't rough house, don't beat the boys.
Early boy message:
Don't act like a sissy, don't hit like a girl, don't cry.
(In fact when little girls are asked what it would be like if overnight they became boys, the little girls were excited about what they could do and be. The little boys, when asked what it would be like if the next day they were girls, were extremely upset and said their lives would be ruined.)

You get the point. The problem is that girls develop different skill sets than boys given those early messages. And they are not the skill sets to win, lead, and be successful in a more competitive world later in life. The messages that boys get set them up nicely to develop into the out-front, be a leader, get resources person as an adult.

In fact, both the skills that women have and that men have are needed to be fully successful and a well-rounded person. Emotional intelligence requires that people build relationships as well as do projects well. The key for both men and women is to learn balance and not to over rely upon the skills received early on.

Progress for Women-What Progress?

January 20, 2007, President George W. Bush was giving his State of the Union address in front of Congress, the Cabinet, the Supreme Court, the Joint Chiefs of Staff and other high level leaders. To state the obvious, the number of women sitting in front of him was still far fewer than the number of men. Some milestones have occurred; in particular, the position of U.S. Speaker of the House has always been held by a man since our government was formed. Today it is held by Nancy Pelosi, who is now third in line in succession to the Presidency. There are nine women governors (the most compelling route to the Presidency) with two women governors holding leadership positions in their associations-Arizona Governor Janet Napolitano, President of the National Governors Association-the role President Clinton played before his presidential nomination-and Kathleen Sibelius (KS) head of the Democratic Governors Association. This speech by President Bush in 2007 didn't look like a meeting of the Taliban leadership, but it did not look like Sweden either. The 2008 presidential election brought two strong women to center-stage.

What do we call the place of women in the United States in this early part of the new millennium? Have we gone farther than expected or disappointingly slow? Are we moving at a rapid pace or a glacial one? What will success look like for women within the realms of what we have normally considered power?

Part of the answer lies in the point of reference. For much of recorded history women have been property, chattel, belonging to a father and then to a husband or elder brother without property rights, control of reproduction, or free of violence. And today many countries still have that description even if laws are in place to counter those prevalent norms.

Other countries, like the Nordic countries, seem to have instilled a far more egalitarian form to their society and though not perfect are far ahead of many other countries in the status of women.

The United States ranks 31rd out of 128 countries in the 2007 World Economic Forum *Gender Gap Report*. Currently, the U.S. has eight women governors (16%), 74 house members (17%) and a record-high 16 Senators (16%). Compare this to Sweden's 47% figure for women in Parliament. So in a relative sense, based on development in other cultures, the U.S. is moving forward but not at a stellar pace.

What have been some of the guideposts for women in the U.S. to measure results? One would argue that intentional acts by the political bodies in the country most accurately reflect steps taken. Scientific discoveries like the pill were hugely instrumental in changing lives, but those inventions came from independent sources not requiring a vote or consensus of opinion.

Women in the U.S. received the vote in 1920, the Civil Rights Act of 1964 provided further legal protections, military academies opened their doors to women in the 1970s. Title IX was passed in 1972 and ensured fairer distribution of funding for athletics for young men and women in school.

A good yard stick is the number of people who say they would vote for a woman president (qualified by the words "qualified candidate"). This number inches higher and higher. In the 1950s, it was around 50%. In the new Sienna/Hearst 2006 poll, that goes to 93%.

The macroinequities have faded on the whole. As I indicated, no more *help wanted* ads for males and females. No more stuck in the typing poo Now noble professions for women include both nurse and doctor. Wome Secretaries of State are appointed and capable. According to the 2007 ACE report on American College Presidents, 23% of presidents of colleges and universities are women, more than double the 1986 rate, but only two percent more than the number in 2001.

And yet in the U.S., persistent stereotypes still undermine women (and other historically underrepresented groups). Social and role expectations are often just as divided as those old "Leave it to Beaver" shows. The number of women at the top of business is abysmal. Power and leadership is still seen as male with male attributes and consistent gender schemas. There are 10 women CEOs of Fortune 500 companies in 2007.

Many thought that it was a pipeline issue--just fill the pipeline and let reverse gravity take effect. Enough time has passed since women entered the major graduate and professional schools-law, medicine, business, military occupational specialties-that there are a wealth of seasoned, experienced women who should be partners, CEOs, chairmen of the Joint Chiefs. This has not happened yet. The pipeline clearly leaks.

As mentioned, these leaks, referred to as "Microinequities" by MIT and Stephen Young, are the small but cumulatively devastating slights that, when added up, create a push/pull feeling for women in positions of leadership. They feel uncomfortable in the environment and not seen and are pushed out. They may also feel pulled out with other responsibilities which they shoulder in the family or elsewhere.

Of course, backlash is always waiting in the wings. When societies change rapidly, many people find themselves untethered. Long-held beliefs provide assurance, comfort, predictability. For many, knowing their own role and place and the role and place of others evokes a sense of order and 'rightness'. Not so long ago, men brought home the bacon and women cooked it.

These traditions are often bolstered by laws, people are influenced by interpretations of religious texts, rituals, sayings, humorous jokes, fairy tales, TV shows, movies and many other ways cultures are communicated and prolonged. So what replaces those fixtures of belief?

For some, when change occurs, particularly in the most basic notions of gender roles, it is the fearful unknown coupled with a huge sense of loss that prevails. Every step that looks like progress for some women may look like a loss of a foothold to others--both men and women.

Progress, unlike technology, is not certain. Bottom line, progress has been made for women (and other underrepresented groups) but around the world, not enough. What would it be like if women ran the world? If women ran the world, as Rosabeth Moss Kantor says, the world would already be different. History still needs to be "hurried."

Appendix A: Interview Questions

Remembering back to your childhood and parents, what values did you acquire then that you use as a world leader today?

Understanding how you rose to power as a leader, what do you feel that you were least prepared to handle as a leader and what do you feel you must uniquely provide to the country?

What is it like to govern? By what standards should a leader be measured?

What skills do you use as the leader of a country? And how have you changed?

You have met other world leaders, mostly men. What do you perceive about their leadership styles in comparison to yourself or to other women?

Have you ever sought the advice of other world leaders? Who inspires you, in the present or in history?

Women have historically played a different role than men in society, often a lesser role. What role should women play in leadership today and why? How can they reach that?

Are the expectations of you as a woman leader different than what you think is expected of men? Give examples if possible.

What advice do you give to young women who see you as a role model?

What role should women in the United Nations play that you see they are not yet performing?

The UN has many issues to deal with: environment, AIDS, national sovereignty. How should it deal with conflicting national pressures to solve world issues?

Describe a typical day of yours. How do you decide the priorities for your energy and efforts?

Here is a Chinese proverb: that no history can be written about an important person until they no longer are present. If you were writing the history of yourself, what would you want it to say?

As you look back, would you have done anything differently? What did you learn through mistakes and efforts made?

What question have you never been asked that you keep waiting to have presented to you?

Is there anything else you would like to add?

Appendix B: Female Presidents & Prime Ministers, 1953-2009

Suhbaataryn Yanjmaa ~ President, Mongolia (1953-1954)

Sirimavo Bandaranaike ~ Prime Minister, Sri Lanka (1960-65; 70-77; 94-00)

Indira Gandhi ~ Prime Minister, India (1966-77; 1980-84)

Golda Meir ~ Prime Minister, Israel (1969-1974)

Isabel Martínez de Perón ~ President, Argentina (1974-1976)

Elisabeth Domitien ~ Prime Minister, Central African Republic (1975-1976)

Lydia Gueiler Tejada ~ President, Bolivia (1979-1980)

Margaret Thatcher ~ Prime Minister, United Kingdom (1979-1990)

Maria de Lourdes Pintasilgo ~ Prime Minister, Portugal (1979-1980)

Mary Eugenia Charles ~ Prime Minister, Dominica (1980-1995)

Vigdís Finnbogadóttir ~ President, Iceland (1980-1996)

Gro Harlem Brundtland ~ Prime Minister, Norway (1981; 1986-89; 1990-96)

Maria Lea Pedini-Angelini ~ Captain Regent, San Marino (1981)

Agatha Barbara ~ President, Malta (1982-1987)

Milka Planinc ~ Prime Minister, Yugoslavia (1982-1986)

Maria Liberia-Peters ~ Prime Minister, The Netherlands Antilles (1984-86; 88-93)

Gloriana Ranocchini ~ Captain Regent, San Marino (1984; 1989-90)

Corazon Aquino ~ President, Philippines (1986-1992)

Benazir Bhutto ~ Prime Minister, Pakistan (1988-90; 1993-96)

Ertha Pascal-Trouillot ~ President (interim), Haiti (1990-1991)

Kazimiera Prunskiene ~ Prime Minister, Lithuania (1990-1991)

Sabine Bergmann-Pohl ~ President (interim), East Germany (1990)

Violeta Barrios de Chamorro ~ President, Nicaragua (1990-1997)

Mary Robinson ~ President, Ireland (1990-1997)

Khaleda Zia ~ Prime Minister, Bangladesh (1991-96; 2001-06)

Edda Ceccoli ~ Captain Regent, San Marino (1991-1992)

Edith Cresson ~ Prime Minister, France (1991-1992)

Hanna Suchocka ~ Prime Minister, Poland (1992-1993)

Susanne Camelia-Römer ~ Prime Minister, The Netherlands Antilles (1993, 98-99)

Kim Campbell ~ Prime Minister, Canada (1993)

Tansu Çiller ~ Prime Minister, Turkey (1993-1996)

Patricia Busignani ~ Captain Regent, San Marino (1993)

Sylvie Kinigi ~ Prime Minister & President (acting), Burundi (1993-1994)

Agathe Uwilingivimana ~ Prime Minister, Rwanda (1993-1994)

Chandrika Kumaratunga ~ President, Sri Lanka (1994–2005)

Reneta Indzhova ~ Prime Minister (int.), Bulgaria (1994-1995)

Claudette Werleigh ~ Prime Minister, Haiti (1995–1996)

Sheikh Hasina Wajed ~ Prime Minister, Bangladesh (1996–2001)

Appendix B: Female Presidents and Prime Ministers
1953-2009

Ruth Perry ~ Council Chairman, Liberia (1996-1997)
Biljana Plavsic ~ President, Bosnia-Herzegovina (1996–1998)
Jenny Shipley ~ Prime Minister, New Zealand (1997–1999)
Mary McAleese ~ President, Ireland (1997–present)
Janet Jagan ~ President, Guyana (1997–1999)
Pamela Gordon ~ Premier, Bermuda (1997–1998)
Jennifer Smith ~ Premier, Bermuda (1998-2003)
Helen Elizabeth Clark ~ Prime Minister, New Zealand (1999-present)
Ruth Dreifuss ~ President, Switzerland (1999)
Rosa Zafferani ~ Captain Regent, San Marino (1999, 2008)
Vaira Vike-Freiberga ~ President, Latvia (1999–2007)
Mireya Moscoso de Arias ~ President, Panamá (1999–2004)
Tarja Kaarina Halonen ~ President, Finland (2000–present)
Maria Domenica Michelotti ~ Captain Regent, San Marino (2000)
Gloria Macapagal-Arroyo ~ President, Philippines (2001–present)
Mame Madior Boye ~ Prime Minister, Senegal (2001-2002)
Megawati Sukarnoputri ~ President, Indonesia (2001–2004)
Maria das Neves ~ Prime Minister, Sao Tome and Principe (2002-2004)
Annelli Jaatteenmaaki ~ Prime Minister, Finland (2003)
Beatriz Merino Lucero ~ Prime Minister, Perú (2003)
Valeria Ciavatta ~ Captain Regent, San Marino (2003-2004)
Luisa Dias Diogo ~ Prime Minister, Mozambique (2004–present)
Fausta Simona Morganti ~ Captain Regent, San Marino (2005)
Yulia Tymoshenko ~ Prime Minister, Ukraine (2005, 2007-present)
Maria do Carmo Silveira ~ Prime Minister, Sao Tome and Principe (2005-06)
Angela Merkel ~ Chancellor, Germany (2005-present)
Ellen Johnson Sirleaf ~ President, Liberia (2006–present)
Portia Simpson Miller ~ Prime Minister, Jamaica (2006-2007)
Michelle Bachelet ~ President, Chile (2006-present)
Han Myung-Sook ~ Prime Minister, South Korea (2006–2007)
Micheline Calmy-Rey ~ President, Switzerland (2007-2008)
Pratibha Patil ~ President, India (2007-present)
Borjana Kristo ~ President, Bosnia Herzegovina (2007-present)
Cristina Fernandez de Kirchner ~ President, Argentina (2007-present)
Zinaida Greceanii ~ Prime Minister, Moldova (2008-present)
Michele Pierre-Louis ~ Prime Minister, Haiti (2008-present)

Appendix C: Network of Women Ministers of the Environment

Recognizing a critical moment for the environmen--and that women bring a unique voice to the challenges and opportunities before the world--22 women ministers of the environment and 28 women leaders of intergovernmental and non-governmental environmental organizations gathered in Helsinki, Finland in March 2002. This historic meeting, attended by women from Africa, Asia, Europe, and North and South America, provided the first opportunity ever for women environmental leaders to come together as a group to address crucial issues for the future and to ensure that gender issues are raised in dealing with environmental issues globally.

Excerpts from the statement of Joint Conclusions on the Environment to inform the 2002 UN World Summit on Sustainable Development:

The elimination of global poverty and the promotion of sustainable development are essential to a fair and equitable world. The current patterns of consumption and production are among the major causes of the degradation of the Earth's resources. If the present trends in poverty growth, population expansion and production and consumption patterns continue, the negative impacts on natural resources, environment and health will only grow worse. And women, who represent a majority of the world's poor, will continue to suffer disproportionately.

Women bring a unique voice to the challenges and opportunities of sustainable development. Their experience, their participation and their leadership are crucial to the success of world environmental efforts.

Appendix D: Excerpts from Interview with Margaret Thatcher

1994 ~ London, England

Liswood: Well, thank you for allowing us to have this interview today. This is for the purpose of interviewing all of the women leaders. You are the last of the 15 current and former presidents and prime ministers that I've met with, so it's a great honor to meet with you today. If you could talk to me about your values and we know your father was very influential.

Thatcher: I think it was my father and my mother. We were brought up to work hard, we had to. We were brought up to be economical. We had to. My mother was very economical in the way she ran the housekeeping and the way we would use up everything, whether it's material from a dress or things from a meal. We were brought up to have organization and method because that's the way in which we managed to get everything into a day. And we were also brought up very much, from my father, that you made up your own mind what you wanted to do and why. Took responsibility for it. And you never, never did things just to follow the crowd or because they were fashionable, that was very, very strongly part of my upbringing and it was extremely valuable. So you see, it was a very well organized household, one which had one foot in business and one foot in housekeeping and, some hand in volunteer work and in local work. You were expected to pull your weight, basically earning your own living as part of a household and as part of the local community and part of the local church. So it's pretty active, pretty busy. And a very, very good background for politics.

Liswood: Some of the other leaders have spoken about the influence of their father, and it seems very interesting to me and intriguing.

Thatcher: I think you'll find that frequently. There is a strong relationship between fathers and daughters and between mothers and

247

sons. But just because you tend to attribute that, to your father, my mother was a massive part of my father's work. She played quite a role in our family grocery business and the work they do enables and frees up the husband to do some other volunteer work as well...it was a family and we were all part of it. And we had to all make our own contribution.

Liswood: Did your mother have certain expectations of you as her daughter?

Thatcher: I have a theory that parents always want to give their children what they feel they've missed in their own childhood. Now, my father, [who] had to leave school at 13 because his family couldn't afford to send him to school any longer, he was actually a very good brain, the best I ever knew. Because he had felt that he missed the education which he longed to have, so he read and read to us and my mother too, both my father and mother were musical and so what did they give us, they very best education possible because they had missed it. The very, very best cultural background possible and so at the age of five I remember, my mother from her savings, buying a piano and I was taught from the age of five to play the piano. We would go always to a musical concert in the town, at a string quartet coming, that was part of your upbringing. You would listen to good music, on the radio, radio was new in our time. We would go to amateur dramatics, again, because these would do some of the best plays and we would go to some of the operettas of Gilbert and Sullivan. So, we had the actual education and we always discussed things. We were taught to read the papers and discuss the issues of the day. Now, when I came to bring up my children, I felt that I have had an extremely good education, I'd worked extremely hard, I wanted them to know something of music and the arts and theater, but I felt that perhaps I had missed out on some of the amusements and sports and entertainment. We only rarely went to a film and it had to be a good film to go to. Not necessarily a terribly learned one, for example we did go to the Astaire/Ginger Rogers [film] because [of the] dancing, was just exquisite and the production was absolutely marvelous. We went once a month that was a lot because you were expected to make your own entertainment. We did again thanks to my mother, who was an extremely good cook, and also thanks God's church, we did entertain one another quite a lot. We went out to tea or to Sunday night supper after service and there was a great deal discussed on the current issues of the day. So, we were brought up to entertain at home. That was a natural thing to do.

Liswood: Your father was very interested in you getting into politics. Was your mother proud of you and had that expectation of you to get into politics?

Thatcher: I don't think we had any expectation. I was a natural debater at school. I was naturally interested in history in debating things because I was so used to listening to argument at home and in the shop. And in these evenings when we had people in, they were very absorbing times. There were times when there was a great depression so we had to be very economical but we always were working hard. We had our own business but we knew some people were out of work. And we did what we could to help. Then you had the rise of Hitler and we watched that with very considerable alarm. So there were very, very interesting times. Another thing in 1935 we had the Sovereign Jubilee of George the first and Queen Mary, which was great outpouring of patriotism. We had a great empire at that time. So we were used to, we were used to people coming to our church because you have a lot of them, different visiting preachers. We're used to people coming from different parts of the Commonwealth.

Liswood: Let's talk about why... it was you who rose to power.

Thatcher: I don't know. Perhaps I just had the combination of talent and abilities that were required plus the upbringing. Plus the opportunity to exercise those talents and abilities. I don't think many children of my generation have the kind upbringing I had with a father not only very prominent in local affairs but again, also a natural debater and a natural speaker. There was a time I've heard at evening meetings when there's been a speaker and they have wanted someone to start off the question or that discussion or they wanted someone, if it was not going very well, they'd say, would you like to say anything else? After my father and without any further ado my father could always get up and make an effective contribution because he got his thoughts worked out, he read and read and read. And worked. We also took the Daily Telegraph every day. And what was called a children's newspaper then, which was a more educative newspaper, we weren't allowed the ones that were rather more full of the comic strips. Those were not permitted in the house.

Liswood: You, when you discuss this I'm thinking that most young women would be more effacing, would not have the courage to step out...

Thatcher: No, no, no. I think that a very old fashioned view and I don't think that our generation, we were more self effacing. They might have been in the end of the last century. There was an enormous change in the lives of women and in the law relating to women in the end of the last century. Particularly the law relating to married women and in the separate property they might have was an enormous change. That was the battle of the last century. That is also the battle to get into politics, it was the battle of the suffragettes to get the vote was greatly enhanced by the role which women had played in World War I. As men and women went to battle and women took over jobs and the offices, they ran things. It is as much as they showed what they could do that justified their right to have the vote. I think that battle was won and I don't think we were suffracating in my time. We were entitled to a good education and we had a good education and we were expected to use our talents. Certainly there were not so many careers open to us then as there are now. And I think in my time as you listen to the news on radio, we didn't have television, we would have thought it very strange if we had a woman news reader. Because we had Stewart Hill we knew their voices. Oh, that would have been very strange...And you would not have had so many women commentators but there were some very distinguished women journalists, there were some very distinguished women aviators, there were distinguished women being pioneers. That battle was over. The thing in my time was to get victories extended to more and more women. But women for a very long time have played an important part in family businesses. They're very good with figures, very good with money as well as some of the, the pictures which some women's magazines might display, but in fact, every married woman is a manager. She has a job as a manager. She has to make decisions, what the family's going to have, what the arrangements are. What, what the clothes are, and usually decorations of the house and I have to say, in countries where there still are not so advanced towards the talents of women, every married women is a manager. Not every woman's job is that of a manager until she's used to making her own decisions.

Liswood: In your experience, have you perceived that there is a style of governance that is different between men and women?

Thatcher: No. I've not found it. The difference is, the real difference that matters is a difference in style between someone who wants to be in politics and in power because they believe passionately in certain principles, and those are the way a country should be governed and therefore the policies both from the principles and sometimes they're different things to do. Many is a time when you're urged to do them because they're the right way to go and the moment the difficulties arise people tend to run away from them and say, oh, no, no, no, go back to the other way. That is the difference between those who have a clear vision and policy, and those who just say, well. I believe in pragmatism, I believe in saying what needs to be done and at the time. Without any principle, that's not good enough that's the differ-ence. And that's why Keith Joseph and I have the same kind of vision and work closely together. This was a personality and approach. We felt to be effective, and to do justice to responsibilities you have, you have to have a clear vision, you had to be committed to it, you had to explain it. There were far too many people I think who think you can do it all just by explaining to the people and not having the vision in the first place. You need to have something to communicate...It's not enough just to be a good communicator and get constantly on televi-sion, particularly in the day when you have things called sound bites.

We used to have detailed arguments, arguments on principle; you can't do this on sound bites. They're deeper and have to be explained.

Liswood: It was quoted that you said when you want something said, ask a man, when you want something done, ask a woman.

Thatcher: I think that's true, I think women often get on with a job that's very hard and are not perhaps quite so much concerned with communications. In our [parliamentary] system we have a certain amount of communication built into it. It was Question Time in the house--Rules are if you're prime minister, that you don't know what question you're going to be asked because the question written down on the order paper is for the prime minister to give details of official duties today. And that is used as a base to ask a question about anything right across the whole spectrum. So twice a week you are in effect communicating. I myself was against television because I knew what would be taken in the half an hour at the end of the day would be a sensational question. I was interested in the real thing and of real things which is much duller than television because of the depths they have to go.

Liswood: When I asked a similar question about style to some of the other prime ministers, Gro Brundtland of Norway, for example, said that she felt that women usually came forward from their own practical experiences in, their own lives, whereas perhaps men were more abstract than that.

Thatcher: I don't like the idea that women are limited to their practical experience. The intellectual woman is every bit as good, sometimes a lot better than men. But it depends from one to another and the brain is there to be used and exercised. The fact that you also have practical experience may make you more methodical, may make you run your day better because you've got to get a lot in it, particularly when you are at home and work, you've got to be able to think ahead. But I have so often said to many young women if you would have had a steak pie for lunch, it's not better because you thought 20 minutes what shall I have than if it's taken you five seconds to decide to have a steak pie for lunch. You learn to make decisions quickly, particularly routine things. But there are many, many men who can do that as well. It's a personality thing, as well. But never underestimate the intellectual power of women. As good a brain as any man.

Liswood: What do you think it might have been like if, if the genders had been reversed in terms of parliament, there had been 98% women and 2% men in your parliament?

Thatcher: Well, I don't think it's much point to speculate on it. It wasn't and isn't very, very likely to be and I'm very much against it, having a quota for women. It's totally and utterly wrong. In my life it's merit and suitability that counts. I would never have liked to be in the position welcoming a new member of our party into the House and say, "Now tell me, my dear, are you a quota woman or a talented woman?" You come in because of your talent and your suitability and the way that you forge an election because people have confidence in you as a personality. Not because you're a quota and have put out someone else who might be more suitable.

Liswood: I've certainly heard that same sentiment in some of the central European women who felt similarly, who have been under quotas.

Thatcher: We are constrained in one way. If you are a young married woman with a young family and your husband has a job, a long, long way away from the capital city. I would never have felt that I could have left my children on Monday morning, travel to London and not gone back until over night on Thursday. I couldn't have done it. I would have felt I was not doing justice to them. I would have missed them. I'd have been worried about them. I'd hope and believe that they would have missed me. That means, you really need to do local politics, in your local town or city in that time, you would always get back home, things go wrong, accidents happen. You must always be able to feel you can get to them within a matter of, let's say, within an hour. Now I was dead lucky, my husband's work was in the London. We lived in the London area. My constituency was in the London area, parliament is in London, so everything just happened to gel. And that was good fortune and there may be many women who shouldn't do it that way or couldn't do it that way and therefore I went into Parliament when I was 35, 36. Others would have to wait too until their youngest child was perhaps in school. And then they could have a different life.

Liswood: Have you sensed that you've changed over time?

Thatcher: Everyone changes with experience, and if you don't change with experience you're a very strange person.

Liswood: I asked that of the former prime minister of Poland

Thatcher: Hannah Suchocka.

Liswood: Hannah Suchocka

Thatcher: She's a great person.

Liswood: She said, she used to sit in a chair for two or three hours and wonder why someone made some remark to her because it was so unjust and then, as she grew in her confidence she'd say when someone would make a stupid remark to her she would say, well you're more stupid than I.

Thatcher: What she was saying was that some of those comments hurt- they do. And when you're prime minister, you find your name's in the paper every day, particularly on comments from those who want to criticize you. Now if you're going to read the papers every day your capacity to do your job will be diminished because we're all human, we don't like to be hurt. And sometimes it is unjust. But you just have to get used to not reading the paper. If I saw my name I would not read it. My first officer would give me a digest of the news so that I knew exactly what was being said, and of course, the days when I went into the House I had to know because I had the same things thrown at me. But then, because I was going into the House, I immediately had to remark, "How am I going to tackle this if it comes up?" So you had something to think about, not to be hurt by the thing, but to just to try to play it away. And, yes, you are hurt. And if you allow it to dominate your life, you will not use you talents to the very best of your ability. This is part of politics. Happens to men, too. They must be hurt just as much.

Liswood: Do you think that what Edith Cresson felt, that the critiques and the cuts were very personal to her, versus to her policy. And she attributed it to many things, including being a woman, that she felt that the criticism was quite personal.

Thatcher: I'm afraid sometimes, yes it is. They spot personal mannerisms you may have, you didn't even know about. Then sometimes they're quite right. And if you're on television you've got to get rid of them because they irritate. If they prevent your message from getting across, then you've got to know about them and change them.

Liswood: Some people have said the comment that men are considered competent until they're proven incompetent whereas women are, considered incompetent until they prove their competency.

Thatcher: Oh no I think sometimes it's the other way around. If she's a woman in that job she must be super competent. Cannot operate the other way around.

Liswood: That in fact she's even better than men?

Thatcher: That's right. In order to get there.

Liswood: So that reminds me of Mary Robinson saying that she would look forward to the day basically when a mediocre woman could get as far as a mediocre man.

Thatcher: Well, sometimes that happens. Sometimes it happens. She's a very distinguished lawyer. As again, women in the professions have made enormous strides. Again, partly I think because of the opportunities and the way in which [women] use them in two world wars when many, many big jobs were filled by well qualified women.

Liswood: I think it will be a challenge though for women who are less than completely super qualified.

Thatcher: Yes, you see. In our system we are chosen to stand for parliament or is it to run for parliament–I'm not sure. In America it's different. You're chosen by your local constituency and it depends then upon the competition...

Liswood: Where was it that overall you look back that you least expected to happen?

Thatcher: What you least expect to happen happened to me. I never expected that I would be faced with the question of putting our armed forces into battle and faced with it very quickly indeed. Faced with it from having news that the Argentine fleet had put to sea and from what they'd taken on board it looked as if they might this time go to invade the Falklands. And then they had actually invaded the Falklands on Friday. So we had to act quickly and obviously the moment one got the news one began to make arms dispositions and to make plans. But it was quick and it is clear that something really rather marvelous occurred I must say about the British Parliament. They were our people and they were invaded and their way of life was taken away by an aggressor. Parliament immediately from all sides, whatever the politics, banded together to support the armed forces to invade to reclaim the lives of those people. The right to live in their own way. And their own islands. That is such a very good thing I had never thought that I would have to take that decision. And it was done with a small group of people who would have been responsible for putting the forces in position to go. We profited very much by being in NATO. The rule in NATO is all your ships, your naval ships, and all your aircraft must be in position with all of the equipment on board to move within 48 hours. So you had all of the military equipment automatically on board which you might need wherever you go. Actually to take that decision and when we heard on the Friday morning, I called together the cabinet in the afternoon and made a clear decision, yes, the armed forces must go even though it's 8,000 miles away. Even though it would take three weeks to get there. So, our enemy or aggressor had three weeks' notice and could increase the forces on the islands and they would arrive there in the deep mid winter, we had only the air cover that could be provided from two aircraft carriers and if we lost one of those it would be fatal. And they had all of their aircraft 400 miles away on airfields on the mainland. If one had all of these facts in a computer decision and said, "Now, do you think we should go?" We should get the answer "no." There's always one other factor, that is the spirit of your people and the shear professionalism of your armed forces. So I recalled parliament on the Saturday morning. Everyone came. There were 650 of us. There were only about six against us going. And we closed ranks in support for the armed forces to go in there fighting. Differences between us [in Parliament] were there. It wasn't so easy when they had actually [to decide] to go into battle because there are some people who wanted to negotiate, reconciliate, Negotiations, negotiations. Beware of too many of negotiations.

Liswood: And certainly in the cases of Benazir Bhutto and several of the others they came to power...

Thatcher: Beware of too many negotiations. The other side will use it and say we're still negotiating and they'll go on and on, never intending to come to an effective agreement. I knew the invader had to be thrown off those islands. I knew that the fleet couldn't go round and round those islands in the deep of winter. So we had a time limit. When they arrived the negotiations had to come to an end. And I said to the military I never expected to have to do this, please understand. Now we put our services, armed forces into battle. Whatever you need to do your job well and to make life more easy for you, you shall have. If you haven't got it, we'll do our level best to get it for you. This to me is crucial.

Liswood: And as you say, having had the experience of being the prime minister, experience in politics, you understood.

Thatcher: I knew exactly how to go about it. But Harold Macmillan came to see me. He said, as the eldest prime minister, "I come to offer you total support on the part of all living ex-prime ministers." I listened to his experience. I should set up an emergency committee, just a few, five or six, not more, with the military and they'll meet every day and don't put the treasury on it. So I didn't. So we met every day. We made all the calls, rules of engagement and then left the military to make the decisions within the policy that we had clearly laid down within limits we'd given them.

Liswood: And you've been said to say that you really do not like consensus politics. I'm not sure I understand that.

Thatcher: Well, let me tell you. What is the difference? I was faced with a situation on Wednesday. A task force of 25 ships left our shores on the Monday fully loaded, not only with equipment but with the men. Later we had to send more because the military wanted it. Now that was quick. There's been a situation in Bosnia which I never expected to see in Europe again. Or anywhere. Two million people – it's called ethnic cleansing – driven from their homes and their homes often destroyed. Between 200,000 and 250,000 massacred. They all got together and said what shall we do? Anything they could agree to do, the first is not to get involved. Secondly was to do humanitarian aid. With ethnic cleansing going on, with the concentration camps we saw on television, the murder, the massacre going on, with schools and hospitals being bombed and people being sniped at on the streets, they couldn't agree on effective action. The United Nations resolutions gives more authority to use force than they employed. Just contrast that with when we were faced with aggression in the Gulf by Saddam Hussein and President Bush and I happened to get together in America speaking to the same conference. Saddam invaded on the Friday. The United Nations resolutions said he had to get out. By the Monday he hadn't gone out and I was again with President Bush. I left the conference, Bush went back to the White House and I went up to the Oval Office with him. We decided what to do. We would both send armed forces and quickly. That was leadership. He didn't call together all the rest of Europe and said, "Now what are we going to do?" It was too urgent. We decided to go and then said to them, "Now we have sent forces and we hope you'll help. Because if Saddam Hussein gets the whole of that Gulf area, he's got 60% of the world's resources of oil and can blackmail us all. Moreover, other aggressors will see what we do, whether we take action or not. We took action. You've seen what's happening in Bosnia. No peace to keep. Safe areas being attacked. I hoped the difference between leadership and consensus is now clear.

Liswood: When I was speaking with Gro Brundtland and with the president of Iceland, President Vigdís, I asked about the balance in their cabinets, particularly Brundtland, because she did have nine women, out of eighteen total [in the] cabinet. Her response to me was that she felt that she couldn't make a wise decision in what she had, without that sense of balance in her cabinet.

Thatcher: I think we must make a clear distinction between women who are the presidents, who are not the executive or sovereignty because they have a prime minister to do that. That is the case in Iceland and also in the Republic of Ireland, a clear difference between that and a person who has executive authority as in the United States and to some extent in France, where the president actually has very, very many powers, though he handed over some of them to a prime minister. There's a great difference between ceremonial president who may have quite important duties, particularly if there's a crisis or whether parliament should continue, and one who has executive authority over prime minister, as well.

Liswood: I think Brundtland was the one with some authority in her position.

Thatcher: She's a prime minister.

Liswood: Yes, she is.

Thatcher: Not a president.

Liswood: Correct. That's the distinction you're making...

Thatcher: She's a prime minister.

Liswood: I understand.

Thatcher: Benazir Bhutto's a prime minister.

Liswood: Right, of course.

Thatcher: Iceland has a president also prime minister.

Liswood: You had one woman I think in your cabinet...

Thatcher: There weren't very many women in the house, this was the trouble. I had to think about more women, a bigger proportion of women in junior minister positions related to their numbers, then we had men in similar positions related to their numbers.

Liswood: Sounds like one of the challenges for women is just to increase the pool.

Thatcher: Well, yes but as I indicated, it isn't easy for the young married woman whose home is a long way away from London to come.

Liswood: What I've found in the group of heads of state and heads of government is that there were fewer married, or they were divorced, single, perhaps precisely because of what you're saying.

Thatcher: Mrs. Brundtland is like me, she's also married...

Liswood: She's married with her family.

Thatcher: Probably able to live in the capital city.

Liswood: I believe so. That's correct. I'm curious about that you were married to a man who is well off, how did that impact your abilities to create your career?

Thatcher: I think politics have changed enormously in our case. You used to have people who had done extremely well in business careers and who retain their business career and they were near the top, very big concerns. One came into parliament because it was very much a part time job. So when you're discussing the motor industries you had someone very high up in the motor industry, right at the top. You're dealing in commodities, someone very high up in dealing with gold, if you were dealing with textiles, someone who knew the wool textiles, someone else who knows the cotton textiles, someone who knew the garment making, all of these people, we had in our party. These days, politics have become much more full time. So in those days you had a variety of occupations and a variety of expertise in almost every subject. These days, young men and women come in much, much more to make a career in politics; they haven't the experience of business. They've perhaps got a good degree and they perhaps have done a certain organization and then they tried to get in and it becomes a full time job. Now, some of those, they will be deterred because they know full well, they'll never carry out their duties as a constituency member and as a good member of their party and in accordance with their interests, they may for no reason of their own lose their seat. Then, they not only lost their seat at election, they've lost their capacity to earn a living. Because they have no other occupation in which they're specialized. Now that will stop quite a number of them, I think, from coming into politics. It will also prevent a number of very good young managers who would like to come into politics from coming in because if they do they may still do their managerial jobs part time but they will forfeit probably the promotion that full time work requires. So, we're going to a very different system. Now, there's another concern. They, I would never have to think, goodness me, if I lose my seat, who's going to keep my wife and children, as it were. I was without that worry. I was also lucky that I had another qualification. I had a scientific qualification and a legal qualification and have done work in both. So I had something to go out to if I wished to take it out. But the fundamental changes taking place in politics now occur because of the kind of experience of people who come which is much more limited. They do not get the advice that we used to from people who are working in the very different industries. This is one advantage to having a House of Lords. And you can in fact put some of these very distinguished people with a life peerage into the House of Lords and you still will get your expertise there. But for me, I never had to worry if I lose my seat, who's going to keep my wife and family. Or my husband and family. I was totally free.

Liswood: I'm so curious in every country that I go to and everywhere I speak and I talk to people, you are the standard, particularly for a woman leader. You're the one that people most reflect upon even with another country's leaders. Kazimiera Prunskiene (Lithuania) was called the Iron Lady, Eugenia Charles (Dominica) was called the Iron Lady after you were. Why is that?

Thatcher: Because I'm decisive by nature and do not shrink from making difficult and courageous decisions. That may sound just a bit much coming from me but that is what it was. I didn't shrink from making decisions and I didn't shrink from tackling difficult problems and for my first three years I had an extremely difficult time. I determined that, the ideological struggle of the century was between socialist/communism, central control and power by the few over the lives of the many, in which it's first cousin is socialism. And our way of life is that governments are there to serve the talents and abilities of so many, many men and women to let them flourish and grow. So that they and their families can profit from their work and make them build up their own future. Government concentrates on doing those things which only governments can do and it's strong to do them. Yes, you have to have a strong rule of law and be responsible for making the framework of law within which industry can operate.

Yes, you have to keep your expenses down because when we got taxation up too much it was taking so much that you were not in fact getting the effort that you needed. Don't forget when I came into office, the top rated tax on earned income left by the socialists, because they spent so much, was 84%. The top rate of tax on savings income, 98%. And people got used to those and the able people have gone away. Prices control, income control, dividend control, foreign exchange control. All went in the first six weeks. It was amazing. It's not politicians who should determine what people are paid. It's how well the industry is doing. Negotiations within them. It's not politicians who would determine what the dividends will be. We have to have general planning because you do have to say when new industries can get set up.

But, I say turn to looking after the finances of the nation, getting down your expenditure and not taxation, keeping your defenses up, making the framework of law in which industry can operate, and the totally independent rule of law and also having a very good education system. Everyone is entitled to that. They're not entitled to be kept from the cradle to the grave by the government, by their neighbor, but they are entitled to a good education which is quite expensive because that gives them the chance to develop their talents and abilities from whatsoever background. Also you need a safety net of social services because life is so specialized these days, you can't have people in great need through no fault of their own. So we need that safety net. Now those are big enough jobs for government to do...But it was quite a revolution because they got used to a central government in control. The managers have got used to not determining their own prices, applying to prices commission and if they could show their costs have gone up so they are no longer competitive. Got used to not making decisions for what they're paid. They got used to not making decisions. What are managers for? Other people's talents and abilities. I say you had to turn around to run a free enterprise society. There's some government good education, safety net, good strong defense. And, the battle is going on between communism with its total negation of freedom, total negation of property. Communism never came from the people. It was imposed after an election which the communists lost. And they took away all liberty. No right even to have a Bible. Let alone freedom of worship. Took away all liberty and the right to choose your own job, no right to own your own home and imposed it from the top. Total central family control. For 70 years the world had unwittingly entered into an experiment. The United States was the outstanding example of a free society and a free enterprise society with a rule of law. Low taxation. Low regulation. And we had to change Britain from what it had become...a socialist state, and back into enterprise thriving example of liberty and taking full responsibilities. And it was tough. Because when you change, I said to Mr. Gorbachev all the difficulties come out first. And it takes three years for the benefits to show. But you've got to stick to it.

Liswood: Such conviction politics and such forthrightness, do you think any of the criticism were fair?

Thatcher: Criticisms. Could you ask the question again?

Liswood: Just do you think that critiques of your political position and your, not the policy, but the style, any of that was fair?

Thatcher: Oh, you don't think about that in politics. Life isn't fair. You're brought up to think it is, then you're not really getting the kind of warnings that you should have. Life isn't fair. And there's no point in getting too sensitive if you're in politics. What you've got to be certain is that what you're doing can be justified by principle, by argument and to put it across. That's the important thing. And you just have to understand that. Yes, some were criticizing our style, they haven't anything good to say about your policy. You don't know your style is so much of it.

Liswood: You don't even realize that you have a style.

Thatcher: No, no.

Liswood: You must be surprised when people observe it.

Thatcher: Well, they criticize. People who could make that criticism on style really don't make very much contribution to politics at all.

Liswood: And yet I think they have a tendency to focus on it?

Thatcher: Yes, I think perhaps they do but my style and whatever it was didn't do so badly for my country.

Liswood: What, do you have any message that you would like to give to young women?

Thatcher: Come into politics if you have a passion for politics because you believe in certain things. That's the only reason for coming in. And it applies to women and to men. It's a tough life, particularly when you start to climb the greasy pole to get to the top. And you will only be sustained because of what you believe and because you're translating into action. When I said earlier my father always told me never do a thing merely to follow the crowd. Make up your own mind what is right to do and get the crowd to follow you because it's right.

Notes for Chapters I through X

Introduction

1.   A few living women have served in these positions for less time, provisionally, or under circumstances that were atypical (for example, their country no longer exists as it was--Yugoslavia).

Chapter I--Politics Sans Intent

1.   Maritess D. Vitug, "Interview with Cory Aquino," *Filipinas*, March 1993, 60.

2.   See Jana Everett, "Indira Gandhi and the Exercise of Power," in *Women as National Leaders*, ed. Michael A. Genovese (Newbury Park, CA: SAGE Publications, 1993), 112.

3.   "During the 1960s and 1970s, when male deputies were removed from office by the military government, their wives were occasionally elected to fill their places, a Brazilian variant of the 'widow's succession.'" Jane S. Jaquette, "Female Participation in Latin America: Raising Feminist Issues," in *Women in the World, 1975-1985, The Women's Decade*, ed. Lynne B. Iglitzin and Ruth Ross (Santa Barbara: ABC-CLIO, 1986), 248.

4.   The latter route was used by Nancy Astor to become the first woman M.P. (in 1919). See Ruth Ross, "Tradition and Women in Great Britain," in *Women in the World: A Comparative Study*, ed. Lynne B. Iglitzin and Ruth Ross (Santa Barbara: Clio Books, 1976), 168.

5.   Linda Witt, Karen M. Paget, and Glenna Matthews, *Running as a Woman: Gender and Power in American Politics* (New York: The Free Press, 1994), 31.

6.　　See, for example, Garry Wills in his book *Certain Trumpets: The Call of Leaders* (New York: Simon and Schuster, 1994): "[The leader] takes others toward the object of their joint quest."

7.　　Jana Everett in *Women as National Leaders*, 127.

8.　　See, for example, the stories of Madeleine Kunin and Ann Richards, two U.S. governors, in Witt et al., *Running as a Woman*, 86.

9.　　Carol M. Ostrom, "Cleaning House in Government," *Seattle Times/Seattle Post-Intelligencer*, Sunday, 2 August 1992, sec. A.

Chapter II--Backgrounds

1.　　In July of 1994, the news media were reporting that India's parliament, hoping to prevent the widespread abortion of females, had passed a law to prevent doctors from telling would-be parents the sex of fetuses.　Girls require a costly dowry at marriage.　India has a long history of female infanticide.

2.　　Nancy Fix Anderson, "Benazir Bhutto and Dynastic Politics: Her Father's Daughter, Her People's Sister," in *Women as National Leaders*, 54.

3.　　Nancy Fix Anderson in *Women as National Leaders*, 45.

4.　　According to Olga S. Opfell, *Women Prime Ministers and Presidents* (Jefferson, NC:　McFarland & Co., 1993), 70.

5.　　Michael A. Genovese, "What Do We Know?" in *Women as National Leaders*, 214.

6.　　Torill Stokland, Mallica Vajrathon, Davidson Nicols, eds., *Creative Women in Changing Societies:　A Quest for Alternatives* (Dobbs Ferry,　NY:　Transnational Publishers, 1982), 23.

7.　　Stokland et al. in *Creative Women in Changing Societies*, 24.

8.   Patricia Lee Sykes, "Women as National Leaders: Patterns and Prospects," in *Women as National Leaders*, 220-24.

9.   Ron Arias and Fred Hauptfuhrer, "Here's to You, Mrs. Robinson," *People*, 26 November 1990, 57.

Chapter III--Through a Different Lens

1.   Stephen Engelberg, "Her Year of Living Dangerously," *The New York Times Magazine*, 12 September 1993.

2.   Claudia Dreifus, "Benazir Bhutto," *The New York Times Magazine*, 15 May 1994.

3.   Michael A. Genovese and Seth Thompson, "Women as Chief Executives: Does Gender Matter?" in *Women as National Leaders*, 4.

4.   For interesting tales concerning women politicians and their problems with dress, see Witt et al., *Running as a Woman*, pages 56-60.

Chapter IV--Leadership Styles

1.   Michael A. Genovese in *Women as National Leaders*, 24.

2.   Lawrence Stone, review of *A History of Women in the West*, *New Republic* (2 May 1994): 34.

3.   Jane Mansbridge in *Harvard Business Review*, 156.

4.   Introduction Speech for International Hall of Fame. Copy provided by President Chamorro's staff.

5.   Michael A. Genovese in *Women as National Leaders*, 198.

6.   Michael A. Genovese in *Women as National Leaders*, 198.

7.   Women are often said to "personalize" politics. Former U.S. President Ronald Reagan became famous for his use--or abuse--of "personal examples" in public performances.

8.   Lyn Kathlene, "Studying the New Voice of Women in Politics," *The Chronicle of Higher Education*, 18 November 1992, B2.

9.   Patricia Lee Sykes in *Women as National Leaders*, 226.

10.   Patricia Lee Sykes in *Women as National Leaders*, 227.

11.   Patricia Lee Sykes in *Women as National Leaders*, 227.

12.   Patricia Lee Sykes in *Women as National Leaders*, 228.

Chapter V--The Toughness Realm

1.   Michael A. Genovese, "Margaret Thatcher and the Politics of Conviction Leadership," in *Women as National Leaders*, 193.

2.   See Witt et al., *Running as a Woman*, 2 and 228.

3.   "Violence is something we women abhor." Corazon Aquino to Maritess D. Vitug, *Filipinas*, March 1993, 59.

4.   Claudia Dreifus, "Benazir Bhutto," *The New York Times Magazine*, 15 May 1994.

5.   Claudia Dreifus, "Benazir Bhutto," *The New York Times Magazine*, 15 May 1994.

6.   Witt et al., *Running as a Woman*, 227.

7.	Witt et al., *Running as a Woman*, 30.

8.	Witt et al., *Running as a Woman*, 30.

Chapter VI--Heroes and Helpers

1.	Social Democratic leader and chancellor of West Germany from 1969-74.

2.	Chairman of the Social Democratic Party in Sweden and prime minister of Sweden (1969-76, 1982-86).

3.	French national heroine, lived 1412-1431.

4.	Leader of Yugoslavia from 1943-1980.

5.	President of Egypt from 1956-1970.

6.	Influential advocate of nonviolence and Indian nationalist leader, assassinated in 1948.

7.	U.S. civil rights leader, assassinated in 1968.

8.	Dissident, playwright, and President of the Czech Republic (1993-2003).

9.	French general and president of the Fifth French Republic (1958- 1969).

10.	Prime minister of Great Britain from 1940-45 and 1951-55.

11.	President of France (1981-1995).

12.	Women in France received the right to vote only in 1944.

13.	In the West, the tradition of arranged marriages is reflected in this passage from the great French writer Michel de Montaigne (from "On Some Verses of Virgil"): "Connections and means have, with reason, as much weight in [marriage] as graces and beauty, or more.

We do not marry for ourselves, whatever we say; we marry just as much or more for our posterity, for our family. The practice and benefit of marriage concerns our race very far beyond us. Therefore I like this fashion of arranging it rather by a third hand than by our own, and by the sense of others rather than by our own."

14. Claudia Dreifus, "Benazir Bhutto," *The New York Times Magazine*, 15 May 1994.

15. Claudia Dreifus, "Benazir Bhutto," *The New York Times Magazine*, 15 May 1994.

16. Lawrence Stone, review of *A History of Women in the West*, *New Republic* (2 May 1994): 34.

17. Lawrence Stone, review of *A History of Women in the West*, *New Republic* (2 May 1994): 34.

Chapter VII--One-Half of the World

1. *Los Angeles Times*, Tuesday, 29 June 1993.

2. *The World's Women 1970-1990, Trends and Statistics* (Social Statistics and Indicators, Series K, No. 8), United Nations, New York, 1991.

3. One such group is the new international women's rights project (directed by Dorothy Thomas) of Human Rights Watch.

4. Most countries of the world use some form of proportional voting. New Zealand has recently converted to one. The U.S., Great Britain, Canada, and France (the last at the national parliamentary level only) are exceptions to the general picture.

5. Jill M. Bystydzienski, "Influence of Women's Culture on Public Politics in Norway," in *Women Transforming Politics*, ed. Jill M. Bystydzienski (Bloomington and Indianapolis: Indiana University Press, 1992), 20-21.

6. Jill M. Bystydzienski in *Women Transforming Politics*, 21.

7. Jill M. Bystydzienski in *Women Transforming Politics*, 21.

8. Jill M. Bystydzienski in *Women Transforming Politics*, 22.

Chapter X—Biographies

1. *Time*, Asian edition, October 11, 2004, Vol. 164 No. 14.
2. From interview with MSNBC
3. From interview with MSNBC
4. *Time*, 25 September 1989.
5. *Wall Street Journal*, 7 May 1987
6. *The New York Times*, 15 July 2003.
7. "Gro Harlem Brundtland," *Scientific American*, Dec 2003, 289:6.
8. *The New York Times*, 15 July 2003.
9. *Daily Telegraph*, 8 September 2005.
10. *The Guardian Weekly*, 16 September 2005
11. *The New York Times*, 3 July 1993.
12. *Lear's*, October 1993.
13. *Guardian*, 7 May, 1991
14. From interview in *The Observer*, 16 June 1991.
15. From interview in *The Observer*, 16 June 1991.
16. *The New York Times*, 8 September 1982.
17. Netherlands Antilles is an autonomous, self-governing region that is part of the Kingdom of the Netherlands, with Holland responsible for defense and foreign affairs.
18. *The New York Times*, 19 August 1985.
19. New York Times, 8/19/85.

Country Notes for Chapter XI

Material for country notes was derived from many sources, including *Country Reports on Human Rights Practices for 1993*, prepared by the U.S. Department of State and published in February of 1994 and the World Economic Forum's *Global Gender Gap Report 2006 and 2007*. Also consulted were data in *The Europa World Year Book*, Volume I, 1994, and Volume II, 1993. Other major sources of information are listed by country. A wide variety of newspaper and magazine articles are not specifically cited, but some references are given in the country histories themselves.

Bangladesh

The quotations cited are all from Najma Chowdhury, "Bangladesh: Gender Issues and Politics in a Patriarchy," in *Women and Politics Worldwide*, eds. Barbara J. Nelson and Najma Chowdhury (New Haven and London: Yale University Press, 1994). See pages 100-1, 102, 105.

Dominica

The one quotation cited is from *The Europa World Year Book*, Volume I, 1994.

France

All quotations except that from Simone de Beauvoir are from Jane Jenson and Mariette Sineau, "The Same or Different: An Unending Dilemma of French Women," in *Women in Politics Worldwide*. See pages 246, 248, 249.

Iceland

The statistics regarding abortion come from the Irish Family Planning Association (IFPA). The quotations cited, except for 1-3, are from Audur Styrkársdóttir, "From Social Movement to Political Party: The New Women's Movement in Iceland," in *The New Women's Movement*, ed. Drude Dahlerup (London: SAGE Publications, 1986). See pages 142, 143, 147, and 155. Other quotes are as follows. 1. *Europa World Year Book*, Vol. I, 1994, 1416. 2. *Country Reports on Human Rights Practices*, 920. 3. *Country Reports on Human Rights Practices*, 920.

Ireland

Except for President Mary Robinson's famous quote, which has been printed in a number of places, the quotations are from *Country Reports on Human Rights Practices*, 924.

Lithuania

Quotations 1 and 2 are from *Europa World Year Book*, Vol. II, 1993, 1806. Any other quotations are from *Country Reports on Human Rights Practices*, 959.

The Netherlands Antilles

The quotation cited is from a telephone conversation with Jacqueline Martis, September 29, 1994.

Nicaragua

The quotations cited, except for 1 and 2, are from Barbara J. Seitz, "From Home to Street: Women and Revolution in Nicaragua," in *Women Transforming Politics*, ed. Jill M. Bystydzienski (Bloomington and Indianapolis: Indiana University Press, 1992). See pages 163, 166, 167, 168, and 172. Quote 1 is from *Country Reports on Human Rights Practices*, 510. Quote 2 is from *Report on the Americas*, XXVI, 4 (February 1993): 13.

Norway

The first two quotations are from Jill M. Bystydzienski, "Influence of Women's Culture on Public Politics in Norway," in *Women Transforming Politics*, 12, 13. The third quotation is from Janneke van der Ros, "The State and Women: A Troubled Relationship in Norway," in *Women and Politics Worldwide*, 535. Updated statistics are from the Norwegian Centre for Gender Equality and Statistics Norway 2003.

Pakistan

All quotations are from *Country Reports on Human Rights Practices*. See pages 1381, 1382, and 1386.

The Philippines

All of the quotations except 1 and 2 are from Belinda A. Aquino, "Philippine Feminism in Historical Perspective," in *Women and Politics Worldwide*. See pages 596, 597, 600, and 601. Quote 1 is from *Europa World Year Book*, Vol. II, 1993. Quote 2 is from *Country Reports on Human Rights Practices*, 721.

Poland

All quotations except 1, 2, and 3 are from Joanna Regulska, "Women and Power in Poland: Hopes or Reality?" in *Women Transforming Politics*. See pages 179-80, 185, and 186. Quotations 1, 2, and 3 are all from Renata Siemienska, "Polish Women as the Object and Subject of Politics During and After the Communist Period," in *Women and Politics Worldwide*. See pages 621, 613, and 616.

Sri Lanka

All quotations not attributed in the text are from *Country Reports on Human Rights Practices*. See pages 1392, 1393, and 1394.

Turkey

Quotations here are from Nermin Abadan-Unat and Oya Tokgöz, "Turkish Women as Agents of Social Change in a Pluralist Democracy," in *Women and Politics Worldwide*. See pages 708, 709, and 716.

United Kingdom of Great Britain and Northern Ireland

Quotations 1 and 2 are from Joyce Gelb, "Feminism in Britain: Politics without Power?" in *The New Women's Movement*, 103, 116. Quotations 3, 4, and 5 are from Joni Lovenduski, "The Rules of the Political Game: Feminism and Politics in Great Britain," in *Women and Politics Worldwide*, 305, 300, 308. Wage gap information came from the Progress of the World's Women 2000 from UNIFEM's Biennial Report.

Bibliography

The following books were particularly helpful in connection with this project:

Bystydzienski, Jill M., ed. *Women Transforming Politics.* Bloomington and Indianapolis: Indiana University Press, 1992.

Capelli, Peter and Hamori, Monika. "The New Road to the Top." *Harvard Business Review.* January 2005.

Carr, David. "To Reach the Heights, First Be Male," *The New York Times.* January 9, 2006.

Carroll, Susan J. "Representing Women: Women State Legislators as Agents of Policy-Related Change." *The Impact of Women in Public Office.* Susan J. Carrol, ed. Indiana University Press, 2001.

Carroll, Susan J. "Women in State Government: Historical Overview and Current Trends." *The Book of the States.* Lexington, KY: The Council of State Governments, 2004.

Catalyst. *Breaking the Barriers: Women in Senior Management in the U.K.* NY: Catalyst, 2000.

Catalyst. *The Bottom Line: Connecting Corporate Performance and Gender Diversity.* NY, 2004.

Catalyst. *Women "Take Care," Men "Take Charge": Stereotyping of US Business Leaders Exposed.* NY, 2005.

Clift, Eleanor and Brazaitis, Tom. *Madam President: Shattering the Last Glass Ceiling.* Scribner, 2000.

Dadzie, Christabel, Torre, Kate, and Valian, Virginia. *Why so Slow?* Boston: MIT Press, 1999.

Bibliography

Dahlerup, Drude, ed. *The New Women's Movement.* London: SAGE Publications, 1986.

Falk, Erica. "The Glass Ceiling Persists: The 3rd Annual APPC Report on Women Leaders in Communication Companies." The Annenberg Public Policy Center of the University of Pennsylvania, December 2003.

Fels, Anna. *Necessary Dreams: Ambition in Women's Changing Lives.* Pantheon Books, 2004.

Freeland, Chrystia. "Women are the hidden engine of world growth," *Financial Times,* August 23, 2006.

Genovese, Michael A., ed. *Women as National Leaders.* Newbury Park, CA: SAGE Publications, 1993.

Hargreaves, Lucy. *The Bottom Line: Connecting Corporate Performance and Gender Diversity.* NY: Catalyst, 2004.

Hausmann, Richard, Tyson, Laura and Zahidi, Saadia. *The Global Gender Report 2006.* World Economic Forum, 2006.

Hewlett, Sylvia Ann and Buck-Luce, Carolyn. "On-Ramps and Off-Ramps," *Harvard Business Review,* March 2005.

Hewlett, Sylvia Ann, Buck-Luce, Carolyn, and West, Cornel. "Leadership in Your Midst: Tapping the Hidden Strengths of Minority Executives." *Harvard Business Review,* November 2005.

Iglitzin, Lynne B., and Ruth Ross, eds. *Women in the World: A Comparative Study.* Santa Barbara: Clio Books, 1976.

Iglitzin, Lynne B., and Ruth Ross, eds. *Women in the World, 1975-1985, The Women's Decade.* Santa Barbara: ABC-CLIO, 1986.

Johnston, Larry. "Making Diversity a Profitable Reality." *Chief Executive.* December 1, 2004.

Kellerman, Barbara and Rhode, Deborah L. "Viable Options: Rethinking Women and Leadership." *Compass.* Fall 2004.

"Keys to the Governor's Office." Barbara Lee Family Foundation.

King, Tonie-Mai, Cappelli, Peter and Hamori, Monika. "The New Road to the Top." *Harvard Business Review*, January 2005.

Lau, Michelle and Carroll, Susan J. "Representing Women: Women State Legislators as Agents of Policy-Related Change," *The Impact of Women in Public Office.* Susan J. Carroll, ed. Indiana University Press, 2001.

Lopez-Claros, Augusto and Zahidi, Saadia. *Women's Empowerment: Measuring the Global Gender Gap.* World Economic Forum, 2005.

Mikulski, Barbara, ed. *Nine and Counting: The Women of the Senate.* William Morrow, 2000.

National Council for Research on Women. *Gains and Gaps: A Look at the World's Women,* March 2006.

Nelson, Barbara J. and Najma Chowdhury, eds. *Women and Politics Worldwide.* New Haven and London: Yale University Press, 1994.

Newton, Alice, Shahrokhi, Katayan and Tannen, Deborah. "The Power of Talk: Who Gets Heard and Why." *Harvard Business Review,* September – October 1995.

Opfell, Olga S. *Women Prime Ministers and Presidents.* Jefferson, NC: McFarland & Co., 1993. This book deserves special acknowledgment for making available biographical information that is difficult to obtain.

Bibliography

O'Toole, James. *Leading Change: Overcoming the Ideology of Comfort and the Tyranny of Custom.* San Francisco: Jossey-Bass, 1995.

Palao, Ana and Fels, Anna. "Do Women Lack Ambition?" *Harvard Business Review,* April 2004.

Shermann, Janann. "Senator-at-Large for America's Women: Margaret Chase Smith and the Paradox of Gender Affinity." *The Impact of Women in Public Office.* Susan J. Carroll, ed. Indiana University Press, 2001.

"Snapshots of Current Political Leadership." The White House Project.

Weisenhorn, Nina. *Who's Talking Now: A Followup Analysis of Guest Appearances by Women on the Sunday Morning Talk Shows.* Washington, D.C.: The White House Project, October 2005.

Witt, Linda, Karen M. Paget, and Glenna Matthews. *Running as a Woman.* New York: The Free Press, 1994. Recommended reading for any woman thinking of entering politics in the United States.

Wondwosen, Tatu, Wellington, Sheila, et al. "What's Holding Women Back?" *Harvard Business Review.* June 2003.

Council of Women World Leaders
Information

The Council of Women World Leaders is a network of current and former women presidents and prime ministers. The Council currently has 37 Members, which represents nearly all of the world's current and former women world leaders.

The Council's mission is to mobilize the highest-level women leaders globally for collective action on issues of critical importance to women and equitable development.

A ministerial initiative that engages sitting and former women ministers and cabinet members is an integral and essential part of the Council structure.

The Council and Ministerial Initiative create a global architecture for giving a collective voice to women at the highest levels of government. Their mission is to promote good governance and enhance the experience of democracy globally by increasing the number, effectiveness, and visibility of women world leaders.

Mary Robinson, President of Ireland (1990-97) is Chair of the Council, and First Vice President of the E.U. Commision Margot Wallstrom is Chair of the Women's Ministerial Initiative.

Beginning in 2002, the Council launched an effort to promote ministerial-level exchange on global issues, identify and address the particular challenges facing women in ministerial leadership positions, and increase their visibility both nationally and internationally. Government ministers and other high-level women leaders representing seven sectors have convened, of which five were formalized into ministerial networks (Environment; Finance, Economics, and Development; Women's Affairs; Health; and Culture).

About the Author

Laura A. Liswood

Secretary General, Council of Women World Leaders

Senior Advisor, Goldman Sachs

In August 1996, Laura Liswood co-founded the Council of Women World Leaders with President Vigdís Finnbogadóttir of Iceland. The Council is now a policy program of the Aspen Institute, in Washington, DC. Ms. Liswood is the Secretary General of the Council, which is composed of women presidents, prime ministers, and heads of government. The work of the Council expands the understanding of leadership, establishes a network of resources for high-level women leaders, and provides a forum for the group to contribute input and shape the international issues important to all people. Individual leaders are also an important resource to students through the Council student fellows program.

In 2002, Ms. Liswood created the Council Ministerial Initiative with the Right Honourable Kim Campbell. The Honorable Madeleine K. Albright is the Funding Chair of the Ministerial Initiative.

Laura Liswood holds the position of Senior Advisor, Goldman Sachs, a premier global investment bank. She was previously Managing Director, Global Leadership and Diversity for Goldman Sachs.

In 1997, Liswood co-founded with Barbara Lee and Marie Wilson The White House Project dedicated to electing a woman President in the United States. Her work with women presidents and prime ministers was the inspiration for the Project to change the cultural message in the United States about women as leaders.

From 1992 to 1996, as Director of the Women's Leadership Project, Liswood identified global leadership contributions by women heads of state. She interviewed the 15 current and former women presidents and prime ministers that comprise the original edition of this book and video documentary, Women World Leaders.

Liswood's professional experience includes CEO/President of the American Society for Training and Development, executive-level consulting to Fortune 500 and international companies, executive positions at Rainier National Bank and Group W Cable, a subsidiary of Westinghouse Broadcasting and Cable. She received the Westinghouse Award of Excellence for her contribution to women and minorities in the work place. She is also the author of a book on service quality, *Serving Them Right.*

Liswood, a nationally recognized speaker, author, and advisor, continues to contribute to leadership in the women's community. Former commissioner of the City of Seattle Women's Commission, Liswood was the owner/publisher of Seattle Woman Magazine. In 2000, the Secretary of Defense appointed her to a three-year term of the Defense Advisory Committee on Women in the Services (DACOWITS). In 2002, she became a Reserve Police Officer (now Sergeant) for the Washington DC Metropolitan Police Department and is a certified mountain bike police officer for the MPD.

Liswood has also held management positions in the airline industry, including general manager for the Pacific Northwest, for TWA, and was a consultant for the Boston Consulting Group. She holds a M.B.A. from Harvard Business School and a B.A. from California State University, San Diego. She holds a J.D. degree from the University of California, Davis, School of Law, and is admitted to practice law in California and Massachusetts.

www.lauraliswood.com